Religion in Environmental and Climate Change

Also available from Bloomsbury

Climate Change and Philosophy, Ruth Irwin
Ecological Imaginations in the World Religions, Tony Watling
Ethics of Climate Change, James Garvey

Religion in Environmental and Climate Change

Suffering, Values, Lifestyles

Edited by
Dieter Gerten and
Sigurd Bergmann

BLOOMSBURY

LONDON · NEW DELHI · NEW YORK · SYDNEY

Bloomsbury Academic
An imprint of Bloomsbury Publishing Plc

50 Bedford Square   175 Fifth Avenue
London   New York
WC1B 3DP   NY 10010
UK   USA

www.bloomsbury.com

First published by Continuum International Publishing Group 2012
Paperback edition first published 2013

© Dieter Gerten, Sigurd Bergmann and Contributors, 2012

All rights reserved. No part of this publication may be reproduced or transmitted in any
form or by any means, electronic or mechanical, including photocopying, recording,
or any information storage or retrieval system, without prior permission in writing
from the publishers.

Dieter Gerten, Sigurd Bergmann and Contributors have asserted their right under the
Copyright, Designs and Patents Act, 1988, to be identified as Author of this work.

No responsibility for loss caused to any individual or organization acting on or
refraining from action as a result of the material in this publication can be
accepted by Bloomsbury or the author.

British Library Cataloguing-in-Publication Data
A catalogue record for this book is available from the British Library.

ISBN: HB: 978-1-4411-6929-7
PB: 978-1-4725-0556-9

Library of Congress Cataloging-in-Publication Data
Religion in environmental and climate change : suffering, values, lifestyles/edited by
Dieter Gerten and Sigurd Bergmann.
p. cm.
Proceedings of a symposium held Jan. 11–13, 2010 at the Potsdam Institute for Climate
Impact Research.
978-1-4411-6929-7 (hardback)
1. Ecology – Religious aspects – Congresses. 2. Global warming – Religious aspects –
Congresses. I. Gerten, Dieter. II. Bergmann, Sigurd, 1956– III. Title.
BL65.E36R45 2011
201'.77–dc23
2011017982

Typeset by Newgen Imaging Systems Pvt Ltd, Chennai, India

Contents

Acknowledgements

The contributions to this book originate in a symposium that was held in January 2010 in Potsdam, Germany. The editors would like to thank the Volkswagen Foundation (www.volkswagenstiftung.de/) for funding this event and Gabriele Götz for her organizational help in conducting it. They are grateful to Nancy Bazilchuk and Andreas Diesel for editorial help, the Norges Teknisk-Naturvitenskapelige Universitet (NTNU) for its generous publication subsidy, and Udo Simonis and the Society of Friends and Promoters of the Potsdam Institute for supporting the research agenda 'religion in climate change'. Thanks also to Konrad Ott, and to Sarah Campbell, Tom Crick, Kirsty Schaper and their colleagues at Continuum who were involved in this project, for their support.

Notes on Contributors

Gulnara Aitpaeva holds a candidate degree in literature from Moscow State University and a doctoral degree in folklore and literature from Kyrgyz State University. In 1999, she created the Kyrgyz Ethnology Department at American University in Kyrgyzstan, then took the initiative of transforming this into the Department of Anthropology and Archaeology with the mission of developing a social anthropology and facilitating connections and collaborations among social scientists of Central Asia. Since spring 2004, she has been leading the Aigine Cultural Research Center with the mission of expanding research into lesser-known aspects of the cultural and natural heritage of Kyrgyzstan, integrating vernacular, esoteric and scholarly epistemologies. Since 2006, she has been editing a series of books (four volumes to date) on sacred sites pilgrimage and related traditional knowledge and practices in Kyrgyzstan. She is a professor of the National State University and teaches courses on history and theory of epics and comparative literature.

Sigurd Bergmann holds a doctorate in systematic theology from Lund University and works as professor in religious studies at the Department of Archaeology and Religious Studies at the Norwegian University of Science and Technology, Trondheim. His previous studies have investigated the relationship between the image of God and the view of nature in late antiquity, the methodology of contextual theology, visual arts in the indigenous Arctic and Australia, as well as visual arts, architecture and religion. He is chair of the European Forum on the Study of Religion and Environment, and in ongoing projects he investigates the relation between space/place and religion, and religion in dangerous environmental/climatic change. His main publications are *Geist, der Natur befreit* (Mainz 1995; Russian ed. Arkhangelsk 1999; rev. ed. *Creation Set Free*, Grand Rapids 2005); *Geist, der lebendig macht* (Frankfurt 1997); *God in Context* (Aldershot 2003); *Architecture, Aesth/Ethics and Religion* (ed.) (Frankfurt, London 2005); *Theology in Built*

Environments (ed.) (New Brunswick, London 2009); *In the Beginning is the Icon* (London 2009); *Så främmande det lika* ('So Strange, so Similar', on Sámi visual arts, globalization and religion, Trondheim 2009) and *Raum und Geist: Zur Erdung und Beheimatung der Religion* (Göttingen 2010). Bergmann was co-project leader of the interdisciplinary programme 'Technical Spaces of Mobility' (2003–2007) and recently co-edited *The Ethics of Mobilities* (Aldershot 2008); *Spaces of Mobility* (London 2008); *Nature, Space & the Sacred* (Farnham 2009); *Religion, Ecology & Gender* (Berlin 2009); *Religion and Dangerous Environmental Change* (Münster 2010); *Religion som rörelse* ('Religion as Movement', Trondheim 2010) and *Ecological Awareness* (Berlin 2011).

Susan Crate is an interdisciplinary scholar specializing in environmental and cognitive anthropology. She has worked with indigenous communities in Siberia since 1988 and specifically with Viliui Sakha since 1991. Her current research focuses on understanding local perceptions, adaptations and resilience of Viliui Sakha communities in the face of unprecedented climate change. Crate is the author of numerous peer-reviewed articles and one monograph, *Cows, Kin and Globalization: An Ethnography of Sustainability* (Alta Mira Press, 2006). She was senior editor of the 2009 volume, *Anthropology and Climate Change: From Encounters to Actions* (Left Coast Press). She is an associate professor of anthropology in the Department of Environmental Science & Policy at George Mason University in Fairfax, Virginia.

Urte Undine Frömming is a junior professor at the Institute of Social and Cultural Anthropology at the Free University of Berlin and head of the environmental anthropology research area. She has undertaken ethnographic fieldwork in Indonesia, Tanzania and Iceland. Besides her interest in environmental anthropology, she specializes in hazards and disasters research. She has published several peer-reviewed articles and a monograph, *Naturkatastrophen. Kulturelle Deutung und Verarbeitung* (Natural Disasters. Cultural Interpretation and Coping), published in 2006 by Campus, Frankfurt am Main. She is one of the principle investigators of the joint research project 'Alpine Naturgefahren im Klimawandel' (Alpine Risks in Times of Climate Change. Pattern of Impacts and Coping Strategies from 18th to 21st Century) funded by the German Federal Ministry of Education and Research (2011–2014). She is chairperson of KatNet (Network of Disaster research) and member of the European Forum for the Study of Religion and the Environment.

Dieter Gerten holds a PhD in freshwater ecology from Potsdam University and is now a researcher at the Potsdam Institute for Climate Impact Research (PIK) in Potsdam, Germany. For more than a decade he has conducted research in areas such as climate change impacts on lakes, global freshwater resources, vegetation–water interactions, global carbon cycle, biosphere dynamics, water and food security, and religious aspects of water at present and in European history. He has published more than 50 peer-reviewed papers in scientific journals and books. Together with Sigurd Bergmann, he recently edited *Religion and Dangerous Environmental Change*, and he is an executive committee member of the 'European Forum for the Study of Religion and the Environment'. He teaches environmental and hydrological courses at the University of Potsdam, the Humboldt University of Berlin and the University of Basel, and has led a number of national and international water-related research projects. In 2007, he was also an Expert Reviewer for several reports of the Intergovernmental Panel of Climate Change (IPCC).

Laurel Kearns is associate professor of sociology and religion and environmental studies at Drew Theological School and the graduate division of religion of Drew University in Madison, NJ. In addition to *EcoSpirit: Religions and Philosophies for the Earth* (co-edited with Catherine Keller), she has contributed chapters to volumes such as the *Blackwell Companion to Modern Theology*; *Religion, Globalization, and Culture*; *Earth and Word* and the forthcoming *Oxford Handbook on Climate Change and Society*. Her research is focused on religious, particularly Christian, involvement in ecological issues and movements; environmental justice; religious climate skeptics; nature spirituality; and religion and animals. In addition to her teaching and research in religion and ecology, she helped found the Green Seminary Initiative and is now serving on the Sustainability Committees of both Drew University and the American Academy of Religion, where she also chaired the Religion and Ecology Steering Committee.

Timothy B. Leduc holds a doctorate in environmental studies and is currently an assistant professor in environmental education at York University's Faculty of Environmental Studies in Toronto. His current research is concerned with questions of interdisciplinarity in Canadian environmental studies and thought. This interest arose out of critiques from his book *Climate, Culture, Change*, which argued interdisciplinary climate research is being limited by disciplinary specialists, and that the physical sciences, social sciences, humanities and religious studies need to be better intertwined. Building upon such critiques, he is now examining trends in Canada's academic approaches to interdisciplinary environmental education and thought, with a particular focus on the value of localizing interdisciplinary knowledge and education. He has published articles on these topics in the journals *Environments, Ethics and the Environment; Worldviews; Climatic Change; Canadian Journal of Environmental Education* and *Ecological Economics.*

Friedrich Lohmann is a professor at the Humboldt University of Berlin (faculty of theology) where he teaches systematic theology with a focus on ethics. After earning a PhD at the Johann Gutenberg University of Mainz (1995), he joined the University of Tübingen and wrote a post-dissertation thesis in which he discusses the possibility of a universal foundation of ethics, especially human rights (*Zwischen Naturrecht und Partikularismus*, Berlin/New York: De Gruyter 2002). He was a member in residence at the Center of Theological Inquiry in Princeton during the academic year 2004–2005. He has held his current position since 2008. Human rights and the foundation of ethics are still the focus of his research. Other fields of interest include the history of Protestant theology and ethics in the twentieth century and economic ethics.

Wolfgang Lucht is a trained physicist and now co-chair of the Research Domain II 'Climate Impacts and Vulnerabilities' at the Potsdam Institute for Climate Impact Research in Potsdam, Germany. Since 2009, he is also Alexander von Humboldt Chair in Sustainability Science at the Department of Geography, Humboldt University of Berlin, Germany. He has led a number of research projects and published numerous papers and book chapters on topics such as global biosphere and agrosphere modelling, climate change impacts, remote sensing of vegetation dynamics, earth system analysis and societal transition to sustainability. He is one of the lead authors of the IPCC's Special Report on Renewable Energy and a contributing author of other IPCC reports. He is a member of the German National Committee on Global Change Research.

Michael Reder studied philosophy, theology and economics in Munich, Tübingen and Fribourg. Since 2010, he is chair of practical philosophy at the Munich School of Philosophy, with particular focus on international understanding. He is also an academic staff member of the Institute for Social and Development Studies at this school. He was the manager of the project 'Climate Change and Justice: Climate policy as a Component of Fair Globalization and Sustainable Poverty Reduction' (2007–2011), and has done research on this issue (e.g. ethics of climate change, human rights as political framework for climate policy). Within a postdoctoral qualification project he is doing research on religion in the current discourse of political philosophy. He is member of several interdisciplinary groups of researchers, for example, on Ethics in the Tension between Science and Public (University of Munich).

Christian Reichel holds a masters degree in social and cultural anthropology and geography from the Free University of Berlin and the Humboldt University of Berlin. His research focuses on past and current human–nature relations, including 'shifting baselines', local knowledge for the prediction, protection and adaptation to climate-related catastrophes, as well as ecosystem services and livelihood analysis. He has undertaken ethnographic fieldwork in Indonesia, Mongolia and Romania and currently works as a research associate on the joint research project 'Alpine Hazards in Climate Change' at the Institute of Social and Cultural Anthropology, Free University of Berlin. As part of his PhD requirements, he conducts research on the mapping and visualization of local environmental knowledge about natural hazards in the Swiss, German and Austrian Alps.

Michael Roberts graduated in geology from Oxford and theology from Durham University and was elected a Fellow of the Royal Historical Society in 2010. After three years as an exploration geologist in Africa, he became an ordained Anglican priest and is now vicar of country parishes near Lancaster. His particular interests are Darwin's Welsh geology and the relationship of British and American Evangelicalism with geology and evolution, as well as creationism. He has published a book *Evangelicals and Science* (Greenwood Press 2008); several book chapters; and various papers on Darwin's geology, Intelligent Design, geology and Genesis, and so on.

Lioba Rossbach de Olmos, a German cultural anthropologist, received her masters from Johann Wolfgang Goethe University in Frankfurt in 1984, and her PhD at Johannes Gutenberg University in Mainz in 1997. Her previous positions include investigations on the Nicaraguan Atlantic Coast from 1984 to 1986 and project management at the 'Climate Alliance of European Cities with Indigenous Peoples of the Tropical Forests' from 1993 to 2004. Afterwards, she joined the staff of cultural and social anthropology at Philipps University Marburg where she is now teaching and doing research on Afro-Cuban religions. She conducted ethnographic fieldwork in Colombia, Nicaragua, Bolivia, Cuba and Germany. Her major research interests are Afro-American cultures and religions, indigenous peoples' rights and environmental anthropology – with focus on biodiversity and climate change.

Martin Schönfeld is a German–American philosopher who teaches at the University of South Florida and conducts annual philosophy workshops in Taiwan. His research aims at integrating the phenomenon of climate change and the concept of climate in philosophy. He organized what appears to have been the first international conference on climate and philosophy (Tampa, 2006), and he edits the yearly *Climate Philosophy Newsletter* (since 2007). He is presently editing a special issue on climate for the *Journal of Global Ethics*, whose contributors explore future trends of climate ethics from the vantage points of Latin American thought, contemporary Canadian philosophy, Japanese philosophy, Neo-Confucianism and Daoism.

Holger Sonnabend teaches ancient history at the Historical Institute of the University of Stuttgart in Germany. He worked for the 'Kommission für Alte Geschichte und Epigraphik des Deutschen Archäologischen Instituts' in Munich and taught ancient history at the University of Saarland in Saarbrücken. The focuses of his research are topics of historical geography and environmental history, especially natural disasters in ancient cultures. On this topic, he has published several books and articles, including *Naturkatastrophen in der Antike. Wahrnehmung, Deutung, Management* (1999). He also deals with issues of the history of religion and the history of mentality.

Markus Vogt is Chair of Christian Social Ethics at the Catholic Department of the Ludwig Maximilian University of Munich, Germany, since 2007. He studied philosophy and theology in Munich, Jerusalem and Luzern. From 1992 to 1995, he worked at the 'Sachverständigenrat für Umweltfragen' (German Advisory Council on the Environment). From 1998 to 2007, he was a professor of social ethics at the theological college in Benediktbeuern and head of the institute for church and environment (cooperation project with the German Bishops' Conference). From 2000 to 2007, he was responsible for the working group for environmental questions of the Council of European Catholic Bishops' Conferences (CCEE). Since 2009, he has been head of the Community of Christian Social Ethics in the German-speaking counties. Since 2010, he has been a fellow and scientific research professor at the Rachel Carson Center for Environment and Society.

Part 1

Setting the Stage

Chapter 1

Facing the Human Faces of Climate Change

Dieter Gerten and Sigurd Bergmann

When faced with enormous quantities,
we lose our sense of proportion and significance.
    —*Mihail Sebastian,* Journal 1935–44, *entry of 12 July 1941*

The Multiple Challenges of Global Climate Change

There is broad scientific consensus that anthropogenic global warming is underway and will continue if greenhouse gas emissions are not drastically curtailed over a rather short time window (Meinshausen et al., 2009). Defining 'dangerous climate change' is less easy, however, even though there is an intense debate within the climate science community about this definition and the related 'reasons for concern' (Schellnhuber et al., 2006; Smith et al., 2008; UNSW, 2009). Largely based on the biophysical and economic impacts expected as a result of climate change, there is now wide agreement that global mean temperature should not rise by more than 2 degrees above pre-industrial levels, so as to keep impacts within a tolerable – and below a 'dangerous' – range.

Local communities, industries, nation-states and society as a whole are consequently in need of great transition in order to face the tremendous challenge of *mitigating* dangerous climate change (however defined) or – if mitigation is not successful – *adapting* to unavoidable changes – an equally challenging issue. Portfolios of adaptive methods have so far been suggested mainly from economic and engineering points of view. However, no one knows today whether these adaptive strategies and techniques will be implemented successfully and in time; we are thus left with a high risk of 'residual' climate change impacts that will almost certainly cause increased suffering for many. How people can cope with large-scale suffering and, ultimately, death as a consequence of climate change (due to short-term extreme events such as floods and gradual processes such as rising sea levels or repeated droughts) is a largely unexplored domain of research. Recent catastrophes – such as Hurricane Katrina in New Orleans and surrounding areas in 2005, the floods in Australia in early 2011 and particularly the earthquake and tsunami in Japan some weeks thereafter – clearly demonstrate that even industrialized societies are poorly prepared for such events and thus highly vulnerable.

The ethical dimensions of these challenges – avoiding dangerous change, managing unavoidable impacts, and coping with the consequences of unmanageable impacts while at the same time trying to meet development goals (Edenhofer et al., 2010) – are obvious, as has been stated in a number of publications (e.g. Altner, 1991; Hösle, 1991; Böhme, 2002; Lienkamp 2009; Vogt, 2009; Bergmann et al., 2010; HRH The Prince of Wales et al., 2010; Ott, 2010). This points to the need for more than merely pragmatic solutions focused on technological and economic energy or water and earth system management (which often entail little more than a continuation of business-as-usual), but also for fundamental changes in prevailing value systems, cultural practices and mentalities. Still, there is a surprising lack of understanding of what *zeitgeist* (historical and present) has laid the foundation for anthropogenic climate change and other environmental problems, what cultural perspectives (either progressive or regressive) on these problems prevail in present times and what cultural techniques may help in adapting to future impacts. A research agenda that addresses these questions requires intensive collaboration between the environmental and climate (impact) sciences and various strands of the humanities, social sciences and cultural sciences. While this kind of collaboration is now in an initial phase (see Crate et al., 2009; Hulme et al., 2009; Voss, 2010; Welzer et al., 2010), the particular role of religion in global climate and environmental change has hardly been addressed in an interdisciplinary manner.

The Multiple Roles of Religion in Climate Change

For a number of reasons, religion is a highly promising analytic lens and an exemplary cultural microcosm for studying the manifold human modes of perception, action and thought (worldviews, moral systems, practices, aesthetics, ethics, lifestyles, hopes and fears) in relation to global change – specifically in relation to climate change (Bergmann et al., 2010). A first reason is that the topic of religion and its socio-political relevance is generally being revived in current debates in philosophy and the humanities (see Michael Reder's chapter in this book). Secondly, religious worldviews and images of nature inform the activities of a large majority of the world population (e.g. Gardner, 2003), which is why, thirdly, they can be crucial driving forces of environmentally relevant behaviour, in both quantitative and qualitative terms (Park, 1994; CSWR, 1997–2003; Stern, 2000).

One has to recognize that this influence of religion is highly ambiguous and can be either positive or negative (Bergmann, 2005; Proctor, 2006). On the one hand, there is a trend for religious organizations and individuals to become 'greener' while screening their traditions for moral imperatives to act against global warming and to respect the natural environment in general (Taylor, 2006). Among the most interesting and dynamic recent developments is the increasing engagement in sustainable lifestyles by members of the Christian church(es) due to the belief in the world as divinely created (e.g. Northcott, 2007). The various world religions have further contributed to the concept of sustainability through, for example, the long ecumenical 'conciliary process' on Justice, Peace and the Integrity of Creation (see Vogt, 2009). On the other hand, the worldviews and practices of religious communities can also influence the perception of environmental changes and their interpretation in a way that essentially ignores them or aggravates them even further. As an example, climate change is sometimes interpreted superficially from a Christian apocalyptic perspective as if it were a God-given, inescapable reality that the faithful cannot and must not prevent (Bloomquist et al., 2009; see also Gerten, 2010, for similar observations in Islamic countries frequently affected by floods). Such fatalist interpretations indicate the theological and practical challenges for religious leaders and communities to re-read the scriptures in a historically and contextually correct way.

The following story provides a glimpse of how important religious belief can be with respect to environmental change in general and natural hazards in particular. In an interview on the Norwegian national broadcast news, only two days after the January 2010 fatal earthquake in Haiti, an aid worker shared her experiences. She reported that, the night after the earthquake, when the shaking slowed and the loss of lives and the damage to buildings and infrastructure was evident, everyone moved into the middle of the street, considered to be the only safe place because of the expected aftershocks. In the streets, people started to sing religious songs and to pray continuously and loudly all night, until sunrise. When everything crumbles into ruins, only belief and hope remain – these feelings need to be expressed, shared and practiced.

This function of religious beliefs, however, is at the outermost edge of what this book is about. The book's focus is on the manifold ways of developing belief-based human feeling, thinking and action *before* climate change further increases the frequency and severity of natural disasters. In doing so, we editors and authors help to prevent society from experiencing the outer edge, among ruins. The scale of perception among religions ranges from so-called climate sceptics (who preach contempt of climate science as well as of the poor victims of climate change) to believers in technocratic 'salvation' and environmentalist activists (who accuse a superior 'system' of not addressing the problem). It includes the established world religions as well as new religiosities, in which images of nature and life mostly work as central drivers in reconstructing spirituality.

Chapters of this Book and Key Findings

This book provides a selection of papers presented and discussed during the symposium 'Religion in Global Environmental and Climate Change: Sufferings, Values, Lifestyles'. The event took place on 11–13 January 2010 (coincidentally at the same time as the Haitian earthquake) at the Potsdam Institute for Climate Impact Research (Potsdam, Germany) and was co-organized by the Norwegian University of Science and Technology (Trondheim, Norway) and the University of Greifswald (Germany) in association with the European Forum for the Study of Religion and the Environment (EFSRE, www.hf.ntnu.no/relnateur/). The contributions carry on in the spirit of previous research dedicated to understanding the interrelations between religion and climate/environmental change, which commenced with workshops held in 2007 and 2008 in Potsdam and Trondheim, respectively. The contributions to those earlier meetings are documented in the book *Religion and Dangerous Environmental Change – Transdisciplinary Perspectives on the Ethics of Climate and Sustainability* (Bergmann et al., 2010). We, as editors of both books, see clear continuity between them: both exemplify religion as a core element of the relationships between humans and the environment. The first book established the agenda for the dynamically growing research field and charted the spread of perspectives ranging from religious and cultural studies to philosophical and ethical discussions. The present book further broadens the ongoing mapping of this 'polycentric' research field (as we described it in the introduction to the previous volume) with a focus on selected functions of religion in climate change, as this now seems to be the arena where most environmental debates and activities of religious groups are concentrated. These functions of religion in climate change are being explored in regional case studies and synthesizing global perspectives. Both books aim for transdisciplinary integration while approaching the phenomenon of religion from different angles, using methods and theories from several disciplines. As such, they mirror the vibrant international dynamics and the emerging figuration of this new research field, the multidimensionality and complexity of the topic, and ultimately the (not least methodological) challenges that lie ahead.

The key conclusions that can be drawn from the Potsdam workshop and this book – beyond the individual conclusions of the authors summarized below – are as follows:

(1) The necessity and urgency of mitigating global climate change and other dangerous environmental changes for humanitarian reasons is emphasized by scientists from a range of disciplines, including earth system science, anthropology, ethnology, sociology, theology, religious studies, philosophy, ethics, environmental history and geography.

(2) Since anthropogenic climate change is by definition caused by specific human practices related to specific attitudes and ideologies (rooted in particular historic developments), and since it will more or less directly affect human societies and cultures, the humanities need to further engage in inter- and transdisciplinary environmental and climate sciences.

(3) As belief systems and religious practices are normative cultural elements for a majority of the world's population, a research focus on religion allows the study of people's manifold modes of actions, perceptions and thoughts when experiencing climate change and coping with its impacts.

(4) The role of religion in mitigating and adapting to climate and other environmental changes is ambivalent and complex, with progressive and regressive tendencies operating at the same time.

(5) There is a strong need for more systematic and comparative interdisciplinary, interreligious and intercultural research on the role of religion – and culture in a more general sense – in global climate change, in order to explore the pros and cons of religion in the face of this change and to identify creative alternatives and correctives to solely economic and technocratic proposals.

This book is structured into three sections. The chapters in Part 1, including this introduction, state reasons for analysing functions of human culture and religion in climate change and other global environmental challenges. Part 2 elaborates more specifically on theoretical and practical developments regarding climate change within Catholic and Protestant Christianity in particular, considering how these and other world religions might evolve in the future in the face of progressing climate change. The chapters in Part 3 explore in yet more detail how worldviews and practices of specific (indigenous) faiths in selected regions are linked with climate and environmental changes, with a brief excursus to ancient times. The key conclusions of the individual chapters can be summarized as follows.

In Chapter 2, Wolfgang Lucht argues from the perspective of earth history and earth system analysis that the anthropogenic pressures upon our planet, particularly the undue material extractions and landscape transformations, have become so pervasive that the closely linked anthroposphere, geosphere and biosphere are at the verge of a no-analogue state. He speculates that new cosmologies (which express themselves in material artefacts – presently cars, power plants and so on – that have ultimately led to the planet's perilous state), informed by state-of-the-art science as well as by archetypical narratives, are a precondition for more sustainable human–environment co-evolution. Lucht furthermore advocates a novel kind of earth system analysis that combines 'macroscopic' computer modelling and earth observation techniques, communicable tableau constructions in the vein of Alexander von Humboldt's grand landscape portrayals, and 'realoscopic' analyses of local socio-ecological developments.

The question of whether religion gains macroscopic, globally relevant influence in the current debate over global climate change is addressed in the subsequent chapters. Michael Reder reflects on the current debate over the social functions of religion in postmodern societies, particularly in relation to global climate change and development policy. He highlights features of religion that may support ethically informed pathways of sustainable development, such as their strong moral orientation (for example, the 'option for the poor' in Catholic social teaching) and a theoretical and motivational basis for building social movements and solidarity networks (as demonstrated by their growing engagement in climate and development policies and their cooperation with non-governmental organizations). Recognizing that religions are ambivalent phenomena – sometimes acting in support of fair and sustainable development, sometimes supporting injustice or fatalism – Reder convincingly argues that religion should have a more prominent role in the public discourse about our common future.

Timothy Leduc offers a religious interpretation of the recent 'Climategate' controversy and, more specifically, the role of the fossil fuel industry in Canada's limited political response to climate change. The central thesis of his chapter is that there is a whole set of beliefs and practices informing the political and public debates on the validity of climate research and the definition of a climate response – beliefs and practices that can be interpreted as religious by nature. By critically assessing a debate on Gaia theory and climate change, the chapter concludes by proposing that religious perspectives can deepen our sense of these paralysing debates while offering a much broader idea of what a comprehensive response to the climate change challenge should entail.

In the first chapter of Part 2, Markus Vogt discusses global environmental problems (of which climate change is only the tip of an iceberg) from the perspective of Catholic ethics. With regard to the traditional social ethics of the Catholic Church, he elaborates a well-grounded proposal to include sustainability as a fourth central 'social principle', in addition to the existing principles of personality, solidarity and subsidiarity. He further explores a threefold aspect of justice – global, intergenerational and ecological – and provides a new and promising definition of wealth as a milestone towards more sustainable societies.

In Chapter 6, Friedrich Lohmann critically and deeply reflects on the notorious controversy in Christian eco-theology about whether an anthropocentric position should be maintained, or whether nature should be ascribed an intrinsic value, thus rejecting the hierarchical idea of human superiority over the rest of nature. He distils from this discourse an intermediate, essentially holistic position (from a Christian perspective) that acknowledges an intrinsic value of nature while preserving the notion of human dignity. Key to this position is the assertion that human superiority does not encourage destructive behaviour towards nature per se, since such superiority implies an 'obligation to serve the whole of creation in a responsible attitude of stewardship'.

In his intriguing analysis in Chapter 7, Michael Roberts charts the spread of recent actions and attitudes of American and British evangelicals – individuals and organizations – concerning the environment and particularly global climate change. Following J. McKeown (John Ray Institute), he characterizes 'green' and 'brown' factions, demonstrating that the latter – including very vocal and influential proponents who mix climate science with pseudo-science and creationist arguments – have gained high visibility in the public discourse. Of course, as Roberts states in his conclusion, the evangelical discourse on climate change is more complex than this simple divide suggests: it develops dynamically, and most evangelicals may well be indifferent to climate change. Nonetheless, these dynamics should be carefully watched, not least because there is a large number of evangelicals and neo-Pentecostals not only in the United States and Great Britain but in many other countries.

Laurel Kearns complements Michael Roberts' analysis by a close look in Chapter 8 at US Evangelicals' modes of thinking and communication with respect to environmental and climate change, with a focus on how these have changed very recently. Her analysis reveals that Christian anti-environmentalists (climate sceptics) often frame their moralistic campaigns by adopting and then abusing economic and scientific arguments. Kearns concludes that while these people and institutions try to undermine the success of environmentalists, there are, however, also 'those of many faiths around the globe who forge ahead in the fight against climate change and its related injustices'.

The exploratory and somewhat provocative essay by Martin Schönfeld suggests that the divergent and partly radicalized positions within evangelical communities (as described by Roberts) and the collective pro-environmental developments in other faith communities (cf. Kearns' conclusion) may well be a harbinger of things to come, as global climate change and its impacts worsen. Schönfeld's argument starts from White's (1967) narrative that Christianity is to blame for the ecological crisis. Schönfeld recognizes this as too simplistic a theory while acknowledging that it is a 'good cartoon' in capturing the dualistic conception, the *gestalt*, of Abrahamic religions: the division of God and nature. He further speculates that, owing to their metaphysical comparative advantage ('the right thing to do is to live in harmony with the natural environment'), 'pagan' belief systems are less vulnerable to fuelling future climate change than Abrahamic religions, which are in need of a revision of their narratives.

While Martin Schönfeld suggests that 'indigenous creeds are poised to come back', Susan Crate (in the first chapter of Part 3) demonstrates compellingly that the livelihoods, worldviews and belief systems of indigenous people are already being adversely affected by climate change. Her ongoing field research focuses on the native Viliui Sakha agropastoralist horse and cattle breeders living in northeastern Siberia, a region experiencing a trend towards milder winters and wetter land surfaces. These environmental changes represent an unprecedented challenge to the mythologies and beliefs of the local people, as they interfere with subsistence living and threaten to undermine settlements and the continued use of the mainstay plants and animals so central to Viliui Sakha livelihoods and spiritual orientation. Crate comes to the conclusion that the cultural and cognitive implications of environmental changes need to be seriously considered in climate impact studies – and that adaptation measures can probably only be successful if the local populations and their worldviews become an intrinsic part of decision-making.

Using examples from different peoples and regions, Lioba Rossbach de Olmos shows that there is a general need for comprehensive ethnological research in order to explore and identify the manifold, culture-specific patterns of response to current and possible future climate change. She emphasizes that 'Western' (climate) scientists and engineers should not expect a priori that cultural scientists will always confirm and support their analyses and suggestions for solving environmental problems. If one contrasts her findings with the normative claims from climate/earth system science and climate policy to mitigate climate change, one could find that, for various reasons, these claims face a lack of understanding and even resistance in different cultural and religious contexts.

Undine Frömming and Christian Reichel have conducted comprehensive ethnological field studies in the Coral Triangle of Indonesia, a region that – due to its high biodiversity and productivity – is home to the most valuable natural resources in the world. However, the region is now prone to impacts of climate change (more frequent and stronger typhoons, rising sea level and continued coral bleaching), which – together with the overuse of (marine) resources – put the habitat at risk of large-scale destabilization. Frömming and Reichel show how the local population has developed various cultural and religious techniques for preventing and coping with natural disasters. Accordingly, in order to design preventive and protective measures more effectively, this local knowledge should be integrated with the currently predominating technocratic practices.

Gulnara Aitpaeva expounds profoundly in Chapter 13 on the Kyrgyz notion *jaichylyk*, which characterizes the traditional ability of spiritual initiates in Kyrgyzstan to change the weather for military and other purposes in a strict, targeted fashion that is limited in both space and time. Analysing the Kyrgyz national epic literature, she first demonstrates how jaichylyk works (though details have always been kept secret). She then reports that this knowledge has gradually disappeared or has been more or less actively suppressed, due to a combination of the increasing influence of Islam and Communism, and the decline of a nomadic way of life. One of the most interesting aspects of this chronology (requiring further research) is how jaichylyk – which implies a moral responsibility for the benefit of people locally and globally – could be revitalized in present times in order to help people mitigate climate change and adapt to climate impacts.

Holger Sonnabend concludes this book by approaching its main topic from the perspective of environmental history. Using examples from pre-Christian antiquity (Romans and Greeks), he provides insights into how people explained environmental changes (particularly disasters) and the coping strategies they had. Sonnabend demonstrates that ancient people usually preferred the security of religious interpretation – attributing responsibility for catastrophes to specific gods – to rational scientific analysis. From a contemporary, rational point of view, one might tend to regard such an attitude as fatalist. Nevertheless, the fact alone that religious interpretations still provide guidance and solace for many people around the world in times of disaster underscores the necessity of inter- and transdisciplinary approaches.

Perspectives for Further Research on Religion in Climate Change

All chapters in this book point out explicitly or implicitly that most, if not all, religions respond very dynamically and ambivalently, in theory as well as in practice, to ongoing global climate change and its foreseeable impacts. As Laurel Kearns and Michael Roberts particularly illustrate, religious organizations and prominent individuals express positions that support or refute the scientific evidence for climate change, and, within a few years, these views can change radically and evolve in different directions. Functions of religion in global climate and environmental change are thus highly diverse and complex, not least in terms of their geographical pattern and scale (global – regional – institutional – individual). In any case, religions – hence the worldviews and practices of their followers – are already in a process of transformation, for good or for bad, in response to current climate change and – perhaps even more so – by the scientific community's projections of possible future changes. In view of this, Schönfeld's question about how, and how strongly, the different religions of the world will continue to transform in a warming world is well posed.

Without doubt, studying the transformation of existing religions (in terms of their moral values, their practices and the interpretation of their traditions) or the rise of new religious forms in the face of progressing climate change is an exciting research topic as such. However, future research should also focus on how these transformations – which certainly reach beyond the sphere of religions into larger cultural settings – may provide either positive (in support of sustainable development) or negative feedback to climate and environmental change in a kind of socio-ecological functional circle (Bergmann, 2008; Schipper, 2010). For instance, it would be highly desirable to have systematic and comparative studies on how the many declarations and activities of religious leaders and communities have entered and are ultimately shaping the public climate change discourse via their cognitive, philosophical and ethical contributions, and how local actions – motivated by religion – are already contributing to mitigation of and adaptation to climate change. While these kinds of influences and feedback have been documented for selected cases (e.g. CWSR, 1997–2003; Chamberlain, 2007; Bedford-Strohm, 2009; Bergmann et al., 2010; this volume), a systematic, interdisciplinary and interreligious documentation and scholarly reflection is still a desideratum for research on the cultural dimension of climate change. Such synoptic analyses need to be complemented by comparative local-scale, 'realoscopic' perspectives (cf. Lucht's suggestions), investigating in detail how mutual human–environment relationships are unfolding, and how coexisting religious communities cooperate or dissent with respect to what an adequate response to climate change is.

By grounding it in the perception of, and respect for, the many human faces of dangerous climate change, we hope that this book can contribute to the ongoing renegotiations of the central topics in environmental science. We would be grateful if it furthermore can fuel the development of what can be called 'the environmental humanities' in synergy with interdisciplinary climate science. Nevertheless, a brief warning should be issued: readers moving into such a landscape of reflection may be challenged to contest conventional convictions, such as the essential difference of science and religion or the individuality of beliefs. By calibrating all their capacities, environmental humanities – and science in general – might improve our human ability to creatively respond to what we have brought unto ourselves. If faith (God) is said to be able to move mountains (Job 9.5; 1 Cor. 13.2), scholars need to explore how belief systems could 'move' climates.

References

Altner, G. (1991), *Naturvergessenheit – Grundlagen einer umfassenden Bioethik*. Darmstadt: Wissenschaftliche Buchgesellschaft.

Bedford-Strohm, H. (ed.) (2009), *Und Gott sah, dass es gut war. Schöpfung und Endlichkeit im Zeitalter der Klimakatastrophe*. Neukirchen-Vluyn: Neukirchener Verlag.

Bergmann, S. (2005), *Creation Set Free: The Spririt as Liberator of Nature*. Grand Rapids: Eerdmans.

— (2008), 'Der Geist unserer Zeit – Zur Verwandlung von Schöpfung, Wissenschaft und Religion im Klimawandel'. *Salzburger Theologische Zeitschrift*, 12, 27–47.

Bergmann, S. and Gerten, D. (eds) (2010), *Religion and Dangerous Environmental Change: Transdisciplinary Perspectives on the Ethics of Climate and Sustainability*. Studies in Religion and the Environment, Vol. 2. Münster: LIT.

Bloomquist, K. L. and Machila, R. (2009), *God, Creation and Climate Change – A Resource for Reflection and Discussion*. Geneva: The Lutheran World Federation.

Böhme, G. (2002), *Die Natur vor uns: Naturphilosophie in pragmatischer Hinsicht*. Baden-Baden: Die Graue Edition.

Chamberlain, G. L. (2007), *Troubled Waters: Religion, Ethics, and the Global Water Crisis*. Lanham: Rowman & Littlefield.

Crate, S. A. and Nuttall, M. (eds) (2009), *Anthropology and Climate Change. From Encounters to Actions*. Walnut Creek: Left Coast Press.

CSWR (Center for the Study of World Religions) (1997–2003), *Religions of the World and Ecology* (10 volumes). Cambridge: Harvard University Press.

Edenhofer, O., Lotze-Campen, H., Wallacher, J. and Reder, M. (eds) (2010), *Global aber gerecht: Klimawandel bekämpfen, Entwicklung ermöglichen*. München: C. H. Beck.

Gardner, G. (2003), 'Engaging religion in the quest for a sustainable world', in Worldwatch Institute (ed.), *State of the World 2003*. New York: W. W. Norton & Company, pp. 152–175.

Gerten, D. (2010), 'Adapting to climatic and hydrologic change: variegated functions of religion', in S. Bergmann and D. Gerten (eds), *Religion and Dangerous Environmental Change*. Münster: LIT, pp. 39–56.

Hösle, V. (1991), *Philosophie der ökologischen Krise*. München: C. H. Beck.

HRH The Prince of Wales, Juniper, T. and Skelly, I. (2010), *Harmony: A New Way of Looking at Our World*. London: HarperCollins.

Hulme, M., Boykoff, M., Gupta, J., Heyd, T., Jaeger, J., Jamieson, D., Lemos, M. C., O'Brien, K., Roberts, J. T., Rockström, J. and Vogel, C. (2009), 'Conference covered from all angles'. *Science*, 324, 881–882.

Lienkamp, A. (2009), *Klimawandel und Gerechtigkeit – Eine Ethik der Nachhaltigkeit in christlicher Perspektive*. Paderborn: Ferdinand Schöningh.

Meinshausen, M., Meinshausen, N., Hare, W., Raper, S. C. B., Frieler, K., Knutti, R., Frame, D. J. and Allen, M. R. (2009), 'Greenhouse-gas emission targets for limiting global warming to 2°C'. *Nature*, 458, 1158–1163.

Northcott, M. S. (2007), *A Moral Climate: The Ethics of Global Warming*. London: Darton, Longman & Todd Ltd.

Ott, K. (2010), 'Ethical claims about the basic foundations on climate change policies', in S. Bergmann and D. Gerten (eds), *Religion and Dangerous Environmental Change*. Münster: LIT, pp. 195–203.

Park, C. (1994), *Sacred Worlds: Introduction to Geography and Religion*. London: Routledge.

Proctor, J. D. (2006), 'Social science on religion and nature', in B. Taylor (ed.), *Encyclopedia of Religion and Nature*, Vol. 2. New York: Continuum, pp. 1571–1577.

Schellnhuber, H. J., Cramer, W., Nakicenovic, N., Wigley, T. and Yohe, G. (2006), *Avoiding Dangerous Climate Change*. Cambridge: Cambridge University Press.

Schipper, E. L. F. (2010), 'Religion as an integral part of determining and reducing climate change and disaster risk: an agenda for research', in M. Voss (ed.), *Der Klimawandel – Sozialwissenschaftliche Perspektiven*. Wiesbaden: VS, pp. 377–394.

Smith, J. B., Schneider, S. H., Oppenheimer, M., Yohe, G. W., Hare, W., Mastrandrea, M. D., Patwardhan, A., Burton, I., Corfee-Morlot, J., Magadza, C. H. D., Füssel, H.-M., Pittock, A. B., Rahman, A., Suarez, A. and van Ypersele, J.-P. (2008), 'Assessing dangerous climate change through an update of the Intergovernmental Panel on Climate Change (IPCC) "reasons for concern"'. *Proceedings of the National Academy of Sciences of the United States of America*, 106, 4133–4137.

Stern, P. C. (2000), 'Psychology and the science of human–environment interactions'. *American Psychologist*, 55, 523–530.

Taylor, B. (ed.) (2006), *Encyclopedia of Religion and Nature* (2 volumes). New York: Continuum.

UNSW (University of New South Wales Climate Change Research Centre) (2009), *The Copenhagen Diagnosis – Updating the World on the Latest Climate Science*. Sydney: UNSW.

Vogt, M. (2009), *Prinzip Nachhaltigkeit – Ein Entwurf aus theologisch-ethischer Perspektive*. München: Oekom.

Voss, M. (ed.) (2010), *Der Klimawandel – Sozialwissenschaftliche Perspektiven*. Wiesbaden: VS.

Welzer, H., Soeffner, H.-G. and Giesecke, D. (eds) (2010), *KlimaKulturen: Soziale Wirklichkeiten im Klimawandel*. Frankfurt: Campus.

White, L. (1967), 'The historical roots of the ecological crisis'. *Science*, 155, 1203–1207.

Chapter 2

Global Change and the Need for New Cosmologies

Wolfgang Lucht

Global Change as a Phenomenon of Co-evolution

The relationship between societies and the environment is entering a critical phase. Their interlinkage has taken on a global dimension, with developments in human culture, economy and number beginning to affect vital functions of our planet (Schellnhuber, 1998). It is possible that earth and the human societies it harbours are in the middle of processes shifting them into markedly different modes of operation: both the climate and the environment's ecology have begun to display qualitatively new properties, while societies are changing at a rate never seen before in human history. The immediate origin of these transformative changes is the hugely increased mechanization of human cultures during the last several thousand years, following in the wake of likely earlier mental transitions to categorical thought in the human lineage, and recently accelerated by the unprecedented availability of large amounts of controlled energy first through agriculture and later through fossil fuel use. Earth's environment and its societies have entered a more profound state of co-evolution than has ever been the case.

The ultimate outcomes of a probably far-reaching social and environmental co-transition in this co-evolution cannot be known, but it is becoming apparent that societies as we know them are in peril as much as some of the iconic features of earth, for example its ice caps and forests. Given these prospects, it is quite urgent that social processes of self-reproduction begin to more substantially interact intellectually and culturally with the mounting body of earth system knowledge that the geosciences have accumulated in the last decades. Otherwise, societies will likely enter this dynamic phase with a lack of knowledge. Awareness about the functioning of and impending change to the earth system has greatly grown over the past 200 years and has become more systematic, particularly in the past 50 years in connection with the rise of global environmental concerns as a public issue (IPCC, 2007a; Weart, 2003). But it has not yet been sufficiently incorporated into the processes of social self-definition and self-reproduction, which continue to operate as if the environmental consequences were a side effect rather than potentially transformational.

I suggest that new forms of cultural self-understanding that are imbued with scientific insights and derived from narratives rooted in cultural mainstreams are now required in order to influence processes of global change. Societal approaches to global change should not only be scientific, technical or economic, but should also reflect the ability of human cultures to resonate with modern global change knowledge. In my view, the current global change debate does not adequately reflect this cultural, mental dimension, at least not the politically relevant parts of it.

Based on our understanding of the history of human social and mental evolution in relation to the environment, I believe there is a case to be made that cultural activity is central to the phenomenon of human existence on the planet, and most likely to global change in this century as well. Humans have interacted with their environment from early on as part of processes of self-definition as conscious social beings, creating individual and collective identities. This may have begun before our brains were capable of verbal language, through a language of material objects in the form of tools and other artefacts. Today, the language of words combined with extensive material expressions of human selves have built a number of world-changing variants of Homo sapiens societies. Becoming aware of the cultural, identity-creating functions of our material artefacts should be an important aspect of trying to understand and manage global change. Unless current social and cultural processes begin to resonate with scientific knowledge, the change set in motion will come as a disruptive, overwhelming surprise.

This essay is meant to provide a few stimulating elements of a larger, as of yet unreconstructed mosaic of interconnections between humans and the world against the backdrop of global change. As such, it does not try to paint a complete and coherent picture and contains speculative elements. It is my hope that, nonetheless, a few directions worth pursuing on this important topic of our time might be discernible from the pieces.

I first give a brief overview over the major phenomena of environmental global change, then discuss the changes that have occurred in the relations of human societies with the environment and their implications for the future. I then discuss, again very briefly, the role of information exchange and self-reflexive culture for the human phenomenon on planet earth, and the role of material and word-based language for human constructions of identity and relations to the environment. Finally, I conclude that, if the cultural constitution of human existence is taken seriously, new cosmologies about the human position in the world are needed in order to face global change successfully. These new cosmologies, however, must be suitably informed and resonate well with the findings of current anthropological and geosciences.

Future No-analogue State of Earth's Geosphere and Biosphere

Where are we presently in the process of environmental global change? Earth is a complex, physico-chemical system fed by the sun's energy. This energy, trapped by the atmosphere's natural greenhouse effect, warms the planet to habitable temperatures. In response, earth's atmosphere and oceans self-organize into complex patterns of wind systems and oceanic currents that transport heat and pattern the regional climates. Plants on land and in the oceans form a thin but dense and vigorous film of life that transforms sunlight into the chemical energy that feeds the whole of life (Vernadsky, 1926). Through its metabolic processes, life is closely linked with the chemical cycles of earth, particularly those of carbon, nitrogen and phosphorus. Life has completely transformed the land surfaces by forming water-holding soils and increasing the weathering of rocks. Overall, life exerts a major influence on the physical and chemical state of the planet and has co-shaped earth's climate since first appearing more than 3.5 billion years ago (Lenton et al., 2011). Biological processes have also triggered some of the largest state changes in earth's history. Among these are the oxidation of earth's atmosphere more than two billion years ago and the subsequent gradual drawdown of atmospheric carbon dioxide levels since the first appearance of multicellular large plants and animals in the Cambrian period. Together, these (bio)chemical processes have kept earth's temperatures within a range supportive of life, even while the aging sun gradually increased its luminosity.

In the past two million years, and therefore during the period in which different species of humans evolved, earth's natural state has been that of an ice-age planet, characterized by spatially extended ice caps and a colder, drier climate than at present. Ice-age climate, itself quite variable, was interrupted only occasionally by short interglacial phases that were warmer and wetter. We currently live in such a warm episode, the Holocene epoch, during which all of the history of more advanced human civilization has unfolded. This phase is expected to last longer than previous interglacial phases, due to unusual properties of the earth's orbit around the sun, which at present is nearly circular rather than slightly eccentric (Berger and Loutre, 2002).

It is within this warm period that greenhouse gas emissions created by humans are now additionally heating up the atmosphere quite strongly, which – if not phased out – will take the atmosphere far outside of its natural range of operation. As a consequence, atmosphere, oceans, cryosphere and lithosphere – which together form the geosphere – are shifting into a *no-analogue state*: a state not seen in earth history since the beginning of the current planetary period of ice ages (Lucht, 2009). If left unchecked, there is a danger of larger-scale restructuring of atmospheric and oceanic circulation patterns, climate zones and sea levels (IPCC, 2007a). Earth is close to loosing its iconic northern ice cap altogether in the warmed Arctic summers of the near future. Large ice sheets in Antarctica and Greenland are in danger of melting and destabilizing (Lenton et al., 2008). In addition to climate warming, anthropogenic CO_2 emissions are increasing the acidity of the oceans, potentially disrupting one of the chemical hearts of earth system functioning and changing the chemical properties of sediments and soils. Conditions somewhat comparable to those expected in the coming centuries have occurred before, such as in the age of dinosaurs, but then earth was very different from the planet we are familiar with (Zachos et al., 2001). Earth's climate and chemical balances are clearly entering new terrain.

At the same time, earth's biosphere is also in transition to a no-analogue state, likewise a direct consequence of human activities. After more than two million years of a hunter and gatherer existence, humans became agriculturalists only a few thousand years ago, clearing the land, planting crops and grazing domesticated animals – a transformation accompanied by often environmentally detrimental population growth and greatly increased resource use. The prairies of North America and the forests of Europe have been converted to farmland, as have the Indian subcontinent and much of arable China. Land use in Africa is now extensive. Deforestation in the tropics is proceeding with the development of roads, industries and global agricultural markets, while logging is diminishing many northern forests. Earth's biosphere is being transformed from a state of widespread forest cover to one of agro-industrial land use.

The current rates of species loss due to habitat destruction as a consequence of this expanding human land use are without precedent in recent earth history and may be compared only to major extinction events driven by natural chemical transitions, massive volcanic activities and large meteorite impacts. Out of direct sight of humans, the abundance of fish in the world's oceans has collapsed due to overfishing in most of the seas. Non-native species are spreading on all continents, having been introduced there by anthropogenic transport. The introduction of genetically modified organisms alongside those transformed by breeding is just beginning. And a great number of chemical substances from human wastes and emissions are accumulating in the environment, causing serious chemical effects to all life forms.

The mosaic of regional degradations (Petschel-Held et al., 1999), in conjunction with increasingly worldwide trade of goods, is producing a global qualitative transformation of the face of the planet. This land use transformation has not yet reached its climax; a growing, prosperous and industrializing world population continues to drive land conversion worldwide, a trend that has strongly accelerated in the past half century (Costanza et al., 2007). Potentially extensive future planting of bioenergy crops to meet the world's energy demands will exacerbate the already precarious change considerably. Additionally, wide-ranging shifts in the vegetation distribution on earth will occur as a consequence of climate warming (IPCC, 2007b).

Past and Future States of Human Societies

The question now, with the geosphere and biosphere shifting into no-analogue states, is whether human societies will also transition qualitatively as a consequence, given how closely interlinked they are with their environments. Cause and effect are here intertwined, as developments in human societies lead to environmental change that will in turn alter those societies: it is a true co-evolution of environmental state (for example, global mean temperature or forest cover) with the development of world societies. A number of these societies have created historically unprecedented forms of organization and material use in the past several centuries, characterized and supported by abundant energy supply; large, densely populated and materially rich cities; and rapidly evolving technologies, transport and communication produced by industrial infrastructure. The large majority of world societies today aim to follow this path to perceived security and wealth. However, in view of the extensive land use, resource extraction and environmental degradation associated with this form of living, the prospect may not be realistic. In fact, quite fundamental departures from the current development pathways may be forced. For already industrialized societies, the preconditions of their existence may become more fragile as environmental change begins to hamper their abilities to adapt and competition for resources becomes stronger. Poorer countries may find it impossible to enter into a similar pattern of global resource footprints. As a consequence, in a few decades, earth's atmosphere, oceans and the biosphere may no longer reflect the world we know today, but societies might also no longer function as they do now.

Three major developments in more recent human history have deeply altered humanity's previous relationship with the environment and have precipitated the global change now affecting the earth system as a whole. First, human relationships to material objects now encompasses living things through the domestication of plants and animals. The invention of agriculture and animal husbandry has made available the energy embodied in their biomass (Haberl and Fischer-Kowalski, 2007). The currently observed worldwide degradation of natural habitats is the environmental consequence, while human societies have witnessed the appearance of villages – a profound social innovation. Hunter-gatherer groups required large territories, but agriculturalists could sustain themselves on rather small areas of land with fertile soil, sufficient water and amenable climate (Mithen, 2003).

Second, the discovery just a couple of hundred years ago of fossil fuels as sources of considerable energy, as well as the technological methods for utilizing them, has also hugely shifted the relationship of societies to the material world. Procuring, transporting and transforming large amounts of materials – both biomass and minerals – from the environment became feasible, not just as the norm but as a precondition for the functioning of industrializing and industrialized cultures (Haberl et al., 2007). The direct results were the expansion of trade and travel, an impressive condensation of living conditions into cities of millions and the appearance of substantial waste streams of materials flowing back into the environment. Landscapes were and are still being transformed at a rapid rate. Global per capita footprints of material consumption continue to grow for harvesting and extraction as well as for waste disposal and emissions.

The third change is the still evolving networking of information through shared language, writing systems, book printing and – more recently – worldwide electronic communication, now reaching a point at which mobile personal devices can readily link into remote information infrastructures. This change directly concerns the relationships among humans and will continue to lead to social change with profound consequences for both.

Against the background of these developments, there nonetheless seems to be a general assumption in the debate that, while the environment changes substantially and societies continue to industrialize and globalize, societies' own principles of functioning and coherence will remain essentially unaltered, with more or less gradual – albeit sometimes rapid – developments leading from the past to the future. However, there is no reason to assume that while the world's natural systems are prone to shifts and transitions, human societies will, with some adaptation, be able to continue through it all without being fundamentally affected as well. In fact, they may be more vulnerable than ecological systems to change because, for example, they operate in a more artificial state regarding the environment on which they depend. Technological innovations will not be sufficient to counter all this, although this is the paradigm of the current political debate. It is quite possible that the co-evolution of both economically poor and rich societies with their regional and global environments could reach critical points in this century.

The future transition of societies could entail changed modes of functioning or different social structures, such as are currently being discussed under terms such as 'low-carbon', 'post-industrial', 'green technology' or 'sustainable' societies – albeit mostly in still vague and largely sectoral rather than comprehensive terms. One may argue that human inventiveness and flexibility cannot be underestimated. These, however, are likely just as much a source of future social transitions as they have been in the past. Transitions could also take the form of collapses of current ways of societal organization, with a strong increase in social misery in degraded environments and undersupplied cities. A good number of historically known societies have undergone major transitions (Takács-Sánta, 2004), sometimes advancing their welfare, more often losing states of civilization previously attained, as happened to the cultures in Mesopotamia or the Maya. Environmental factors often played a role in these developments, when variations in crucial environmental factors proved too much of a strain on social organizations (Tainter, 1988).

The often called-for 'great transition of humankind to sustainability', if it is possible, would clearly be a change of a most fundamental nature, definitely more than merely a process of optimization and adaptation (Raskin et al., 2002; Schellnhuber et al., 2005). While the earth's environment is changing as a consequence of the development of human societies and abilities, human societies will also be facing transformational change in this century.

On the scientific side, the immediate tasks at hand are manifold. Macroscopy through a combination of concerted earth observation across natural and social systems on the one hand and advanced computer modelling of earth system dynamics on the other hand are required for monitoring current and charting potential future pathways (Schellnhuber, 1999). Continued development of scientific insights into earth system processes is required, such as exploration of potential tipping points in the climate system, that is, the mechanisms and thresholds for nonlinear change – especially regarding the stability of ecosystems (Lenton et al., 2008). Furthermore, there needs to be a focus on 'realoscopy', which is to confront generalized macroscopic insights with concrete local realities: place-based action requires that scientific notions of global change are re-injected into everyday contexts so that they acquire concrete meaning in concrete contexts (cf. Lucht and Pachauri, 2004). Only from this can workable solutions emerge that make sense for a given location and social situation. All the while, such local realities must in turn be distilled back into images amenable to human thought processes through tableau construction in the vein of Alexander von Humboldt (Graczyk, 2004) – carefully arranged, selective but precise images that convey the essence of systemic interconnections in landscapes, their life forms and human inhabitants (von Humboldt, 1807). Such a new science of the earth – resulting from macroscopy, realoscopy and tableau construction – would examine in a new methodological manner the co-evolutionary dynamic interaction between geosphere, biosphere and anthroposphere (Lucht, 2010).

On the social side, it is paramount that global institutional mechanisms are developed to progress towards a global civil society that controls its macroeconomic instruments. It is also paramount that technological progress will continue to provide new opportunities for advancing lifestyles without increasing the environmental burden disproportionately. A wide array of research into development options for social infrastructure – from energy to transport to living arrangements – is required, as well as advances in ways of implementing and managing policies in these areas. Social costs and trade-offs have to attain a new importance in environmental debates. But that is not enough. Additionally, a new understanding of the sociocultural substrate on which societies are built is required. The material and communicational infrastructures of societies are closely entwined with the self-images they pursue in establishing their identities in the world. It is here that awareness of problematic developments and opportunities for altered perceptions may perhaps be found. The world of values, religions and spiritual relationships is likely as central to societies as their economic self-organization. Study of these topics in ethnology, anthropology, religion and related disciplines should self-consciously take their place alongside the organizational and natural scientific analyses of global change.

Narratives of the Self

What is the nature of human self-organization into complex social structures? Life, having arisen on our planet quite early in its history, is characterized by a continuous stream of information inheritance between generations of organisms and underlying evolutionary natural selection of variations (Jablonka and Lamb, 2005). The link of life through time has for the most part been genetic and epigenetic. Only higher animals use behavioural imitation as a third mode of information transfer.

It is in this system of life's information inheritance that the appearance of language in humans may be seen as a most profound innovation, one of the rare transitions in the state of the planet (Maynard Smith and Szathmáry, 1995). Language opens up what appears to be a fourth viable pathway of information inheritance between generations of organisms, realized at present in one species. It allows an accumulation of knowledge into self-reflexive cultures that are consistent but fluid and that are not genetically encoded, at least not directly. The amplification of information networking through the current internet and wireless communication to handheld computing devices is bringing a whole new dimension to the organization of this information flow, creating collective phenomena with a potentially substantial impact on social and environmental developments of the future. The language transition – which is rather an information flow transition to networked, grammatically structured information – is still very much under way. As in previous major transitions in earth's biological information flow systems, transformational changes in the planet's energetic state and chemical cycles are the consequence, now in the form seen as anthropogenic global change.

Self-aware, symbolic and categorical representation of information in a brain processed into structured thought through grammatical language is an ability that seems to have arisen particularly in hominins. It likely occurred as a consequence of the complex social intelligence that primates share. With regard to language as a form of interaction with the environment, expressions of a social self through bodily actions perhaps came first, followed by expressions of the bodily self in external material objects used as tools and later by language proper at an unknown period in human evolution, quite possibly at a stage well before Homo sapiens.

Evidence for the mental engagement of conscious humans with the phenomenon of their existence in the environment can perhaps be seen in the unexplained symmetry and care in production of many early tools, particularly the ubiquitous handaxes. Humans, from the early tool users in Eastern Africa to the late Neanderthals in Eurasia, manufactured these for the impressive time span of about 1.5 million years (Ambrose, 2001). Their properties have never been satisfactorily explained by functional considerations (Wynn, 1995). They ranged from minute sizes to huge instruments that were unwieldy for work. Their symmetry and frequently very careful production cannot be explained merely by their use as a multi-purpose cutting, pounding, digging or throwing tool, functions which would have been equally fulfilled by sharp-edged stone flakes, which were much less demanding to produce, particularly in a situation where heavy stone tools would not have been carried far for absence of good carrying containers. There is an uncanny aesthetical and perhaps symbolic quality to them that attracts admiration even today, even when the results of micro-wear analysis confirm their use in the processing of meat, wood and bone. They could well have been expressions of self as social actors in the landscape, acquiring their meaning instantaneously in manufacture and use.

A comparison may be made with the functions of the polished stone axes of the more recent, late phases of the Stone Age in the Neolithic Denmark. These very regular flint axes were ground to often mirror-smooth surfaces, either on all sides or just on the faces (Petersen, 1993). Arguments have been made that the polishing enhances the durability and utility of a flint axe, but this has not been convincingly shown to be the case. Rather, it is quite possible that here, too, an aesthetic or symbolic element is strong. There are long periods in the northern post-glacial Stone Age when polishing was absent, superficial or badly executed, showing it to perhaps be a cultural phenomenon not strongly driven by utility. And while most of these axes were used for felling trees and producing wooden tools and structures, some were also produced specifically for sacrificial offerings. Polished axes were typical grave goods of males. It is obvious that while these axes, as the tools that allowed the early farmers to clear the land, were the tools of beginning global change, they were also clearly viewed as spiritually interconnected objects. They express a particular relationship these early farmers had to the land, their world and their identity in it. These polished axes were formulations of cultural dimensions beyond their practical use.

These merely indicative observations serve as examples from the material domain. Not only recently, but nearly from the origins of human tool use, human self-expression manifested itself in material objects (Gamble, 2007). Human self-expression used a language of objects before and after developing a language of words. This is significant because I would like to suggest what is almost obvious: the material artefacts of our cultures – the leading cause of global change, given the amount of fossil energy available for creating them – are expressions of our cultural and spiritual identities as well. Our cars, buildings, airplanes and furniture, so intimately part of the processes leading to the current transformational global change, both express who we are as cultural beings today and fulfil practical functions.

There is a whole language of self-expression in the form of tools, implements and objects. This should be taken seriously when considering the problems of global change: it is not merely a matter of changing to other material patterns in view of unsustainable practices, of lessening the material extractions and emissions that characterize our transformative exchange with the environment. It is not just a matter of management of resources. It is also a matter of reflecting upon our material self-expression as cultures embedded in landscapes and exploring pathways for altering our impact on the environment. It seems that in the current perilous planetary situation, cultural evolution of our relation to the artefacts surrounding us requires as much attention as economic steering and technological progress.

Narratives of Symbolic Meanings

Homo sapiens also possesses language through words. The ability of modern humans to produce generalized categories in grammatically structured thoughts, and to produce these as sounds, has led to a far-reaching fusion of social, technological and environmental domains of intelligence, allowing to imbue objects with relations and living things with properties of objects (cf. Mithen, 1996). I think in this context it is significant that the very first examples of art preserved from prehistory, taken here as a somewhat uncertain proxy for the mental processes of symbolic language and thought, are highly abstract and clearly non-realistic in nature.

While the earlier Neanderthal and Homo erectus predecessors of Homo sapiens were intelligent beings that inhabited their landscapes successfully for hundreds of thousands of years, the extensive emergence of drawings, paintings, sculptures, ornaments, jewellery, engravings and other forms of pictorial expression did not occur in Europe before the advent of anatomically modern humans some 40,000 years ago. Whether members of homo sapiens produced such culture much earlier in Africa and the Near East remains disputed, as archaeological evidence is still scattered. But in Europe, the earliest examples are impressively rich.

The oldest figurine currently known is the Aurignacian so-called Venus of Hohle Fels from south-western Germany. It is at least 35,000 – perhaps 40,000 – years old, and therefore considerably older than the better-known Gravettian Venus figurines, engravings and decorative artworks from across Eurasia. Discovered in a cave during excavations in 2008, it depicts a large-breasted, squat, wide-hipped woman without a head, with pointed legs and prominent sexual attributes, as well as incisions that may indicate some form of clothing wrap or ornamentation. The figure might have been worn as a pendant. The piece clearly shows that the oldest known example of figurative art in the world was already abstract, highly symbolic, perhaps spiritual and obviously an instrument of highly constructed communication. Clearly, abstract symbolic representations imbued with meaning are not an invention of the twentieth century.

Another indicative example of the early origins of this mode of human self-expression is the famous lion-headed figure (also from south-western Germany), found in the Stadelhöhle and dated to 32,000 years ago. It is a humanoid figure with a lion head made in ivory. The magical or mythical nature of this figurine is self-evident. One can also think of the very realistic but also highly abstract depictions of animals in the famous caves of the Upper Palaeolithic in south-western France, and of the abstractions common in ethnic art from indigenous tribes around the world.

As with material self-expression in handaxes and polished flint axes, so also in art (taken here somewhat speculatively as a proxy for symbolic language) a high degree of fusion existed between utility and naturalism, and abstraction, aesthetics and spiritual meaning. And this seems to have occurred not as the product of a slow, long evolution from simple beginnings to such abstract mental dimensions, but rather in a highly developed form from the very beginnings of the respective phases of human history. My conclusion is that it is a convincing hypothesis that this manner of relating to the world through the language of symbolic as well as material (tool) objects – through art and words – is an ancient and constitutive part of the human phenomenon. They are narratives of the conscious human self, which is interpreting its bodily existence in the external environment, through symbolic representation in social contexts.

Narratives of Humans in the World

Today, as before, human societies continue to abound with narrations of who we are and what and why. These stories go along with our material artefacts and form our identities as individuals and societies. Our cities are described in terms of what they offer and what kind of atmosphere they provide to social self-definition. Our landscapes are the substrate of regional characters and larger cultures. Nations define themselves through the history of their lands, with narrations of how people settled in, shaped and used that geography to build social and political realities that were inherited and modified over generations. These narrations take on many forms from ancient stories of mythical foundation and pivotal events to projections of futures rising out of the dynamic present. They form a rich tapestry of constructions of identities through the power of infrastructure, artefacts and language (cf. Cosgrove, 1984). The increasingly networked system of communications between humans and social groups is producing the broad flow of concurrent human cultures and ways of living.

In an interconnected but somewhat parallel, rationalistic development of engagement with the environment, the modern geosciences – having emerged from the historical process of enlightenment in Europe – are now formulating dramatic messages to the public. The earth, these sciences conclude, is on the threshold of large-scale environmental changes that will directly and indirectly affect its human societies by altering the foundations upon which they are built – and humans themselves are the cause of this change. These insights are the product not of cultural reinterpretations, but of rational analysis, observation, theorizing and modelling, which renders them somewhat peripheral to the core dynamics of human societies.

How then can the mainstream of human cultural self-reproduction respond to this message from the sciences? Does science even have a place in the world of social self-definition, originating as it does from a highly rationalistic and partial view of realities, albeit one that has proven very powerful in its ability to describe and predict phenomena, and in producing technologies? Indeed, even in the rationalistic Western cultures, the position of science and the scientific expert in public debate is contested. The credibility of the scientific process and its position within the human world of values remains unclear. Between expert knowledge so complicated that few will be able to judge it and a large public hunger for knowledge about the fascinating workings of the world, there is unease as to the extent to which scientific knowledge should and can be the basis for concrete social decisions.

I suggest (and am not the first to do so) that what is now adequate and needed in the sociocultural process are new cosmologies. Cosmologies have long been created that fuse scientific understanding of the world with systems of thought defining human freedom and reflecting on the place of humans in the world and in the cosmos (von Bingen, 1151). Cosmologies transcend more practical modes of human self-understanding because they address issues of meaning. They provide more than an analysis by being frames of reference. For the era of global change, they should be built using archetypical narratives present in human societies, most of which are very old. At the same time, they now should be scientifically well informed: world stories that neglect what the modern geosciences are telling us are not responsible stories in our times. If they are to work, these cosmological narratives should be socially intelligent – and therefore culturally compatible – while being scientifically accurate (i.e. in accordance with the scientific state of the art). They should re-address the oldest questions: who we are, who we want to be, and what we can and will do with our freedom, as conditioned by our embedding in increasingly dynamic cultural traditions and environmental characteristics. This would link the current challenge of achieving sustainability to the deeply rooted prehistoric human enterprise through addressing our world-changing artefacts in a mode of language, both material and linguistic.

The problem is that time is running out. Perhaps only 50 – at most, 100 – remain for achieving a sustainability transition. Considerable societal and technological self-evolution is required if such transition is to be achieved. My suggestion is that to approach this challenge through consciously constructing new cosmologies is to attempt to transcend the modern natural sciences while taking their message seriously, and at the same time to acknowledge the fundamental nature of human self-expression through material objects in the world, which have taken on a volume in industrialized societies that is endangering the grounds upon which they were built.

Culture makes human histories interesting and meaningful. This is likely also the case when approaching the problems of global change. Cosmological expressions of the human self should be put back with other things into the centre of the global change debate.

References

Ambrose, S. H. (2001), 'Paleolithic technology and human evolution'. *Science*, 291, 1748–1753.

Berger, A. and Loutre, F. M. (2002), 'An exceptionally long interglacial ahead?' *Science*, 297, 1287–1288.

Cosgrove, D. (1984), *Social Formation and Symbolic Landscape*. London: Croom Helm.

Costanza, R., Graumlich, L., Steffen, W., Crumley, C., Dearing, J., Hubbard, K., Leemans, R., Redman, C. and Schimel, D. (2007), 'Sustainability or collapse: What can we learn from integrating the history of humans and the rest of nature?'. *Ambio*, 36, 522–527.

Gamble, C. (2007), *Origins and Revolutions: Human Identity in Earliest Prehistory*. Cambridge: Cambridge University Press.

Graczyk, A. (2004), *Das literarische Tableau zwischen Kunst und Wissenschaft*. München: Fink.

Haberl, H. and Fischer-Kowalski, M. (eds) (2007), *Socioecological Transitions and Global Change*. Cheltenham: Edward Elgar Publishing.

Haberl, H., Fischer-Kowalski, M., Erb, K.-H., Gaube, V., Bondeau, A., Plutzar, C., Gingrich, S., Lucht, W. and Fischer-Kowalski, M. (2007), 'Quantifying and mapping the human appropriation of net primary production in the Earth's terrestrial ecosystems'. *Proceedings of the National Academy of Sciences of the United States of America*, 104, 12942–12947.

IPCC (2007a), *Climate Change 2007: The Physical Science Basis*. Cambridge: Cambridge University Press.

— (2007b), *Climate Change 2007: Impacts, Adaptation and Vulnerability*. Cambridge: Cambridge University Press.

Jablonka, E. and Lamb, M. J. (2005), *Evolution in Four Dimensions*. Cambridge: MIT Press.

Lenton, T. M., Held, H., Kriegler, E., Hall, J. W., Lucht, W., Rahmstorf, S. and Schellnhuber, H.-J. (2008), 'Tipping elements in the Earth's climate system'. *Proceedings of the National Academy of Sciences of the United States of America*, 105, 1786–1793.

Lenton, T. M., Held, H., Kriegler, E., Hall, J. W., Lucht, W., Rahmstorf, S., Schellnhuber, H.-J. and Watson, A. (2011), *Revolutions that Made the Earth*. Oxford: Oxford University Press.

Lucht, W. (2009), 'Air, a planetary hybrid', in B. Hermann and C. Dahlke (eds), *Elements – Continents. Approaches to Determinants of Environmental History and their Reifications*. Halle: Nationale Akademie der Wissenschaften.

— (2010), 'Earth system analysis and taking a crude look at the whole', in H.-J. Schellnhuber, M. Molina, N. Stern, V. Huber and S. Kadner (eds), *Global Sustainability, A Nobel Cause*, Cambridge: Cambridge University Press.

Lucht, W. and Pachauri, R. K. (2004), 'The mental component of the Earth system', in H.-J. Schellnhuber, P. Crutzen, W. C. Clark, M. Claussen and H. Held (eds), *Earth System Analysis for Sustainability*. Cambridge: MIT Press, pp. 341–365.

Maynard Smith, J. M. and Szathmáry, E. (1995), *The Major Transitions in Evolution*. Oxford: Oxford University Press.

Mithen, S. (1996), *The Prehistory of the Mind: The Cognitive Origins of Art, Religion and Science*. London: Thames & Hudson.

— (2003), *After the Ice. A Global Human History 20,000–5000 BC*. London: Weidenfeld & Nicolson.

Petersen, V. P. (1993), *Flint fra Danmarks Oldtid*. Copenhagen: Høst & Søn.

Petschel-Held, G., Block, A., Cassel-Gintz, M., Kropp, J., Lüdeke, M. K. B., Moldenhauer, O., Plöchl, M. and Schellnhuber, H.-J. (1999), 'Syndromes of global change – a qualitative modelling approach to assist global environmental management'. *Environmental Modelling and Assessment*, 4, 295–314.

Raskin, P., Banuri, T., Gallopin, G., Gutman, P., Hammond, A., Kates, R. and Swart, R. (2002), *Great Transitions. The Promise and Lure of Times Ahead*. Boston: Stockholm Environment Institute.

Schellnhuber, H.-J. (1998), 'Earth system analysis. The scope of the challenge', in H.-J. Schellnhuber and V. Wenzel (eds), *Earth System Analysis: Integrating Science for Sustainability*. Heidelberg: Springer, pp. 5–195.

— (1999), 'Earth system analysis and the second Copernican revolution'. *Nature*, 402 (Supp.), C19–C23.

Schellnhuber, H.-J., Crutzen, P. J., Clark, W. C., and Hunt, J. (2005), 'Earth system analysis for sustainability'. *Environment*, 47, 10–25.

Tainter, J. (1988), *The Collapse of Complex Societies*. Cambridge: Cambridge University Press.

Takáscs-Sánta, A. (2004), 'The major transitions in the history of human transformation of the biosphere'. *Human Ecology Review*, 11, 51–66.

Vernadsky, V. I. (1926), *Biosfera*. Leningrad: Nauchoe Khimikotekhnicheskoe Izdatelstvo (English edn (1991): *The Biosphere*. New York: Springer).

von Bingen, H. (1151 [1986]), *Scivias*. Salzburg: Otto Müller.

von Humboldt, A. (1807), *Ansichten der Natur*. Tübingen: Cotta.

Weart, S. R. (2003), *The Discovery of Global Warming*. Cambridge: Harvard University Press.

Wynn, T. (1995), 'Handaxe enigmas'. *World Archaeology*, 27, 10–24.

Zachos, J., Pagani, M., Sloan, L., Thomas, E., and Billups, K. (2001), 'Trends, rhythms, and aberrations in global climate 65 Ma to present'. *Science*, 292, 686–693.

Chapter 3

Religion in the Public Sphere: The Social Function of Religion in the Context of Climate and Development Policy

Michael Reder

The Paradigm of Secularization

Religions offer an important cultural background for societies all over the world. In post-war Europe, however, they seemingly have lost their public role. As a corollary of the sociological debate on secularization, religions in Western countries seemed destined to lose ever more of their importance in light of progressive modernization and individualization (cf. Pollack, 2003). Yet this hypothesis has not been confirmed; on the contrary, religions today play an extremely important role in Western societies and worldwide. The idea of secularization ran rampantly (cf. Dobbelaere, 2002; Martin, 2005): religion is no longer seen as a mere temporary phase in the history of modern societies. The 'revival of gods' is now taking place on different levels, from political and cultural levels to that of society in general. Essentially, religions 'take positions on political questions or engage in public debates' (Reder and Schmidt, 2010, p. 1).

Thus, the discourse over secularization has undergone a pronounced change. In this context the debate over the social role of religions in post-modern societies started again about ten years ago and is still ongoing. This debate is also underway in political theory and philosophy. In these discussions, two different ways of interpreting the social functions of religion, the liberal and the post-secular model, are prevalent. On the one hand, liberals such as John Rawls (Rawls, 1971) or Richard Rorty (Rorty and Vattimo, 2005) tend to reduce religions to the private sphere. From their perspective, religions could be a foundation for individual schemes of life and private worldviews. But religions should not play a role in the public sphere. In democratic societies, secularized reasoning replaces religion in a broad communication process intended to bring about a consensus. Religion seems to block this 'communicative action' (Habermas, 1984–1987). Rorty even interprets religions as 'conversation stopper(s)' (Rorty, 1994), which is why – according to the liberal model – religions should be overcome.

On the other hand, a post-secular model has developed over the last decade among a number of academics who once favoured the hypothesis of secularization. Habermas is probably the most well known of these individuals. He sees modern societies as being in danger of being 'derail(ed)' (cf. Habermas and Ratzinger, 2007; Habermas, 2008). In his view, deliberative democracy needs sources for motivation, and religions could provide such a moral impetus. He also states that democracy depends on moral stances that stem from pre-political sources, such as religious ways of life. Thus, religions play an important role for democracy as a background and a source of motivation, even though they cannot serve as normative guidelines for democratic procedures (Habermas, 2010). 'In this context, the concept "post-secular" – which in the interim has exerted a major influence on the debate over the social role of religion – expresses the fact that modern societies should also expect that religions will continue to exist and should seek to engage them in a constructive dialogue.' (Reder and Schmidt, 2010, p. 7)

Given the convincing nature of this hypothesis, it follows that there should be a discussion of the ways in which religion could play a role in different political fields. The Worldwatch Institute describes five aspects that distinguish religions from other social actors: ability to create meaning, moral authority, a large following, significant material resources and the ability to form communities (Gardner, 2003).

This chapter analyses these functions of religion with respect to climate and development policy. In doing so, two different aspects are discussed: first, what a convincing general interpretation of religion in the public sphere entails and, secondly, three dimensions of religions public role – their moral orientation, particular worldview and social capital – in relation to climate and development policy.

Religions in Post-secular Societies

Social sciences started discussing a 'cultural turn' about 20 years ago. Similar to the 'linguistic turn' in the 1960s when philosophers focused on language, today cultural conditions of social phenomena are taken into

account and analysed in ever more detail. Hence, culture is a special category to be analysed and evaluated as a serious aspect of the diversity of
society in the age of globalization. Much emphasis is placed on the fact
that the world society is not a homogenous body, but is characterized by
dynamic interactions between different cultural perspectives and even cultural reasoning (cf. Walzer, 1994).

This theoretical background can be used to develop a comprehensive
understanding of a theory of pragmatism. The main idea of pragmatic theory is that norms and politics are always connected to cultural beliefs. For
example, moral values are not (only) accepted because of an abstract reason
but because they are incorporated in common beliefs, which themselves
are influenced by cultural practices. Therefore, the aim of pragmatism is
not to provide an abstract moral reason, as Kant did. Pragmatism means
instead to look at cultural and social practices and to analyse how people
realize morality from a practical standpoint (cf. Honneth, 2004; Reder,
2009a). This perspective enables the interpretation of moral and political
orientations, such as human rights. Today, human rights provide a basis
for a universal (global) morality. From a pragmatic view they are accepted
because they are incorporated in various global practices (cf. Müller and
Reder, 2009). Global discourses regarding issues such as the Millennium
Development Goals or sustainable climate policy are both examples of this.
In the fight against poverty and climate policy, global practices were established in which human rights function as a moral guideline. This incor-
poration of moral standards in global practices mostly takes place when
disadvantaged people and groups refer to standards (Reder, 2009a).

But moral standards such as human rights never exist independently of
cultural contexts. Rather, they have to be interpreted in various cultural
contexts and practices. Religions can be regarded as cultural practices
under which people live and interpret their lives (cf. Stegemann, 2003). The
history of religions is closely connected with cultures from which the internal plurality of religions also emerged. Even the sources of religion have
always been embedded in particular sociocultural contexts. The idea of a
pure beginning for a religion is nothing other than an imagined construction. Hence, religions always reflect the strengths and weaknesses of their
respective cultures, even though they claim universal worldviews and ethical imperatives that indeed may transcend any particular culture and enable them to drive internal reforms (cf. Reder, 2009b). Thus, there seems to
be no 'Ur-Religion', as Friedrich Schleiermacher pointed out as early as the
beginning of the nineteenth century (see Schleiermacher, 1799/1984). The
common characteristic of all religions is that they establish a comprehensive

practice that enables discussion and reflection on a transcendent dimension of reality. But the way they realize this practice depends on the different cultural backgrounds involved. Therefore, from Schleiermacher's perspective, religion and culture are always interconnected.[1]

One factor that distinguishes religions from other cultural systems is the reference to an absolute authority, an authority that by definition cannot and should not be questioned or even challenged (Geertz, 1966). In general, religions pretend or at least presuppose that there is no contradiction between their truths and the results of human reasoning. Religion is concerned with the relation between transcendence and immanence without being able to objectify it. Authors like Nicholas of Cusa convincingly expressed this idea in the fifteenth century (Nicholas of Cusa, 2002; Bulhof, 2000). The conclusion for authors like Nicholas of Cusa was that this authority – God – is interpreted in different cultural ways. The plurality of religions emerged from their interconnection with various cultural systems (Reder, 2009b).

Summarizing the previous argumentation, religions should be understood as a comprehensive cultural practice, which express a transcendent dimension of reality that cannot be objectified (cf. Derrida and Vattimo, 1998). Religions express this transcendence in differentiated rites and semantic forms by which a comprehensive worldview is founded. The different social forms of religions emerge from their irreducible relations to cultural backgrounds (cf. Müller, 2007a).

What does this mean for a convincing understanding of religion as an actor of social change in times of climate change and global poverty? Answering this question requires that three different dimensions of religions be distinguished: their strong moral orientation, their particular worldview and their 'social capital' in terms of providing a theoretical and motivational basis for social movements.

Social Functions of Religions Facing the Impacts of Climate Change and Global Poverty

Moral Values Concerning Climate and Development Policy

Religions create a strong emotional adherence among their believers. Having a transcendent authority in the background always motivates a great number of people to follow this authority with conviction. Religion proves to be an important moral resource, according to Habermas, because religious citizens have special access to the potential for justifying moral attitudes. Its meaning-endowing function provides a moral basis for public discourses and thereby plays an important role in the public sphere.

This can have destructive as well as constructive consequences. On the one hand, one could even speak of an inherent tendency or openness of religions to (fundamentalist) instrumentalization (Meyer, 1995). On the other hand, religions could guide people to think about moral aspects of social change in a constructive way.

In that perspective, religions include both ideas of a flourishing life and instructions for ethically acceptable behaviour. They motivate their followers in a particular way because they justify moral values with reference to a comprehensive interpretation of reality and an absolute. For instance, moral values could be based in the idea that the world was created by God. Thus, religious people will be motivated to preserve creation in terms of sustainable environmental policy or solidarity against poverty. 'Indeed, the world's religions have many assets to lend to the effort to build sustainable progress, including moral authority, a long tradition of ethical teachings, and the sheer political power that comes from having many adherents' (Gardner, 2006, p. 6). However, concerning the ethical dimension of religions, their (more or less) universal values are always connected and embedded in cultural contexts. This means that there is an irreducible constellation of tensions between the claim of universal validity and the realization of religious values in cultural contexts.

Two examples of religious ideas are helpful to understand the public role of religions concerning climate and development policies: the idea of inter-generational justice and the 'option for the poor' (a similar religious idea is 'eco-justice', cf. Deane-Drummond, 2004). First, intergenerational justice is a central value in many religious traditions all over the world, guiding believers to take care of their children and future generations because they are also loved by God. From this perspective, intergenerational justice functions as a convincing reason for climate protection. Second, solidarity with poor people is another important value in almost all religious traditions. Under the principle of solidarity, religious people might focus especially on the social impacts of climate change on poor people in the south. Climate change impacts could be spelled out as human rights violations, as was done by the Human Rights Council of the United Nations in 2008, which stated that it was 'concerned that climate change poses an immediate and far-reaching threat to people and communities around the world and has implications for the full enjoyment of human rights' (Human Rights Council, 2008). Religions emphasize these impacts because they have a negative influence on the living standard of poor people. The advantage of religions (especially the major world religions) is their focus on social impacts on people worldwide.

> They stand up for an integral development of the whole person and of all mankind. Likewise, you find the idea of human solidarity and compassion with and support for the plight of needy people, especially the poor in all religious heritages.
>
> (Müller, 2007b, p. 202)

This moral orientation of religions is related to both the individual and the institutional level (cf. Müller and Reder, 2009). First, a moral orientation provides ethical arguments for a political design of global processes. Religious leaders and organizations can participate in these discussions about globalization as they reflect on ethical aspects of global processes and institutions. Second, religious values such as intergenerational justice or the option for the poor could guide personal ways of living. An emphasis on the close binding between humans and god(s), religions tend to be supportive of lifestyles that ensure the well-being of all humans. Religious people are asked to take such values into account as they live their own lives. For example, religions draw attention to the need for respect of the environment in the individual's choice of life and consumption style (Gardner, 2010, p. 25). Religious citizens are asked to choose a lifestyle that goes along with the religious interpretations of humans and creation.

The social teachings of the Catholic Church are an example of a religion's ethical justification for both poverty reduction and climate protection. Personality, solidarity and subsidiarity are the main principles of the social doctrine, which forms the ethical basis for the option for the poor.

> The *priority option for the poor*, the weak, the disadvantaged and the excluded . . . forms an essential nucleus of the Christian faith. This is why the Church – in light of the denied or threatened justice – stands up in solidarity for God's creation and for the victims of climate change, especially the poor, the old, the sick, children, the unborn and the coming generations . . . and supports their interests in public negotiations.
>
> (German Bishops' Commission for Society and Social Affairs and Commission for International Church Affairs, 2006, no. 40)

The consequence of the idea that humans are images of God is that all have equal dignity. The love of God is transferred into the call for solidarity. The option for the poor is an obligation of solidarity. 'The normative key criteria from a Christian perspective are *the dignity of the human being* as the image of God . . . and the (graded) *intrinsic value of creation*'. (German Bishops' Commission for Society and Social Affairs and Commission for International Church Affairs, 2006, no. 35) Therefore, Christian believers are asked to see the image of God in all fellow beings and to engage actively in social processes to show solidarity with them. Climate protection is an important test for this attitude. Because the world/earth is God's creation, it is worth protecting and not simply to be used as a resource.

This moral orientation of religions could be criticized from two perspectives: First, historically, religion has been a source of injustice, violence and inhumanity – not only a source of justice, peace and human rights. This applies to all the great religious traditions, including Christianity, Islam and Buddhism. In that way, the sources for motivation, which are founded in the reference to the transcendent dimension of reality, were and still are being exploited in some regions (cf. Müller and Reder, 2009). The main roots of this ambiguity will presumably not be found in the religions themselves. Political, economic and social conditions are always other important influences. Religions have often been exploited to improve the social conditions of particular groups or to strengthen a political order in favour of such groups. Nevertheless, religions and religious beliefs themselves contribute to this dichotomy. This is most obvious in internal religious conflicts, such as the wars between Catholics and Protestants in the sixteenth and seventeenth centuries. Hence, the ambiguity of religions is also a characteristic from an internal point of view. But this is no reason to disregard general religious values in public discourses.

Secondly, some authors tend to focus too much on the moral function of religions. The moral implications are important, of course, but they are always rooted in the worldview or metaphysics of the respective religion, which is reinterpreted in different times and contexts. Therefore, religions are multidimensional phenomena. It is not convincing to reduce them to one (e.g. a moral) function. If we take note of the continuous process of change in religions, we can see that religions have various functions for different groups and that these functions also change throughout history (e.g. the Indonesian history and the dynamic process between the Javanese and the Islamic tradition with their different religious functions; cf. Magnis-Suseno, 1981; see also the contribution of Frömming and Reichel in this book). These other functions (e.g. cultural functions) are also important in their understanding of, and advocacy for, justice. This aspect leads to the next step: religion as a comprehensive worldview.

Religions Imply Specific Interpretations of Reality

As has been shown above, the moral values of religions – one of their important functions – are rooted in more general worldviews. These world-views could serve as a basis for people to be aware of the impacts of climate change. As Gardner pointed out, the idea of 'sacred ground' plays an important role in almost all religions (Gardner, 2006, pp. 67ff.). Both the interpretation of nature as God's creation in the Christian and Jewish traditions and the idea of man as the caliph of God in the Islamic tradition are examples of this. From that perspective, it is obvious that religions shape worldviews and could influence the way in which global problems are interpreted. Not only world religions but also natural religions and their spirituality are important in such processes. 'Indigenous peoples, drawing on an intimate and reciprocal relationship with nature, help people of all cultures to reconnect, often in a spiritual way, with the natural world that supports all human activity' (Gardner, 2010, p. 24).

Liberals such as Rawls or Rorty argue that worldviews like these are only private and not reasonable in a secular way (cf. Rorty, 1994). Very often, religious beliefs are seen as non-rational decisions, which imply a strong separation of faith and reason. Authors such as Habermas stress that we have to distinguish clearly between faith and reason (Habermas, 2010). But to be religious means to think about transcendence in an understandable and reasonable way. Religions cannot objectify God or transcendence. But the worldviews that are connected to the idea of transcendence are reasonable for religious people. Therefore, it does not make sense to separate faith and reason in a distinct way. From that perspective, religions are in fact reasonable cultural practices.

This way of understanding religions has various consequences for the inter-religious dialogue about climate change and its social impacts. Inter-religious and intercultural dialogue about worldviews could help to strengthen religious activities concerning climate protection and the fight against poverty. The aim of such dialogues is to facilitate an exchange between different worldviews concerning the impacts of climate change. These concrete dialogues are based on common cultural practices. Inter-religious dialogue is most successful when people share everyday life in the form of such cultural practices. The 'dialogue of action' primarily takes place locally, at the grassroots level, as can be seen in development processes. 'The main aim of such "inter-religious development co-operation" in a broader sense is human development and fight against poverty' (Müller, 2007b, p. 201).

Two examples might be helpful to demonstrate the function of cultural and religious worldviews in addressing global challenges. In the project 'Climate Change and Justice' (www.climate-and-justice.de), the Potsdam Institute for Climate Impact Research, the Institute for Social and Development Studies at the Munich School of Philosophy, the Munich Re Foundation and Misereor analysed the interactions between the mitigation of dangerous climate change and the reduction of worldwide poverty (Edenhofer et al., 2010). The crucial political question of the project was how to organize a fair burden sharing with respect to climate protection in the context of a global agreement for climate and development policy. The dangerous impacts of climate change for poor people were an important focus of the analysis. From an ethical point of view, questions of justice were dominant (Wallacher and Reder, 2008).Dialogue with representatives of different cultures about climate impacts and adaptation played an important role in the project.

Additionally, in the autumn of 2009, a dialogue forum entitled 'Climate Change and the Religions in Indonesia' was held in Yogyakarta. The aim of the forum was to discuss concrete environmental projects with climate policy relevance and to explore possibilities for cooperation between Muslims and Christians in terms of climate policy. All participants agreed that religion plays an important role in this particular field. In his presentation, the rector of the State Islamic University in Yogyakarta pointed out the moral resources of religions concerning the social impacts of climate change. In his view, both Christianity and Islam offer theologically similar arguments for a strong ethical commitment to climate and development policy. Therefore, he argued further, it is important to not get caught up in theological discussions, but to build on common ground to engage society. The Archbishop of Semarang supported this point of view explicitly.

On that basis, the participants began to form interfaith alliances on various climate and development issues. A number of concrete programmes were initiated to support these issues (e.g. in education). These programmes will be developed further in an inter-religious direction. Going forward, both Christian and Islamic schools and universities will offer environmental education programmes.

Religions as Social Capital in the Context of Climate Change and Development

The third important aspect of how religions can influence climate change and poverty is as a provider of social capital. This term describes norms, mentalities, social relations and networks that promote cooperative behaviour and solidarity in a society.

'The core of this is formed by the norms of mutual relations (behavioural reciprocity) which support trust and therefore citizens' willingness to join forces in mutually coordinated ways to benefit the personal interests of the partners involved, such as increasing the general welfare of society' (German Bishops' Conference Research Group on the Universal Tasks of the Church, 2001, p. 11).

Three different forms of social capital can be distinguished: Social ties in the form of family or friends (bonding social capital); social networks between various communities (bridging social capital); and relations between individuals, social groups and institutions (linking social capital) (Wallacher, 2001).

With their close value-related and social ties, religions can both be a provider as well as a representative of social capital. Their social capital is based on religious values and worldviews. From that perspective, religions could play an important role both on the micro- and meso-level to strengthen cooperative processes. Thus, religions are regarded as actors in civil society today.

> Religious groups have become active in direct political activity on behalf of the environment as well. Sometimes advocacy is motivated by a deep concern for the integrity of the natural environment. Other times it is a response to the religious imperative to advocate for justice.
>
> (Gardner, 2006, p. 81)

An important reason for the political influence of religions (understood as social capital) is the fact that they have many followers worldwide: 'Roughly 85 percent of people on the planet belong to one of 100,000 or so religions, and 150 or so of these faith traditions have at least a million followers each' (Gardner, 2006, p. 49).

The main function of religions from the perspective of social capital is to build solidarity networks in order to adapt to the impacts of climate change or to strengthen the ability of the poor to act. The exchange of knowledge, money and human capital can support this. For instance, education is an important aspect of society, in which religions function as social capital and strengthen both awareness of the impacts of climate change and social justice. 'At the most basic level, religious leaders are engaged in disseminating environmental teaching through statements and declarations to the faithful and to the public at large' (Gardner, 2006, p. 72).

Religion as a provider of social capital is able to empower the local people, particularly those in developing countries who face the social impacts of climate change. But religious communities can also be political actors on the national and international level by, for example, protecting the rights and interests of the poor. In addition, many partnerships between municipalities and communities in the north and south, which are often far away from each other, could support this public engagement.

As environmental problems are global, the solutions must be global. At the same time ethical principles such as solidarity can guide political action on the local level. The churches have a special obligation and common opportunity because they are present at all levels.
        (Umweltbeauftragte der Europäischen Bischofskonferenzen, 2004)

Religions are more and more aware of their social and political power in relation to climate change and empowering the poor. To strengthen this competence, they have started various cooperative efforts with different non-governmental organizations all over the world. 'These partnerships tend to work best when religious groups are seen as full partners, and when groups appreciate the unique perspective – and unique value – that religious groups bring to the table' (Gardner, 2006, p. 52).

Conclusion

Liberals such as Rawls or Rorty tend to reduce religions to the private sphere. And religions certainly do provide a foundation for individual ways of life. But this approach to religion and its role in society is far from sufficient and, indeed, misleading. The embedded interrelation between the secularization, privatization and de-politicization of religion is not a causal one, as sociologist José Casanova, among others, underscores (Casanova, 2010). Religions function as social actors; they play an important role not only in the private but also in the public sphere, providing social capital and moral background or functioning as cultural actors. They could help prevent modern societies from losing their bearings in these areas.

Therefore, religions should be integrated and taken seriously in public debate. As actors in the global civil society, religions also participate in the public debate surrounding climate change and development (Bergmann and Gerten, 2010). They thus manage to create an awareness among their members (and often far beyond) of related problems and to develop suggestions for political solutions. Of course, religions represent ambivalent phenomena. Sometimes they tend to support injustice rather than justice. But this is no reason to reduce them to the private sphere, rather it is an even stronger reason to include them in the public discourse over our common future.

In sum, moral values and political solutions are not (only) accepted for abstract reasons but because they are incorporated in common beliefs, which motivate citizens to engage in social discourses and political processes. This is also the case concerning climate and development policy strategies. Political programmes will only be effective if people integrate climate issues into their own cultural and religious practices. In this way, religions provide an important foundation that is crucial for the success of mitigation and adaptation policies.

Note

[1] Of course, the term 'religion' is a quite modern invention and emerged from the Western tradition, as Jacques Derrida has pointed out clearly (cf. Derrida et al., 1998). Nevertheless, it is used today in almost all regions of the world to express and reflect the transcendent dimension of reality.

References

Bergmann, S. and Gerten, D. (eds) (2010), *Religion and Dangerous Environmental Change: Transdisciplinary Perspectives on the Ethics of Climate and Sustainability.* Studies in Religion and the Environment, Vol. 2. Münster: LIT.

Bulhof, I. N. (ed.) (2000), *Flight of the Gods. Philosophical Perspectives on Negative Theology.* New York: Fordham University Press.

Casanova, K. (2010), 'Religion in modernity as global challenge', in M. Reder and M. Rugel (eds), *Religion und die Umstrittene Moderne.* Stuttgart: Kohlhammer, pp. 1–16.

Deane-Drummond, C. (2004), *The Ethics of Nature.* Malden: Blackwell.

Derrida, J. and Vattimo, G. (1998), *Religion. Cultural Memory in the Present.* Stanford: Stanford University Press.

Dobbelaere, K. (2002), *Secularization. An Analysis at Three Levels.* Brussels: Peter Lang.

Edenhofer, O., Wallacher, J., Reder, M. and Lotze-Campen, H. (eds) (2010), *Global aber gerecht: Klimawandel bekämpfen, Entwicklung ermöglichen.* München: C. H. Beck.

Gardner G. T. (2003), 'Engaging religion in the quest for a sustainable world', in Worldwatch Institute (ed.), *State of the World 2003.* New York: W. W. Norton & Company, pp. 152–175.

— (2006), *Inspiring Progress. Religions' Contributions to Sustainable Development.* Washington: Worldwatch Institute.

— (2010), 'Engaging religions to shape worldviews', in Worldwatch Institute (ed.), *State of the World 2010: Transforming Cultures from Consumerism to Sustainability.* New York: W. W. Norton & Company, pp. 23–29.

Geertz, C. (1966), *Religion as a Cultural System. Anthropological Approaches to the Study of Religion*, M. Banton (ed.). New York: Praeger, pp. 1–46.

German Bishops' Commission for Society and Social Affairs and Commission for International Church Affairs (eds) (2006), *Climate Change – A Focal Point of Global, Intergenerational and Ecological Justice.* Bonn: Secretariat of the German Bishops' Conference.

German Bishops' Conference Research Group on the Universal Tasks of the Church (ed.) (2001), *Social Capital. One Element in the Battle against the Poverty of Societies.* Bonn: Research Group on the Universal Tasks of the Church.

Habermas, J. (1984–1987), *The Theory of Communicative Action.* Cambridge: Polity Press.

— (2008), *Between Naturalism and Religion.* Cambridge: Polity Press.

— (2010), 'An awareness of what is missing', in M. Reder and J. Schmidt (eds), *An Awareness of What is Missing. Faith and Reason in a Post-secular Age.* Cambridge: Polity Press, pp. 15–23.

Habermas, J. and Ratzinger, J. (2007), *The Dialectics of Secularization: On Reason and Religion.* Ignatius Press: San Francisco.

Honneth, A. (2004), 'Gerechtigkeit und kommunikative Freiheit. Überlegungen im Anschluss an Hegel', in B. Merker, G. Mohr and M. Quante (eds), *Subjektivität und Anerkennung.* Paderborn: Mentis, pp. 213–227.

Human Rights Council (ed.) (2008), *Human Rights and Climate Change (Resolution 7/23).* http://ap.ohchr.org/documents/E/HRC/resolutions/A_HRC_RES_7_23. pdf .

Magnis-Suseno, F. (1981), *Javanische Weisheit und Ethik. Studien zu einer östlichen Moral.* München: Oldenbourg.

Martin, D. (2005), *On Secularization. Towards a Revised General Theory.* Aldershot: Ashgate.

Meyer, T. (1995), 'Fundamentalismus und Universalismus in Moral und Politik', in W. Kerber (ed.), *Religion: Grundlage oder Hindernis des Friedens?* München: Kindt, pp. 165–183.

Müller, J. (2007a), 'Religionen – Quelle von Gewalt oder Anwalt der Menschen? Überlegungen zu den Ursachen der Ambivalenz von Religionen', in J. Müller, M. Reder and T. Karcher (eds), *Religionen und Globalisierung.* Stuttgart: Kohlhammer, pp. 119–137.

— (2007b), 'Interreligious cooperation for human development', in J. Müller and M. Reder (eds), *Africa and Europe.* Münster: LIT, pp. 198–203.

Müller, J. and Reder, M. (2009), 'Religions and global justice. Reflections from an inter-cultural and inter-religious perspective', in M. Schramm (ed.), *Absolute Poverty and Global Justice. Empirical Data – Moral Theories – Initiatives.* Aldershot: Ashgate, pp. 91–99.

Nicholas of Cusa (2002), *Vom Frieden zwischen den Religionen.* Frankfurt am Main: Insel.

Pollack, D. (2003), *Säkularisierung – ein moderner Mythos? Studien zum religiösen Wandel in Deutschland*. Tübingen: Mohr Siebeck.

Rawls, J. (1971), *A Theory of Justice*. Cambridge, MA: Belknap Press.

Reder, M. (2009a), 'Menschenrechte als ethische Grundlage der Klimapolitik. Ein Beitrag der politischen Philosophie'. *GAIA*, 4, 315–323.

— (2009b), 'Religion als kulturelle Praxis an der Grenze zwischen Glauben und Wissen. Anregungen von F. Schleiermacher und J. Derrida', in K. Wenzel and T. N. Schmidt (eds), *Moderne Religion? Theologische und religionsphilosophische Reaktionen auf Jürgen Habermas*. Freiburg: Herder, pp. 128–152.

Reder, M. and Schmidt, J. (2010), 'Habermas and religion', M. Reder and J. Schmidt (eds), *An Awareness of What is Missing. Faith and Reason in a Post-secular Age*. Cambridge: Polity Press, pp. 1–14.

Rorty, R. (1994), 'Religion as conversation stopper'. *Common Knowledge*, 3/1, 1–6.

Rorty, R. and Vattimo, G. (2005), in S. Zabala (ed.), *The Future of Religion*. Columbia: University Press.

Schleiermacher, F. (1799/1984), 'Über die Religion', in G. Meckenstock (ed.), *F. Schleiermacher, Kritische Gesamtausgabe Bd. I/2*. Berlin and New York: De Gruyter, pp. 185–326.

Stegemann, W. (ed.) (2003), *Religion und Kultur. Aufbruch in eine neue Beziehung*. Stuttgart: Kohlhammer.

Umweltbeauftragte der europäischen Bischofskonferenzen (2004), Ergebnisse der sechsten Konsultation der Umweltbeauftragten der europäischen Bischofskonferenzen zu 'Gemeinsame Schöpfungsverantwortung der Kirchen und Religionen'. Namur: Consilium Conferentiarum Episcoporum Europae (CCEE).

Wallacher, J. (2001), 'Das soziale Kapital'. *Stimmen der Zeit*, 219/5, 306–318.

Wallacher, J. and Reder, M. (2008), 'Principles of justice. Climate negotiations need a precise ethical concept'. *Welt-Sichten*, 5, 14–15.

Walzer, M. (1994), *Thick and Thin. Moral Argument at Home and Abroad*. Notre Dame: University of Notre Dame Press.

Chapter 4

Contemplating Climategate: Religion and the Future of Climate Research

Timothy Leduc

Introduction

On 8 December 2008, the front page of the *New York Times* displayed an image that symbolizes for me the role religion can play in climate change. The full-colour picture showed an altar of a Pentecostal Christian congregation in Detroit, Michigan, and upon it was a choir, a young girl in ritual dance and two large white American-made sport utility vehicles (SUVs). At the time, the 2008 economic crisis was hitting America's car culture hard; the caption read 'Praying to Save the Auto Industry'.[1] This image raises critiques like that of Lynn White, Jr (1967) on the Judaeo-Christian roots of modern society's unsustainable relation with the planet. Many researchers have since clarified that White's seminal analysis may have been too broad and general in application, though not totally flawed (e.g. Scharper, 1997; Gardner, 2003). In the 2003 *State of the World Report*, Gary Gardner drew upon White and various other researchers of religion and ecology to argue that religious motivations not only underlie the contemporary environmental crisis, but also have much to contribute to a sustainable response. Highlighting research that indicates 83 per cent of the world's population adheres to some spiritual tradition, Gardner states, 'A sustainable world cannot effectively be built without full engagement of the human spirit' (Gardner, 2003, p. 153). This is no romantic assertion, for Gardner and others clarify that world religions contain both adaptive and maladaptive potentialities (e.g. Rappaport, 1999). Though I am here concerned with the general role of religion in researching climate change, this chapter will focus on a Canadian case study – with international dimensions – that I hope broadens our sense of religion to include the more secular beliefs and practices of a fossil fuel-based culture.

Underlying the symbolic purity of those white SUVs on the Christian altar is the black oil that, over the twentieth century, fuelled North American car culture, today's global climate changes and – increasingly – also the Canadian economy. The past decade has seen Canada surpass Saudi Arabia as the largest supplier of oil to the United States, based on its development of the Alberta tar sands. Canadian Prime Minister Stephen Harper (2006) has described the investment required to convert the tar sands into crude oil as 'an enterprise of epic proportions, akin to the building of the pyramids or China's Great Wall. Only bigger'. Contrasting such an optimistic, perhaps even delusional, vision is Andrew Nikiforuk's description of tar sands as not only 'the world's dirtiest hydrocarbon' but also 'what a desperate civilization mines after it has depleted its cheap oil' (Nikiforuk, 2008, p. 16). The US Department of Energy supports such a critique, estimating that on average one barrel of oil can 'pump out anywhere between twenty and sixty barrels of cheap oil', while the same amount only yields between four and five barrels in the tar sands (Nikiforuk, 2008, p. 15). In contrast to politicians like Harper who describe these developments in positively 'epic' terms, Nikiforuk argues that the tar sands endeavour 'distracts North Americans from two stark realities: we are running out of cheap oil, and seventeen million North Americans run their cars on [it]' (2008, p. 16). In other words, fossil fuel-based practices are deeply influencing the beliefs of North Americans and their capacity to make a balanced assessment our climatic situation. This is what I think is symbolized so poignantly in the Christian-SUV ritual of that *New York Times* image.

In this chapter, I make the case that the ability of climate change deniers to continue undermining climate research (the Intergovernmental Panel on Climate Change (IPCC) specifically) and climate policy is related to the contemporary hold fossil fuel life-ways have on our minds, hearts and bodies. I will do this by first offering a Canadian view on the role of fossil fuels in the recent Climategate controversy and Canada's limited political response to climate change, as represented at the 2009 Copenhagen Climate Conference. This social uncertainty that surrounds climate research and policy discussions will then be contemplated from the perspective of Anne Primavesi's Gaian theology. My goal is to highlight the importance of more fully incorporating religious considerations in a post-Climategate research initiative.

Friends of Climate Research?

In the month prior to the 2009 Copenhagen Climate Conference, the Canadian media became enamoured with a Climategate story that was tied to stolen emails from the University of East Anglia's Climate Research Unit in the United Kingdom – a major source of IPCC research. Based on some correspondence that at first glance suggested researchers were obscuring problematic data, sceptics of climate research claimed the IPCC was exerting too much global political influence. Just prior to the Climategate story, one could also hear on Canadian radio an ad by 'The Friends of Science' denouncing climate research and calling on the Canadian government to show policy restraint at the Copenhagen meeting. The ad asserted it would be irrational for Canada to make any policy changes in a time of economic uncertainty, especially when evidence suggests there has been no warming since 1998. This debatable 'no warming' story – one which we will return to later – coalesced with Climategate in suggesting to Canadians that climate change was more fiction than fact. It should be noted that The Friends of Science is a Canadian group which largely consists of oil geologists, Conservative government insiders and oil industry professionals (Montgomery, 2006). By taking a closer look at the role of fossil fuels in these social uncertainties, we can begin to get a sense of why cultural and religious perspectives may be so vital to the future of climate research.

Back in 2001, David Demeritt offered a penetrating analysis of climate debates that in many ways foretold the difficulties of Climategate. He was concerned that the IPCC's effort to win political trust by focusing on scientific facts and certainty may in the end increase public uncertainty because it will, in his words, 'invite political opponents to conduct politics by waging war on the underlying science (and scientists!)' (Demeritt, 2001, p. 328). As supporters of the IPCC have noted in relation to Climategate, the stolen emails have been blown out of proportion; in reality, they only raise questions 'about one or two lines of evidence out of several hundred lines of evidence which show that man-made climate change is taking place' (Monbiot, 2009; Suzuki and Moola, 2009). Demeritt's analysis points out that, because 'the leading cause of increasing GHG concentrations is fossil fuel consumption', it is not surprising that climate research and politics has been 'closely intertwined with the politics of energy and the policies of development' (Demeritt, 2001, p. 308). He rightly points out that such fossil fuel-based scepticism has been a prominent feature of the American climate-change debate. These influences were highlighted in a 2004 report by the 'Union of Concerned Scientists' that found the 'misrepresentation of science by the Bush administration is unprecedented', pointing to evidence that the administration watered down the domestic 2003 *State of the Environment* report, limited the scope and validity of the *Arctic Climate Impact Assessment* and actively discredited the IPCC's research – and thus the research reviewed by the IPCC (see Kennedy, 2004, p. 95). This scepticism also had a small contingent of supporters in Canada whose influence increased with the 2006 election of Prime Minister Harper.

A few months following the Conservative victory, the denial critique of climate change was presented to Canadians in a national newspaper in the form of an open letter to the prime minister signed by 60 researchers from The Friends of Science (National Post, 2006). The letter expressed concern about the way in which inconclusive climate research had led Canada's preceding Liberal government to ratify the Kyoto Protocol and related policies that squandered billions of dollars. While the Republican administration of George W. Bush actively used public uncertainty to confront climate research during its 8 years of power, Canada's previous 12 years of Liberal government meant that, even if Prime Minister Harper wanted to, mainstream science could not be totally dismissed. In this context, the cultivation of public uncertainty concerning climate research fell on the shoulders of non-governmental organizations like The Friends of Science. They had lots to work with, as a 2006 poll reflected that four out of ten Canadians attributed climate change 'to natural warming and cooling patterns rather than human influences' (Montgomery, 2006).

Drawing upon the climate's complex uncertainties, the signatories to the newspaper letter argued not only that it 'may be years yet before we properly understand the Earth's climate system' but that if the international community knew in the mid-1990s what is known now, Kyoto would have been seen as unnecessary (National Post, 2006). Referencing the climate science debate of the 1970s, they reminded the prime minister and Canadians that only 30 years ago 'many of today's global warming alarmists were telling us that the world was in the midst of a global-cooling catastrophe'. Interestingly, of the 60 scientists that signed the open letter, only one-third were Canadian and many were economists and geologists who had 'received money from the oil, gas and coal industries in the United States' to conduct their research (Montgomery, 2006). Supporting this point, Demeritt writes that many sceptical critiques of the IPCC have been largely 'paid [for] by the fossil fuel industry' (Demeritt, 2001, p. 328). One of the Canadian signatories promoted by The Friends of Science was climate scientist Timothy Ball (Montgomery, 2006). In a cross-country speaking tour to governmental representatives and newspaper editorial boards,

Ball argued that 'Environment Canada and other agencies fabricated the climate change scare in order to attract funding' (Montgomery, 2006). These presentations neither revealed The Friends of Science as a funding source, nor mentioned that Ball had not published a climate research paper in a decade and a half. It is a point consistent with Spencer Weart's finding that the research critics of the IPCC often tout is generally so limited as to be unacceptable to 'peer-reviewed journals where every statement was reviewed by other scientists' (Weart, 2003, p. 166).

Writing about the pre-Copenhagen Climategate and 'no warming' stories, editorialist Rex Murphy (2009) of the Canadian Broadcasting Company and a national newspaper presented The Friends of Science view to the public when he wrote that the BBC – which had broken the 'no warming' story – 'is not the only voice showing sprigs and shoots of independent thinking on global warming', and then offered Ross McKitrick as another 'mind outside the herd'. Back in 2001, this economist and signatory to the open letter wrote a popular non-academic book on climate change with applied mathematician Christopher Essex, another signatory. The book argued the IPCC and Environment Canada were creating a 'convection of certainty' to support ratifying the Kyoto Protocol (Essex and McKitrick, 2002, p. 231). While conceding it may eventually be proven that humans are affecting the climate, they conclude – as did the open letter – that politicization is undermining climate research and that this represents a 'loss of nerve' in economic rationality. The writings of McKitrick continued to stir up debate in the United States when his critique of the iconic 'hockey stick' diagram – an image of rising average northern hemisphere temperatures that supported the IPCC's claim of a human climate influence – was considered by the Republican-led House Energy and Commerce Committee (see Demeritt, 2006 for review of debate). The deniers of human climate influence have received media and governmental attention because, as Demeritt writes, their views 'have been greatly amplified by the deep pockets of multinationals with vested interests in the consumption of fossil fuels' (Demeritt, 2006, p. 453). I would go one step further and suggest that this mindset resonates with historically deep American and Canadian practices, one important reason why The Friends of Science can continue to fuel public uncertainty about climate research and policy.

The predisposition of Canadian political economics towards a resourcist economy is a significant cultural tradition which, it can be argued, underlies my nation's approach to the tar sands and climate change. It was the eminent Canadian economic theorist Harold Innis who first clearly articulated the extent to which Canada's political economy is shaped by our colonial approach to the land's resources. From the seventeenth-century fisheries and fur trade to the time of his writing in the mid-twentieth century, he found that cheap and accessible 'water transportation favoured the rapid exploitation of staples and dependence on more highly industrialized countries for finished products' (Innis, 1995, p. 135) – first France, then Britain and now the United States. From its colonial beginnings, Canada has approached 'the environment as an infinite supply of resources and a bottomless sink for wastes', with the most difficult problem considered humans' limitations to utilizing the land's abundant resources (Hessing et al., 2005, p. 16). It was only in the 1960s that this frontier economics approach became more concerned about 'the destruction of the environment' as awareness about the relation between environmental issues and a sevenfold growth in Canada's resource-based economy – not to mention global consumption patterns – forced a deeper consideration of regulatory options (Hessing et al., 2005, p. 16). Despite this rising concern, the Canadian environmental response had limited success even prior to the election of Prime Minister Harper's Conservatives in 2006.

While Canada's preceding Liberal government actively pursued international leadership in sustainability through actions like ratifying the Kyoto Protocol, Anthony Perl and Eugene Lee explain the nation actually continued reaping the 'rewards of ever-closer economic integration with the United States' (2003, p. 253). The mismatch of a growing fossil fuel industry and largely voluntary climate policies made it impossible for the Liberals to even approach Canada's Kyoto commitments, as evidenced in the fact that Canadian emissions in 2005 had increased by 24 per cent in comparison with the 13 per cent increase by the United States – a nation that had not ratified the Kyoto Protocol. A few years prior to Liberal electoral defeat, Canada was given an international environmental ranking that was 'second worst among twenty-eight Organisation for Economic Cooperation and Development member nations, followed only by the United States' (Lee and Perl, 2003, p. 23). With the election of Prime Minister Harper's Conservatives Canada's unsustainable frontier economy tendencies have accelerated. This is symbolized in tar sands developments that produce oil which not only releases 2.5 times more emissions than conventional reserves but also require companies to 'mow down hundreds of trees, roll up acres of soil, drain wetlands, dig up four tons of earth to secure two tons of bituminous sand, and then give those two tons a hot wash' (Nikiforuk, 2008, p. 13). It is in this frontier economic context that Canada's environment minister re-announced at the Copenhagen Conference the Conservative government's half-hearted proposal of a

20 per cent reduction in greenhouse gases below 2006 levels by 2020 – a pledge that means Canada will at best meet its Kyoto commitments well after 2020. Even more significantly, Canada proposed giving special treatment to the tar sands so as not to hamper economic development.

This powerful frontier economy influence is not confined to Canadian politics and climate sceptics like The Friends of Science for conservationist John Livingston (2007) argues the failure of Canadian environmentalism over the twentieth century has cultural roots as well. While Canada's political-economic tendencies have impacted the nation's environmental record, Livingston observed that environmental initiatives were also being compromised by the public's embrace of frontier economic ideas like stewardship, sustainable harvest and wise-use – all of which define ecology as a 'human asset' (Livingston, 2007, p. 166). These tendencies continue today as the National Sciences and Engineering Research Council – the main source for Canadian research funding – increasingly requires matching grants from industry and commercial interests, an approach that raises concerns about the capacity of academics 'to examine the consequences of new technologies openly and critically' (Bocking, 2004, p. 198). It was announced in 2009 that even funding for social science and humanities research will be preferentially given to those with business-related degrees. Such trends are reflective of Demeritt's (2001) survey of leftist critiques that suggest the demand for international and national policy relevance has subtly influenced the IPCC and climate research generally. As he later states, 'Climate change shows the difficulties of distinguishing strictly scientific questions for experts alone to decide from associated value-laden and often politicised matters of concern for the lay public to debate' (Demeritt, 2006, p. 474). This is a more nuanced critique than the whole-sale rejection of climate research epitomized in the approach taken by The Friends of Science and the Climategate debate. In Canada, the historic grounding of the population, including politicians and academics, in a frontier economy can be seen as defining cultural practices and beliefs which fuel debates that are limiting climate research and policy responses.

While documenting Canada's frontier economy, Innis began expressing concern about the potential influence of industrialism on our cultural ways of thinking. In his words, Canadian culture and education was being 'disciplined by the spread of machine industry' (Innis, 1995, p. 473). Raising similar concerns as Livingston, Innis observed signs of a narrowing 'mechanisation of knowledge' in academia's skewed preference for factual information, classification strategies and increasing professionalization (1995, p. 475). Canadian engineer and peace activist Ursula Franklin

(1999) subsequently provided a more detailed outline of this industrial concern. She began by discriminating between holistic technologies which are associated with forms of craft work that allow people to be involved in the creative process from inception to final product, and prescriptive technologies which require people be involved in only one element of a production process that coordinates many people. These latter technologies have proliferated since the industrial revolution and have given us 'a wealth of important products that have raised living standards and increased well-being' (Franklin, 1999, p. 19). What concerns her is that this technological power has also 'created a culture of compliance' that mechanizes our knowledge right down to the way we are educated (Franklin, 1999, p. 19). As she states, even though we 'know that a person's growth in knowledge proceeds at an individual rate, schools and universities operate according to a production model' that turns out students with a narrow and increasingly professionalized expertise (Franklin, 1999, p. 23). Left out is a broader sense of the context to which this technical knowledge is being applied, as well as a holistic experience that could raise critical questions about the place of technology in a sustainable response to climate and environmental changes. In the present context, we could say technology drives Canadians away from questions about a frontier economy increasingly propelled by the tar sands and a government focused on carbon sequestration as a climate change response.

The environmental and climatic implications of Franklin's research have been clarified by her engineering colleague, Willem Vanderburg (2005), who characterizes our environmental crisis as a mismatch between proliferating expert technological know-how and an interconnected ecological reality. Prior to the Industrial Revolution, Vanderburg argues, cultural tradition and ecological experience offered a diversity of ways for contextualizing knowledge. The ensuing century and a half has seen knowledge become dominated by 'information that is decontextualised from culture-based connectedness and recontextualised in relation to technique-based connectedness' – that is, knowledge which can manipulate the environment for political-economic benefits (Vanderburg, 2005, p. 377). As does Franklin, he identifies today's great danger as the capacity for technical knowledge to alter 'our consciousness so as to make us almost unaware of our condition' and thus weaken critical cultural insights which could help us 'escape from it' (Vanderburg, 2005, p. 421). This difficulty extends into almost every facet of life, as Toronto urban ecologist Michael Hough clarifies when he writes that urban roadways 'structure the experience of the environment and separate us physically and in time from the world through which we pass' – thus impacting both the ecological integrity of these places and our conscious relation with them (Hough, 1995, p. 101). Using similar automotive imagery, Vanderburg compares modern society to an individual who has decided to drive 'a car by concentrating on its performance as indicated by the instruments on the dashboard as opposed to watching the road' (2005, pp. 307–308). Such perceptual tunnel vision may not only partially explain Canada's ineffective climate response, but also the paradox of the Copenhagen Conference – ostensibly focused on climate change – requiring the shipment of 1200 limousines from neighbouring nations for dignitaries and having over 140 private jets parked in the airport. The thought of Vanderburg, Franklin and Innis suggest such contradictions are due to the fact that industrial technologies are not simply tools, but powerful organizers of human relations that can create beliefs and dependencies which limit the larger vision required for considering a sustainable response.

The promotion of climatic uncertainty by groups like The Friends of Science may appeal to people not only because no one wants to think their personal, familial, national and cultural behaviours are undermining their children's future but also because our cultural practices make it difficult to recognize those deep-seated beliefs which resonate with their ads. This difficulty with practice-based beliefs goes far beyond sceptics denying climate research or a populace assured by such arguments, for, as Demeritt (2001) points out, climate research has taken another extreme position that denies any social influence in its findings. He states that the main reason for this denial is that any disclosure of social relations informing science 'has become grounds for discrediting both that knowledge and any public policy decisions based upon it' (Demeritt, 2001, p. 309). Such a position runs counter to both fossil fuel-informed sceptics and leftist critics of the IPCC who suggest 'the demand for and expectation of policy relevance has subtly shaped the formulation of research questions, choice of methods, standards of proof, and the definition of other aspects of "good" scientific practice' (Demeritt, 2001, p. 308; also see Hallman, 2000; Leduc, 2010). If there is a silver lining to Climategate, it may be based in the need to formulate a response to such absurd denials. Professor Hulme, one of the non-implicated climate researchers from East Anglia's Climate Research Unit, similarly proposes that a response to the political compromise of climate research requires making raw data 'available to everyone, including climate-change sceptics' (see Saunders, 2009). This sounds remarkably similar to Demeritt's view that the black-and-white debates between climate sceptics and researchers need to be replaced with 'a more reflexive understanding of science as a social practice' (Demeritt, 2001, p. 329). More transparency so that climate research can be less ideological and properly contextualized in a broader social dialogue is perhaps the future of climate research.

There are clearly difficulties with the IPCC process, but – like Demeritt – I am of the view that its interdisciplinary and international networking effort is to date the most effective climate research response. Despite the IPCC's great coordination of physical science and economic adaptation research, its effort has not yet considered the complementary value of the world's diverse cultural and religious perspectives on climate change. This is partly due to the way in which IPCC decision-making has structurally depended upon nation-states, and to the fact that the cultural and religious dimensions of climate change have not been coordinated in as comprehensive a manner as the IPCC's science and policy. In Gardner's (2003) *State of the World* analysis, he argues that one of the pivotal blocks to enacting such a broad environmental response has been the West's historic separation of irrational religion from rational scientific research following the Enlightenment. It may not even be unreasonable to suggest the IPCC's denial of social influences is rooted in the modern view of science as a rationally verifiable endeavour – one that differentiated it from the West's preceding Christian worldview. In much the same spirit as Gardner, I argue that enlightened beliefs continue to limit our appreciation of how contemporary religious perspectives can broaden international climate research. By contemplating one Christian perspective on climate research, I will now offer a religious view on the social issues highlighted by Demeritt, the recent Climategate controversy and Canada's fossilized frontier history.

From Frontier Resources to Gaian Gifts

In her recent book *Gaia and Climate Change*, ecotheologian Anne Primavesi suggests, as in White's previously discussed analysis, that Christian beliefs have played some role in today's climate changes. The analysis of White had proposed that our environmental issues are historically grounded in Christianity's marginalization of the pagan view of the world as spiritually animated. He characterized this mental change as the greatest psychic revolution in Western history because it 'not only established a dualism of man and nature but also insisted that it is God's will that man exploit nature for his proper ends' (White, 1967, p. 1205). Though by no means following White's argument that humans are commissioned to exploit the earth's resources, Primavesi similarly contrasts the dominant Christian view of God as transcendent 'and non-locatable in relation to the earth' with an immanent 'understanding of God as emerging from earthly knowledge and firmly situated there' (Primavesi, 2009, p. 17). Drawing upon the insights of both Gaian science and ecotheology, Primavesi describes the latter immanent approach as being absolutely pivotal if Christianity is going to offer an alternative vision that can respond to climate change. She concludes that any sustainable religious response to the present crisis will have to be based on 'a conviction that we would not, and cannot, exist without [Gaia's] gifts' (Primavesi, 2009, p. 35). These gifts are in fact the basis of Canada's frontier economy and tar sands developments, and yet the industrious nature of twenty-first-century life offers little space for considering the divine grounding of our everyday practices and those denials which support them. From such a view, climate change challenges us to transform our relation with the planet from one that is primarily focused on extracting frontier resources to one that recognizes Gaian gifts. Let's now reflect on what this religious change could mean for climate research.

The impetus for Primavesi's work is drawn from various developments in climate research that have moved our understanding of earth history towards an increasing recognition '*of our place within it*' (Primavesi, 2009, p. 10). Though she discusses the role the IPCC has played in opening space for this change of thought, the book's title reflects its indebtedness to James Lovelock's theory on a Gaian climate system that, in her words, 'binds all our lives and our fates together' (Primavesi, 2009, p. 126). The implication of such interconnectedness for climate research has also been written about by climate physicist Spencer Weart. After displaying the extent to which the IPCC has significantly increased knowledge but 'scarcely narrowed the range of uncertainty', he explains that this paradox is due to the way in which climate changes are related to rising greenhouse gases that 'depend less on geochemistry and biology than on human actions' (Weart, 2003, p. 191). He concludes that the future climate 'actually does depend in part on what we think about it', for our response is deeply intertwined with how we think about human–climate relations (Weart, 2003, p. 198). This linking of climate change to our thought is in many ways the starting point of Primavesi's book; she leads us through various inquiries on both the present impact of prevailing cultural beliefs and practices, and the potential value of religion in re-thinking our political-economic responses.

In Primavesi's previous book *Gaia's Gift*, she assesses the planet's challenge to our ways of thinking by historically interconnecting Lovelock's theory to those Copernican and Darwinian scientific revolutions that similarly required marginalizing the belief in human centrality. She writes that, despite these revolutions, 'the scientific homocentrism against which every other species was and is measured, and their relative unimportance established, went relatively unchallenged and has remained so' (Primavesi, 2003, p. 68). Ecotheologian Stephen Scharper has made a case that even Lovelock has in the past been afflicted by such scientific homocentrism – though less so in the present according to both Scharper and Primavesi. After considering Lovelock's dismissal of the ozone depletion problem in the 1980s, Scharper concluded that the theories of scientists can lead them to 'ignore data and minimise mammoth problems which belie their visions' (Scharper, 1994, p. 212). It is an issue that Lovelock himself alludes to in the foreword to Primavesi's *Sacred Gaia* when he states, 'Science has developed a dangerous tendency to be certain' (cited in Primavesi, 2000, p. xi). Beyond highlighting the cultural limits to scientific objectivity, Scharper's deeper concern is that scientific conceptions of Gaia display a severely limited appreciation of social justice issues – a point that Primavesi also makes. As Scharper states, there is next to no critique of 'existing power structures as well as historical patterns of inequality' that are the social context of today's climate changes (Scharper, 1994, p. 218). This does not mean Gaia research cannot contemplate injustices, only that an interdisciplinary project built on scientific and economic assumptions has just begun to consider how social and environmental issues interact. With a human-centered and economizing mentality continuing to block our conception of climate change, Scharper and Primavesi challenge all of us to enact a 'change of mind' that will have practical consequences for human relations with Gaia and its regional ecologies. In *Gaia and Climate Change*, Primavesi characterizes this 'new context for human history' as a 'global compass whose effects now call for change in us too', for it is the dominant mental focus on the homocentric utility of Gaian resources that is at the core of today's climate changes (2009, p. 130). Such anthropocentrism is clearly a prevalent cultural belief that underlies Canada's frontier economy, The Friends of Science view, Demeritt's constructionist critique and much climate research.

To consider the relevance of Primavesi's 'change of mind' to climate research and climate sceptics, it is worthwhile to bring her thought into dialogue with a recent scientific debate on Lovelock's Gaia theory and climate change. In 2002, the journal *Climatic Change* hosted three articles by prominent biospheric theoreticians and an editorial commentary by biological scientist Tyler Volk on the value of Gaian science for elucidating principles about the planetary climate system. The commentary by Volk is a good place to begin, not only because he analysed the dominant themes discussed in the three articles, but also because his books *Gaia's Body* (Volk, 1998) and *What is Death?* (Volk, 2002a) influenced Primavesi's thought. In looking at the papers by Axel Kleidon (2002), Timothy Lenton (2002) and James Kirchner (2002), Volk sketched out what he saw 'as tasks for the future of Gaia theory' (2002b, p. 423). Though he was sympathetic to aspects of all three papers, he agreed most with Kirchner's assessment that evidence of the climate's potentially detrimental negative feedbacks suggests 'biological effects are not necessarily stabilising' (Kirchner, 2002, p. 426). Considering the relation of rising atmospheric CO_2 to climate change, Kirchner clarified that documentation of only 'a modest increase in terrestrial photosynthetic uptake of CO_2' refutes Gaian notions of homeostasis because it reveals atmospheric CO_2 to not be tightly regulated at an optimal biological set point (Kirchner, 2002, p. 405). While Kleidon and Lenton offer evidence for a more classic conception of Gaian self-regulation, Volk opined that 'a few conforming examples drawn from the wealth of interactions within the biosphere' cannot be held up as a scientific basis for Gaia theory (2002b, p. 424). Despite rejecting aspects of the theory, he concluded that Gaia is conceptually important because it requires being 'mindful of the biggest scale' and, following Lovelock's example, asking 'big questions' (Volk, 2002b, p. 428). This leaves Volk with one concluding question that Primavesi's religious analysis helps us contemplate: 'What do we have if Gaia theory is a way of generating hypotheses and not a specific hypothesis about the way the biosphere works?' (Volk, 2002b, p. 428). In broader terms, what can a religious sensibility offer climate research?

Considering just such a question, Primavesi draws inspiration from a passage where Volk talks about the way in which oxygen came together with primordial hydrogen to create the water that 'now nourishes algae and my life' (cited in Primavesi, 2009, p. 67). As Volk watches creek water flow over his hand, he contemplates its ultimate source in a way Primavesi finds has religious implications. Far beyond the melting snow of some distant mountains are the atoms of this water which came into existence some 13 billion years ago when hydrogen, in a sense, died 'to form oxygen' and then coalesced into life (cited in Primavesi, 2003, p. 108). Of particular interest to Primavesi is Volk's assertion that to view this process whereby death nurtures life it is necessary to shift our perspective towards the larger-scale entities that encompass human living. In her words, the symbiotic nature of Gaia 'means that each being is generated with, chemically modulated through and sensitive to other modes of being, whatever, whoever and wherever they may be' (Primavesi, 2009, p. 68). Such an analysis clarifies for Primavesi that humanity is indebted to the biological beings and ecological processes of the past, as is apparent today in our inheritance of those fossilized biological beings that are the source of the tar sands and other oil deposits fuelling Gaia's changing climate. Reflecting on Primavesi's Gaian theology, Sigurd Bergmann observes that the environmentalist vision of planet–human relations that is being oriented to money accumulation, thus destroying 'relationships between organisms and their surroundings', 'stands out as a critique of civilisation of unexpectedly large proportions' (Bergmann, 2005, p. 5). This recognition of planetary interconnectedness leads Primavesi to a religious question concerning the inheritance humanity is passing on to all life forms. As Primavesi states, will our 'raised awareness of climate change' not only increase our understanding of this biological inheritance, but also make us more 'able, willing and competent to act wisely' (2009, p. 73)? It is a query not far off Volk's assertion that 'gratitude for life is the self-conscious response for dealing with the fears engendered by death' (cited in Primavesi, 2003, p. 103).

The climate change debate continued in 2003 with not only responses by Lenton and Kirchner to Volk and each other, but also a letter by Lovelock that continued asking 'big questions' that resonate with Primavesi's theological view. With the support of bioscientist David Wilkinson, Lenton responded to the critiques about Gaian self-regulation by writing that 'a combination of positive and negative feedback does not preclude regulation' as there are many examples of complex systems that regulate through a mixture of these feedbacks (Lenton and Wilkinson, 2003, p. 4). Responding to this nuanced view of Gaian regulation, Kirchner agreed that coupling the atmosphere and biosphere should result in feedbacks and emergent behaviours like self-regulation, but he worried the theory of Gaia can 'lead to a false confidence that once one accepts that biological systems are intrinsically self-regulating, understanding the Earth system is easy' (Kirchner, 2003, pp. 22, 42). In his opinion, a check against research complacency is needed because the progress in developing climate knowledge 'is still dwarfed by what we don't know' (Kirchner, 2003, p. 42). It was a view consistent with his earlier argument that we must continue to promote 'thinking mechanistically' in a world where natural selection favours life forms that most effectively exploit the planet's environmental services (Kirchner, 2002, p. 399). Lovelock's letter would critique Kirchner's proposal by comparing the complexity of Gaia's multiscalar climate system to quantum indeterminism.

To stress the importance of making this comparison, Lovelock wrote that just as '[q]uantum theory is incomprehensible because the universe itself is far stranger than the human mind can contemplate', Gaia 'is difficult to understand because we are not used to thinking about the Earth as a whole system' (2003, p. 1). Just as Primavesi calls for a change in mindset, Lovelock states that because 'reductionist science cannot offer a rational explanation of quantum phenomena like entanglement, nor of whole systems phenomena such as emergence, does not mean that these phenomena do not exist' (Lovelock, 2003, pp. 1–2). In fact, the complex uncertainties of a planetary climate system that is responsive to humanity's biological and cultural behaviours 'confirms the limitations of the Cartesian view of the universe'. For researchers and sceptics who are finding it difficult to make such a shift in thought, Lovelock advises them to leave Cartesian scruples aside and consider that 'you do not need to know the details of a friend's biochemistry to know them as a person and in a similar way you can envisage Gaia without knowing the recondite details of its geochemistry' (Lovelock, 2003, p. 3). This 'need for' or 'belief in' certainty can be seen to underlie both Climategate and the pre-Copenhagen 'no warming' story that received so much interest among climate change deniers, as well as responses from climate research proponents.

Prominent Canadian environmentalists Suzuki and Moola (2009) point out that the time period for the 'no warming story' was cherry-picked by 'starting with the warm 1998 and ending with the cold 2008'. Other popular environmental thinkers like George Monbiot (2009) and Thomas Homer-Dixon and Weaver (2009, p. 15) similarly argue that choosing 'this year as the starting point for a trend is misleading at best and dishonest at worst'. Despite choosing this cooler period, Suzuki adds there is still evidence for 'a warming trend of $0.11°C$ per decade' (Suzuki and Moola, 2009). Raising these critiques of the sceptics does not require denying the difficulties of Climategate and climate modelling. As Demeritt's review clarifies, where a lack of knowledge persists, the variables have tended to be hypothesized based on modeller assumptions. For example, he states modellers tend to concentrate on simulating the most likely outcomes based on 'a subjective judgment about risk tolerance' and the potential of system variability (Demeritt, 2001, p. 325). Highlighting a similar point, Weart (2003) explains climate models often assume smooth and gradual climate changes, despite paleoclimatic evidence that suggests interacting feedbacks have the potential to result in abrupt changes – a projection that each succeeding IPCC report has found to be increasingly probable to occur in the future as well. At the same time, such limitations do not mean sceptics are justified in a wholesale rejection of climate research. In fact, it seems quite clear that the approach taken by groups like The Friends of Science is at best based on a long-outdated mechanistic belief in scientific certainty, and at worst on a political agenda of economic self-interest and an unsustainable fossil fuel economy. In contrast to such a compromised approach, what is needed today is climate change research that socially engages human, ecological and divine indeterminacies.

While more science will definitely help in clarifying aspects of Gaian climate change, Lovelock is of the view that such physical research may not be the most essential way of coming to know such a socially indeterminate reality. He concludes that 'humans have the ability to recognize whole systems instinctively, and this ability makes the Earth understandable outside science and it can make Earth System science more comprehensible to scientists' (Lovelock, 2003, p. 3). There is an indeterminate complexity to Gaian climate change which transcends a scientific law-based approach to planetary economic management. As Weart writes, 'When you push on something steadily it may remain in place for a while, then move with a jerk' (Weart, 2003, p. 138). We are neither talking about a smooth linear warming trend from one year to the next nor changes that will be similar across all regions. Based on the modelling issues and sceptical critiques, Demeritt proposes it is better for proponents of the IPCC to appreciate the partial insights climate 'models provide without falling into Reductionism and losing sight of the limitations of physical process modelling' (Demeritt, 2001, p. 314). For him, the aim of demystifying scientific knowledge by highlighting its social construction is not – in contrast to the sceptics – to deny our knowledge of a very real and troubling climatic situation but rather to raise important questions about how we understand and live with this complex reality in a more inclusive way. Consequently, Demeritt argues the attempt to alleviate public doubt by increasing their climate research knowledge needs to be replaced with an initiative that increases 'public understanding of and therefore trust in the social process through which those facts are scientifically determined' (Demeritt, 2001, p. 329). In other words, we need to educate people about a climate research process that is valuable because it can increase our knowledge and adaptability to the current situation, though there will continue to be intractable uncertainties.

The question of how we can comprehend something like climate change without complete knowledge is central to Primavesi's analysis, for, as a theologian concerned with Gaian and divine gifts, she recognizes that unknowability is different from ignorance when contemplating realities that reveal 'an absolute limit to what we can say we know' (Primavesi, 2003, p. 45). In this sense, the concerns raised by Lovelock open the larger global debate on the IPCC's climate research to religious sensibilities like that of Primavesi's theology and, I would argue, the myriad of cultural and religious views that inform most people around the planet (see Gardner, 2003). This is not only necessary because of the need to build grass-roots regional responses in a context of continued international political inaction, but also because religious perspectives can provide a complementary view on the role of beliefs in our seemingly more secular fossil fuel consumption practices. Responding specifically to the pervasive belief in economic self-interest, Primavesi proposes climate change can be seen as a force that is moving us, in almost regulatory fashion, to a response based on 'acts of forgiveness' (Primavesi, 2009, p. 133). Her religious view highlights the point that it is not merely humans who are socially constructing a complex reality, but that our research and debates are arising in response to the more encompassing social dialogue of ecological, climatic and divine indeterminacies. Transcending our anthropocentric, economistic, resourcist and industrializing beliefs may require not simply a demystification of climate research so that it can be socially engaged, but also its re-sacralization so that the planet's gifts can animate our ways of living and researching.

Conclusion: An Intercultural Companion

The preceding analysis leads me to the conclusion that we are in need of some kind of intercultural and inter-religious companion to the IPCC process – a broader networking endeavour aimed at replacing unsustainable beliefs and paralysing scepticism with scientifically knowledgeable and interculturally relevant climate responses. While this research project will need to be pragmatically grounded in a low carbon footprint, it will simultaneously have to, in Gardner's words, 'reunite our civilization's head and heart' (2003, p. 153). It is an initiative whose horizon goes beyond an IPCC agenda that has predominantly focused on objective physical properties of greenhouse gases while marginalizing ethical questions about the underlying social relations. In Demeritt's words, IPCC models have tended to 'conceal, normalise, and thereby reproduce those unequal social relations' (2001, p. 316). This critique is consistent with Primavesi's view that science often seems too closely aligned with dominant political-economic beliefs. As she states, science has tended to presuppose 'our entitlement to handle global resources as though they are nothing but an inexhaustible supply of material for gratifying our desires' (Primavesi, 2009, pp. 10–11). That said, the IPCC is clearly light years ahead of deniers like The Friends of Science in providing a knowledge base that can support a socially and ecologically aware change of mind.

In contemplating Climategate, Canada's frontier economy, the climate change debate and Primavesi's ecotheology, I have attempted to exemplify how one religious perspective can clarify the value of a broader intercultural approach to climate research and policy. As with Lovelock's letter, Primavesi partially blames our continued failure to meet this challenge on the inability of people – including politicians, scientists, sceptics and theologians – to conceive of themselves as part of those Gaian processes that have gifted our lives. But she also adds to this debate a much-needed theological questioning of the human-centred mentality and related global economic drive that are fuelling today's climate changes. As she states, our economizing and industrializing mentality educates 'us to ignore what we are now slowly and painfully learning about our earth-centredness: that without earth's givenness built up over deep time, and without the present gifts of life-support systems made possible by it, we would not exist, could not exist' (Primavesi, 2003, p. 135). In confronting this narrowing worldview, she challenges us as researchers and earthly citizens to more actively intertwine religious, scientific and political-economic understandings in a way that can have practical consequences for personal, national, cultural and, more broadly, biological behaviour. It is a spirited change of perspective that seems very much in line with Lovelock's view on the ultimate value of Gaia as being for those 'who like to walk or simply stand and stare, to wonder about the Earth and the life it bears, and to speculate about the consequences of our own presence here' (Lovelock, 1979, p. 12). Based on such planetary inspiration, I conclude some kind of intercultural companion to the IPCC is needed, one that can help people appreciate both the historic challenge and the cosmic, yet anthropogenic, wonder of climate change.

Note

[1]   Photo and article at www.nytimes.com/2008/12/08/us/08pray.html. Accessed 31 January 2011.

References

Bergmann, S. (2005), 'Space and justice in eco-spirituality', in V. N. Makrides and J. Rüpke (eds), *Religionen im Konflikt*. Münster: Aschendorff, pp. 212–225.

Bocking, S. (2004), *Nature's Experts: Science, Politics, and the Environment.* New Brunswick, New Jersey and London: Rutgers University Press.

Demeritt, D. (2001), 'The construction of global warming and the politics of science'. *Annals of the Association of American Geographers*, 91, 307–337.

— (2006), 'Science studies, climate change and the prospects for constructivist critique'. *Economy and Society*, 35, 453–479.

Essex, C. and McKitrick, R. (2002), *Taken by Storm: The Troubled Science, Policy and Politics of Global Warming.* Toronto: Key Porter Books.

Franklin, U. (1999), *The Real World of Technology.* Concord: Anansi Press.

Gardner, G. (2003), 'Engaging religion in the quest for a sustainable world', in Worldwatch Institute (ed.), *State of the World 2003.* New York: W. W. Norton & Company, pp. 152–175.

Hallman, D. G. (2000), 'Climate change: ethics, justice, and sustainable community', in D. T. Hessel and R. R. Ruether (eds), *Christianity and Ecology: Seeking Well-being of Earth and Humans.* Cambridge: Harvard University Press, pp. 453–471.

Harper, S. (2006), *Harper's Index: Stephen Harper Introduces the Tar Sands Issue.* www. dominionpaper.ca/articles/1491.

Hessing, M., Howlett, M. and Summerville T. (2005), *Canadian Natural Resource and Environmental Policy* (second edition). Vancouver and Toronto: UBC Press.

Homer-Dixon, T. and Weaver, A. (2009), 'Responding to the sceptics'. *The Globe and Mail*, 7 December, A15.

Hough, M. (1995), *Cities and Natural Process.* London and New York: Routledge.

Innis, H. (1995), *Staples, Markets, and Cultural Change,* D. Drache (ed.). Montreal: McGill-Queen's University Press.

Kennedy, R. F. (2004), *Crimes Against Nature: How George W. Bush and His Corporate Pals are Plundering the Country and High-Jacking our Democracy.* New York: HarperCollins.

Kirchner, J. W. (2002), 'The Gaia hypothesis: facts, theory and wishful thinking'. *Climatic Change*, 52, 391–408.

— (2003), 'The Gaia hypothesis: conjectures and refutations'. *Climatic Change*, 58, 21–45.

Kleidon, A. (2002), 'Testing the effect of life on earth's functioning: how Gaia is the earth system?' *Climatic Change*, 52, 383–389.

Leduc, T. B. (2010), *Climate, Culture, Change: Inuit and Western Dialogues with a Warming North.* Ottawa: University of Ottawa Press.

Lee, E. and Perl, A. (2003), 'Introduction: institutions and the integrity gap in Canadian environmental policy', in E. Lee and A. Perl (eds), *The Integrity Gap: Canada's Environmental Policy and Institutions.* Vancouver: UBC Press, pp. 3–24.

Lenton, T. M. (2002), 'Testing Gaia: the effect of life on earth's habitability and regulation'. *Climatic Change*, 52, 409–422.

Lenton, T. M. and Wilkinson, D. M. (2003), 'Developing the Gaia theory: a response to the criticisms of Kirchner and Volk'. *Climatic Change*, 58, 1–12.

Livingston, J. A. (2007), *The John A. Livingston Reader: The Fallacy of Wildlife Conservation and One Cosmic Instant.* Toronto: McClelland and Stewart.

Lovelock, J. E. (1979), *Gaia, a New Look at Life on Earth.* Oxford and New York: Oxford University Press.

— (2003), 'Gaia and emergence: a response to Kirchner and Volk'. *Climatic Change*, 57, 1–3.

Monbiot, G. (2009), 'Canada's image lies in tatters: it is now to climate what Japan is to whaling'. *The Guardian*, www.guardian.co.uk, 30 November.

Montgomery, C. (2006), 'Nurturing doubt about climate change is big business'. *The Globe and Mail*, 12 August, F4–F5.

Murphy, R. (2009), 'Through Copenhagen's looking glass'. *The Globe and Mail*, 19 December, A25.

National Post (2006), Open Kyoto to debate: sixty scientists call on Harper to revisit the science of global warming. 6 April.

Nikiforuk, A. (2008), *Tar Sands: Dirty Oil and the Future of a Continent*. Vancouver, Toronto and Berkeley: GreyStone Books.

Perl, A. and Lee, E. (2003), 'Conclusion', in E. Lee and A. Perl (eds), *The Integrity Gap: Canada's Environmental Policy and Institutions*. Vancouver: UBC Press, pp. 241–270.

Primavesi, A. (2000), *Sacred Gaia: Holistic Theology and Earth System Science*. London and New York: Routledge.

— (2003), *Gaia's Gift: Earth, Ourselves and God After Copernicus*. London and New York: Routledge/Taylor & Francis Group.

— (2009), *Gaia and Climate Change: A Theology of Gift Events*. London and New York: Routledge/Taylor & Francis Group.

Rappaport, R. A. (1999), *Ritual and Religion in the Making of Humanity*. Cambridge and New York: Cambridge University Press.

Saunders, D. (2009), 'Copenhagen summit: breach in the global-warming bunker rattles climate science at worse time'. *The Globe and Mail*, 5 December, A1, A22.

Scharper, S. B. (1994), 'The Gaia hypothesis: implications for a Christian political theology of the environment'. *Cross Currents*, 44, 207–221.

— (1997), *Redeeming the Time: A Political Theology of the Environment*. New York: Continuum.

Suzuki, D. and Moola, F. (2009), 'Canada must do more to confront climate crisis'. *Canoe Network*, http://cnews.canoe.ca, 20 November.

Vanderburg, W. H. (2005), *Living in the Labyrinth of Technology*. Toronto: University of Toronto Press.

Volk, T. (1998), *Gaia's Body: Toward a Physiology of Earth*. New York: Copernicus Books/Springer.

— (2002a), *What is Death? A Scientist Looks at the Cycle of Life*. New York: John Wiley and Sons.

— (2002b), 'Toward a future for Gaia theory: an editorial comment'. *Climatic Change*, 52, 423–430.

Weart, S. R. (2003), *The Discovery of Global Warming*. Cambridge: Harvard University Press.

White, Jr., L. (1967), 'The historical roots of our ecologic crisis'. *Science*, 155, 1203–1207.

Part 2

Sketching Sustainable Futures: Recent Dynamics in World Religions

Chapter 5

Climate Justice from a Christian Point of View: Challenges for a New Definition of Wealth

Markus Vogt

The Gap between Knowledge and Belief

Responsibility in climate change is – in the first place – not a problem of knowledge, but a problem of faith: we do not believe what we know about climate change because we cannot sufficiently imagine what it means for us, people all over the world and life on earth. We are not able to react adequately, because we have never had any experience with such a deep, complex change in life conditions. The consequences are – for most decision makers – too far away. The UN climate conference in Copenhagen showed that we are 'atheists of the future' (Sloterdijk, 2009, p. 10). To enable us to realize what climate change means and to react adequately, it is necessary to translate the scientific data we have into descriptions of what they mean for society in terms of suffering, values and lifestyles. Thus, social sciences would be of crucial help in overcoming that deep gap between knowledge and belief in this very specific situation.

To support such an embedding of empirical facts into a context that enables us to realize what climate change means in terms of global life conditions, I will illustrate in the following an understanding of climate change from an ethical point of view.

- Global climate change is, primarily, an anthropogenic phenomenon. So, from an ethical point of view, it has to be classified not as a result of fate, but as a question of justice (Lienkamp, 2009, pp. 358f.). The scale of climate change is so vast that it affects every aspect of the ongoing phenomenon of globalization.

- Humankind has never before interfered so extensively with the biosphere, with such far-reaching spatial and temporal consequences (IPCC, 2007; Rahmstorf and Schellnhuber, 2007, pp. 29–52; Schönwiese, 2008, pp. 17–21; also see Lienkamp, 2009, pp. 49–155; Vogt, 2009, esp. pp. 44–49 and 415–419).
- Climate change will have truly shocking consequences. The world we used to know will no longer exist if the worst of the climate change scenarios comes true. An axial age of radical transformation lies ahead (see Leggewie and Welzer, 2009, pp. 13f.).
- Climate change will lead to the creeping destruction of the homes and food and water resources for countless people in subtropical regions. It will undermine the existence of 2.5 billion people worldwide who make their living from agriculture (Santarius, 2007, p. 21).
- Climate change is a direct attack on the economic, social and cultural rights of several hundred millions of people. The right to live under humane conditions can only be safeguarded by climate protection measures (UNDP, 2007, pp. 1–16).[1]
- The unresolved problem of emission level rights poses one of the greatest opportunities for injustice in our present phase of global development (Baer et al., 2007a, pp. 19–21).
- Climate change and the associated debates about access to resources, the destruction of habitats and the migration of many hundreds of millions of people are all central questions for the foreign and security policies for different nations (WBGU, 2008, esp. pp. 15–42 and 169–190; Lienkamp, 2009, pp. 144–149).
- Climate change represents what is most likely the greatest threat to the existence of current and future generations, and to the continued existence of non-human life on earth' (German Bishops' Commission for Society and Social Affairs and Commission for International Church Affairs, 2007, No. 1).

Justice and peace cannot be realized in the twenty-first century without climate protection. In the specific ethical debate about climate change, the human rights approach might be the most important because it generates close ties between moral and legal assessments. The right to physical integrity forms the foundation for human rights; therefore, lowering the level of greenhouse gas emissions protects human rights (Santarius, 2007, p. 21; Oxfam International, 2008, p. 6). Within all that discussion is a profound conflict between climate protection and the fight against poverty, as the familiar and financially viable methods of economic development largely depend on access to fossil fuels (Ostheimer and Vogt, 2008, pp. 10–13). However, there is no remaining capacity in the atmosphere for the CO_2 that developing countries would emit if they progressed along the same path as the industrialized nations. The technical potential for fighting poverty and protecting the climate – and for integrating these two aims – is in theory relatively good. Realizing these aims is primarily a question of overcoming political and institutional obstacles, as the necessary investments can only be made in conditions that facilitate a fair, cooperative and long-term sharing of the burden. Currently, from the point of view of developing countries, there are hardly any consensual and attractive suggestions on the table for climate protection that involve fair and equitable 'burden sharing'.

The particular nature of ethical problems that arise as a result of climate change lies in the temporal and spatial distance between initiators and victims.[2] This distance can be defined in three ways: Climate change is having a profound and negative impact on future generations, the poorer countries in the southern hemisphere and the habitats of fauna and flora – thereby also on the relationship between humans and nature. It can be regarded as a threefold externalization of the costs of our way of life: its consequences fall and will continue to fall on future generations, on the poor and on the natural world. For these reasons, the German Conference of Catholic Bishops has referred to climate change as the 'crossroads of global, intergenerational and ecological justice' (German Bishops' Commission for Society and Social Affairs and Commission for International Church Affairs, 2007).[3]

Climate change and its consequences offer an exemplary field for justice research, encompassing new dimensions of justice, solidarity, the protection of wealth and responsibility for the natural world in the twenty-first century. 'Climate change will undermine international efforts to combat poverty' (UNDP, 2007, p. 1)[4] and will make the achievement of the Millennium Development Goals (MDGs) impossible in the long run. The awareness of global warming gives the fight to reduce poverty a new focal point and a new dimension of complex interrelations. Climate change exacerbates many distribution problems and has provoked a struggle for access to resources and habitats that is no longer resolvable through traditional models of growth. Ecological problems overwrite social conflicts without erasing them.

The ethical–political problem is particularly complex, featuring an opaque web of winners and losers, both in terms of climate change and in terms of our climate-hostile economic system. Since climate change affects people differently – in terms of geography, immediacy, and the nature of the impact itself – a broad range of interests and perspectives is at stake.

Moreover, on a fundamental level, there are the dilemmas of ecological versus social and economic interests, short-term versus long-term issues and national versus global concerns, all of which are often not directly resolvable by individual agents or political movements. The dilemmas are so deep that it was unrealistic to expect that they could be resolved at the 2009 Copenhagen Climate Conference. They are connected to the cultural and ethical foundations of our society, which simply cannot be changed by a UN conference. We have to speak about our values and our understanding of wealth, both of which guide the economic development of modern and postmodern society.

Climate protection needs a code of ethics that draws attention to the opportunities for injustice, analyses dilemmas and provides firm criteria on which to base political decisions. We have to talk about a philosophy of nature; about anthropology and the complexity of human wishes, hopes and conflicts; and about the cultural reasons and obstacles of changing behaviour. Without a deeper understanding of these various dimensions of responsibility for climate change and the required cultural transformation, it will not be possible to solve the problems of climate justice.

Ethical Bearings in the Conflict between Development Rights and Climate Protection

Managing climate change is a challenge facing all of society. This assertion has a legal and an ethical basis in the 1960s concept of nature as the 'common heritage of mankind'.[5] The ethical challenge posed by climate change involves three kinds of solidarity:

- Long-term solidarity, incorporating measures of prevention or mitigation of climate change through the rejection of fossil fuels. Since everyone would be affected, climate change here is a question of cooperation or *con-solidarity*.
- Medium-term solidarity and adaptive measures are the main priority (e.g. water provision, resettlement, ecological and agricultural adaptation).
- Short-term solidarity is mainly a question of disaster response, hitherto something that society has provided relatively well, partially due to pity-inducing media images. The ever-intensifying scale of disasters calls for

these reactive measures to be backed up by the establishment of international funds. This kind of help can be termed *pro-solidarity*.

The pressure to cooperate as a result of climate change requires a different kind of solidarity, one that does not fit into existing structures; it demands engagement with a distant crisis. On the level of global climate protection there is a serious lack of legal controls, which generates a freeloading mentality and a collective inertia, thus blocking all initiatives. Institutional reforms at the United Nations that would result in a greater degree of legal control have therefore become a matter of urgency. We need a new way of *global governance* in order to balance market-orientated ideas (such as trade-offs), solidarity-based ideas (fair distribution of resources) and a stable legal framework of global development.[6] To form a firm basis for inter-departmental multilateral negotiations, it would be necessary to create an independent organization for environmental concerns, equipped with the power to impose sanctions, under the umbrella of the United Nations (Epiney, 2007, p. 38). The idea of an Environmental Court of Justice is also gaining popularity, in order to impose sanctions on those whose actions are in breach of international regulations and affect a large sector of the population. The critical ethical and political challenge is to overcome short-term thinking and activate moral, political and economic solidarity in order to move from mere reactive disaster 'aftercare' to preventative climate protection and innovative energy technology. That move from a reactive to a preventative concept is also necessary in the context of security and peace policy: Pope Benedict XVI's message for the Day of Peace on 1 January 2010 was: 'If you want to cultivate peace, protect creation' (Benedict XVI, 2009).

Despite the initiatives of the Kyoto Protocol, there has still been about a 40 per cent increase in CO_2 emissions worldwide since 1990. It is imperative that we act decisively and quickly. At the same time, the *global deal* calls for a much stronger cooperation with developing countries to achieve reduction targets, since their share of CO_2 emissions is rising, in some cases very quickly (Edenhofer and Flachsland, 2008, pp. 24–33; Petermann, 2008). Coal poses one of the major problems for climate protection. Climate change is the greatest collective problem humanity has ever had to face. We will only succeed if we can negotiate a new balance between freedom and justice. Enforcing efficient climate protection measures requires us to abandon our inward-looking national political perspectives and establish new institutions (Ekardt, 2008, pp. 17–29).

Green Development Rights

Key to understanding the possible conflict between climate protection and the fight against poverty is the recognition of the right to develop. Global climate protection is only acceptable to the majority of developing countries if it is combined with recognition of a country's right to develop, encompassing (a) the meeting of basic human needs, (b) freedom from deprivation and vulnerability and (c) a basic degree of safety and well-being. The right to develop is not the same as the right to economic growth; it is a right to the conditions that support the sustaining of life in dignity.

The Heinrich Böll Foundation's study *The Right to Development in a World Threatened by Climate Change* combines the indicators of the responsibility for and capacity to influence climate protection to form a 'responsibility and capacity indicator' (RCI) (Baer et al., 2007a, p. 11).[7] The study assumes that responsibility and capacity can only be freed from that portion of income and emissions that is not directly necessary for existence.[8]

This is similar to the basic principle of tax law, which states that a subsistence level of income must be free from state payments – that is to say, at a particular level, there are no payments due to the state. In this way, the requirement to contribute towards international climate protection is conceived as a kind of luxury tax on the global consumer class (cf. Baer et al., 2007a, p. 32: '"luxury" emissions'). Only those people who belong to the global consumer class have the responsibility, and indeed the capacity, to pay their dues to a political climate emergency programme.[9]

The million-dollar question – almost literally – with regard to this concept is how to define the threshold between basic subsistence and luxury.[10] The responsibility and capacity model can calculate the actual quantitative reduction in emissions that is required; according to the model, a third of the efforts towards climate protection should come from the United States and a quarter from Europe (Baer et al., 2007a, pp. 5, 12).[11]

Another concept for a common contract on CO_2 justice is currently being debated under the title *Contraction and Convergence* (C&C) (Ott, 2010). This combines a contract that fixes an upper limit for global CO_2 emissions (contraction) with a gradual introduction of a distribution of emission rights according to egalitarian principles (convergence) (Baer et al., 2007a, pp. 23–45; Baer et al., 2007b, pp. 14–18). The basis for the fixing of a global upper limit is a consensus within society about the level of justifiable ecological risk. The grandfathering principle[12] eases the transition for countries with a high level of emissions. It can be justified ethically as property protection and pragmatism.

An important axiom of the human rights and the developmental ethics-based approaches to climate protection as discussed here is the fact that global climate justice is enacted on a per capita basis, rather than per nation–state. The principle of an equal distribution of emission rights is ethically justified by the fact that the climate is something we all share. All of the earth's inhabitants must in principle have equal access (Santarius, 2007, p. 24). Egalitarianism in terms of climate politics can be interpreted using the 'golden rule': we can talk about having achieved CO_2 justice when no individual produces more CO_2 than he or she tolerates others emitting. But aiming for absolute equality between human beings is problematic in two respects. Geographical and cultural differences result in different needs; in justice theory, this can be described as treating equals equally and unequals unequally.[13]

The principle of *proportionality* argues for a higher contribution from those who emit most. The 'polluter pays' principle demands that industrialized nations, which produced more than 90 per cent of harmful gases in the last 150 years, contribute the lion's share towards climate protection measures. But this begs the question of the extent to which the past should form the basis for a contemporary concept of justice. As a result, there is a plethora of very different points of view, all of which are worthy of consideration in terms of justice theory. In spite of many problematic issues, the per capita distribution of emission rights can be seen as an acceptable and workable approach to climate justice. It should serve to give us our ethical and political bearings, at least as long as the ethical and political discourse and the provision of reliable data on the costs of climate change and climate protection do not reach any other broad consensus.

Particularly controversial from an ethical point of view are those parts of the global deal on climate protection called the 'flexible mechanisms'. These are joint implementation, the clean development mechanism and – in particular – the trade in emission allowances. The trade in emission allowances requires a functioning market, something that exists only in certain places, such as the European Uunion, and then only to a limited extent. The rules for allocating allowances are often unclear. Procuring allowances should not become a substitute for structural reforms, neither on a national nor a business level. For this reason, the German Catholic Bishops' Conference suggests that at least 50 per cent of the agreed rate of reduction must be achieved within the home country, which requires a real change in energy supply and would not allow the purchase of additional emission rights (German Bishops' Commission for Society and Social Affairs and Commission for International Church Affairs, 2007, No. 54).

'If the average cost of reducing emissions is less in a developing country than the price of emission allowances – something that is evidently the case – then the developing countries will be able to profit from the sale of allowances. The profits from the trade in allowances could for example easily top the sums spent on developmental aid in Africa' (Edenhofer et al., 2008, p. 11). But despite all this, ethical safeguards must be in place. In the trade in emission rights, the power of market forces must not be higher than the commitment to human rights. The major challenge will be to channel the flow of money from the northern hemisphere (the industrialized countries) to local communities in the poor countries, hereby ensuring that benefits reach the right people.

Sustainability from a Christian Point of View: A New Definition of Welfare

Climate change is a situation that lies at the very edge of society's ecological, social and economic experience. It is not just a challenge for political negotiation and technical innovation, but also a question of changing society's values. 'Faster, higher, further' has proved to be an inadequate ideal of progress. The situation demands individual and collective answers to genuinely ethical questions about the goals, limits and conditions of our lifestyles. How much is enough? What are the priorities in striving for progress? How can we ensure fair chances for people all over the globe? How can we ensure that long-term interests are properly represented in the democratic system?

In the search for answers to these questions, which are profoundly relevant to the twin goals of fighting poverty and protecting the climate, churches and religious communities can make a substantial contribution. Their competence is especially based on the fact that they embed moral claims into a cosmology and a symbolic and ritual communication that has the ability to change individual behaviour (Gardner, 2003; Vogt, 2009, pp. 482–494). Christianity is the oldest global player on earth, and the Catholic Church in particular administrates an influential global institution and network; it therefore has a specific duty and opportunity to fight for the globalization of solidarity. All religions identify themselves as embodying long-term thinking. On this basis they offer a very fundamental approach to thinking about sustainability.

Managing Contingency: Future Ethics between Fear and Utopia

The ethical and political principle of sustainability is a new definition of the conditions, limits and aims of progress; instead of a permanently increasing tally of goods and speeds,[14] safeguarding the ecological, social and economic stability of human habitats has prime place in the development of society and in political planning. Only wealth built on fewer resources, and open to as many people as possible, is capable of providing justice.

Sustainability is not the byword for a social and economic programme for conserving resources, but instead involves an ethical and cultural reorientation. The contemporary paradigm of progress as unlimited growth needs to be replaced by a concept of development governed by the cycles of resources and the rhythms of nature. Long-term economic success needs to be measured by how well it is integrated into the whole, in other words, the economy of creation. The Index of Sustainable Economic Welfare can serve as a means of measuring and checking progress, evaluating prosperity not merely in terms of a country's gross national product but according to criteria of sustainable development (Diefenbacher, 2001, pp. 133–170; Miegel, 2010).

Our current model of progress is based on the nature philosophy of Newton's mechanics, which describes time and space as empty vessels, lacking both direction and structure, both a beginning and an end. Time and space are merely obstacles to be overcome. Our accelerated society – which is managing to use up myriad resources at a breakneck speed and defines the pace of our lives by the maxim 'everything, now, forever' – is a consequence of this interpretation of nature. Christian belief in creation leads us to search for alternatives to this view of nature and can today base its natural philosophy on process theology.[15] Sustainability needs new concepts of time and space and thus a cosmology that draws on the consequences of Albert Einstein's theory and the new theories of the development of complex adaptive systems (Vogt, 2009, pp. 305–372).

Sustainability is a precaution for the future, its motivating hope not belief in everlasting progress but in the vision of a well-led life within the limits of nature. The Christian faith offers such a vision. It is not founded on the idea that things are constantly improving and that humans will be able to build a perfect society but the opposite, on the existential awareness of the limits of humanity, which can be turned into hope if humans recognize that human life is a gift and everyone depends on the existence of a human community.

This ethos should serve as a corrective to some interpretations of sustainability that have become the main twenty-first-century utopian underpinning for global, ecosocial and economic management. Without the profound insights of critical anthropology and natural philosophy, sustainability represents a deeply ambivalent utopia (Reis, 2003). Seen from a theological perspective, sustainability demands a rejection of the utopia that politics and science will manage all problems. Even the agreements reached in the UN Conference on Environment and Development in Rio (1992) need critical analysis; they offer deeply ambivalent promises that paper over the cracks of these existential boundaries and do not clearly address the limits of growth. We are promised a utopian, global management of ecological and social problems, while – behind the scenes – the same old models and power networks are pursued. The talk is of sustainability, but what is really meant is the traditional prosperity model, which, according to the trickle-down principle, makes the supply for and accommodation of the poorest in society dependent on the growth and surplus of society's rich. The experience of the last two decades shows that this is a misleading promise. The rejection of the fossil fuel-dependent economy and way of life are just the beginning.

The utopian excess of this model of sustainability, as it is currently communicated politically, is open to question. We have to realize that CO_2 emissions are still increasing – especially in China and India – and the likelihood that we can achieve the 2 degree Celsius target in climate politics is declining. Methane emissions from melting permafrost have exceeded various worst-case scenarios, and we are well on the way to accelerating this process further.[16]

Given this and other pertinent facts, there has been a return in sustainability debates to the apocalyptic visions of the 1970s. How can Christian theology, based on its gospel of good news, negotiate a path between Scylla and Charybdis, between playing down the danger on the one hand and a discourse of fear on the other? Christian faith has nothing in common with a belief in progress. It is a hope that is quite different from the expectations of security and prosperity we are used to in the West. It is a way of managing contingency in the face of the ambivalence of progress and setbacks, security and risk, joy and suffering, life and death.

If we assume that managing contingency is a primary function of religion (Lübbe, 1998, pp. 35–47; Luhmann, 2000), then it is also here that we find the specific competence of theological ethics in the discourse on sustainability. Managing contingency is vital to answering the postmodern breakdown of the belief in progress – the starting point of debates on climate change and sustainability – without resorting to scenarios of eco-logical apocalypse or to a new version of the utopia of permanent growth.

Christian ethics of sustainability does not constitute a closed system of self-serving nature ontology, a guarantee of equality or a utopia of human progress; rather, it offers a way forward in the dialectics of progress and risk.

And this is exactly what Hans Jonas meant with his responsibility princi-ple as a counter-argument to the principle of hope as formulated by Ernst Bloch. Jonas demands an ethics of caution, the acceptance of limits and the 'heuristics of fear' (see Jonas, 1994, pp. 63f.).[17] Others talk about 'intel-ligent self-restraint' (Offe, 1989), for it is not the limits of nature, but the seemingly limitless desire of humanity in connection with the extreme rise in knowledge about availability of natural resources that today pose the main threats to our future. The ability to enact self-restraint is a precondi-tion for the redirection of technical and economic development to serve the well-being of humanity and creation.

The Principle of Sustainability: Its Place in Catholic Social Ethics

Sustainability has not until now been a systematic part of Catholic social doctrine. The term 'sustainability' does not appear in papal documents. There have been impassioned calls for a 'return to ecology', but these have not made it past the level of individual ethical virtues. On the level of political systems, there has been no orderly reflection on the relation-ship between environment and development. This is why I would like to postulate an extension of social principles – that sustainability should be recognized as a fourth social principle along with personality, solidarity and subsidiarity. This is the core argument of my book in terms of the sys-tematic aspects of Catholic social ethics (Vogt, 2009, pp. 456–494).

Sustainability is the 'missing link' between belief in creation and social discourses on climate change. Just as the Christian idea of charity was for centuries only understood ethically on the level of a personal virtue, and only became politically effective in connection with the solidarity princi-ple, belief in creation needs a translation into ethical categories so that it can become politically viable and justifiable and can clarify concrete consequences of organizational structures and economic decisions in the context of climate change. Belief in creation without sustainability is, in terms of structural and political ethics, a form of blindness. Sustainability without belief in creation (whether Christian or not) runs the risk of losing out on ethical depth.

A crucial factor in the acceptance of sustainability as one of the fundamental principles of Catholic social teaching is, at the end, that it effectively summarizes the social and ethical diagnosis of the 'signs of the times'[18] and gets to the heart of the associated challenges for society and the Church. Sustainability is a synthesis of the social–ethical diagnosis of social questions at the start of the twenty-first century, and on this basis is also a barometer for how welfare and justice will fare in future development.

Sustainability highlights loopholes in the execution of justice. It is the issue at the interface of all the main questions about the future, often displaying surprising parallels and structural similarities to different dilemmas in different contexts. Sustainability opens the way for new analyses and solutions for the complex interplay between local and global phenomena. Such a central function can only be realized by a discourse of sustainability when this submits to ongoing questioning of its boundaries, however. This is where theology can be a useful tool to enforce sustainability's search for hope and meaning, which stretches beyond human, societal or technical effort can achieve. Facing climate change means facing contingencies that demand not only a political but also a cultural answer. The religious and spiritual understanding of sustainability opens a critical view of the risk of the sustainability discourse closing itself off and mistaking its integral nature for an omnipotent power to solve. Sustainability needs an accompanying critical ideology, to be provided by philosophy, theology, sociology, and cultural and historical studies to solve all sorts of problems.

Notes

1   Oxfam published research regarding the human rights abuses resulting from climate change (Oxfam International 2008, esp. the table on p. 6); according to this, the rights to life and to security of person, and access to food and health care of many hundred million people are under threat or have been negatively affected.
2   For analysis of the unequal distribution of climate damage, cf. Santarius (2007), pp. 19f.; UNDP (2007), pp. 3–5, 24–31; Lienkamp (2008), pp. 4–6.
3   There are different ways of understanding the term 'ecological justice' in the American and the German debate; cf. Leist (2007).
4   'Some 262 million people were affected by climate disasters annually from 2000 to 2004, over 98 per cent of them in the developing world' (UNDP, 2007, p. 8).
5   For different concepts of nature and their theological and ethical implications, cf. Bergmann (2005); Vogt (2009), pp. 216–372.
6   This is also a claim in the new encyclical of Pope Benedict XVI, *Caritas in veritate*, (2009a, no. 67). Ethical bearings regarding to environment: No. 48–52.

[7] Even more fundamental reflections about the conflict of climate protection and the fight against poverty, which is especially important for the Christian ethics approach, are published by Edenhofer et al. (2010).

[8] 'We define capacity as income, excluding all income below the development threshold. We define responsibility as cumulative CO_2 emissions, excluding all emissions deriving from consumption below the development threshold' (Baer et al., 2007b, p. 11). Income below this is termed 'survival income' or 'survival emission' respectively and cannot be claimed for political purposes related to climate.

[9] Cf. Baer et al. (2007b), p. 33: 'Countries cannot be asked to incur any mitigation costs as long as they are developing'. *On the Quantification of Global Development Rights*, see pp. 23–44.

[10] The authors assume that an annual income of US$9,000 (purchasing power) is usually enough to meet basic needs and is therefore the passport to the 'global middle class' (Baer et al., 2007, pp. 82–84). Income is calculated in terms of purchasing power.

[11] The burden is shared as follows: US 34.4 per cent, EU 26.6 per cent, Russia 5.5 per cent, China 7 per cent. An optimistic estimate, which calculates the costs for emergency assistance at 1 per cent of the world's gross national product, the following costs per inhabitant are incurred over the 'development threshold', ca. US$780 annually in the US, $372 dollars/year in the EU, $142/year in China.

[12] The term 'grandfathering' means that with respect to the history and the tradition of earlier generations, a gradual rather than an abrupt transition will be required. For more on this, see Baer et al. (2007a), pp. 14f.; Rahmstorf and Schellnhuber (2007), pp. 18f.

[13] For an ethical and philosophical discussion of the legal aspects of egalitarianism, which has rather unexpectedly become highly relevant as part of the climate justice debate with respect to equal rights to CO_2 emissions, cf. Pauer-Studer (2009), pp. 207–231.

[14] For reflections about the phenomenon of permanent acceleration ('*kinetischer Imperativ*'), see Höhn (2010).

[15] Process theology has its roots in a new concept of time and space and all reality as a complex interrelated process; its starting point is Whitehead's philosophy of nature (Vogt, 2009, pp. 323–330; Faber, 2003); other approaches come from Trinitarian Cosmology or from theology of liberation; see Bergmann (1995), pp. 57–171, 269–321.

[16] See www.umweltbundesamt.de/klimaschutz/veroeffentlichungen/permafrost.pdf.

[17] The 'heuristics of fear' as suggested by the religious philosopher need further differentiation in my opinion, in terms of society and of decision theory. We need different models to enable analysis and to manage different kinds of risk. Ortwin Renn illustrates this under the heading of 'risk maturity' (Renn, 2008; Vogt, 2009, pp. 369–372).

[18] The term 'signs of the times' is a key for understanding the theology of the Second Vatican Council (1962–1965); see Hünermann (2006, pp. 122–145) for a reflection on 'the cry of creation as a sign of our times'.

References

Baer, P., Athanasiou, T. and Kartha, S. (2007a), *The Right to Development in a Climate Constrained World. The Greenhouse Development Rights Framework*, commissioned by the Heinrich Böll Foundation (www.ecoequity.org/docs/TheGDRsFramework. pdf).

Baer, P., Athanasiou, T., Kartha, S. and Athanasiou, T. (2007b), *Frameworks & Proposals. A Brief, Adequacy and Equity-Based Evaluation of Some Prominent Climate Policy Frameworks and Proposals*, commissioned by the Heinrich Böll Foundation (www.boell.de/alt/downloads/global/global_issue_paper30.pdf).

Benedict XVI (2009), *If You Want to Cultivate Peace, Protect Creation.* Message for the celebration of the world day of peace on 1 January 2010, Vatican.

Bergmann, S. (2005), *Creation Set Free: The Spirit as Liberator of Nature.* Grand Rapids: Eerdmans.

Bergmann, S. and Gerten, D. (eds) (2010), *Religion and Dangerous Environmental Change: Transdisciplinary Perspectives on the Ethics of Climate and Sustainability.* Studies in Religion and the Environment, Vol. 2. Münster: LIT.

Diefenbacher, H. (2001), *Gerechtigkeit und Nachhaltigkeit. Zum Verhältnis von Ethik und Ökonomie.* Darmstadt: Wissenschaftliche Buchgesellschaft.

Edenhofer, O. and Flachsland, C. (2008), 'Ein Global Deal für den Klimaschutz. Herausforderungen an die Energie- und Klimapolitik'. *Amos-international*, 2, 24–33.

Edenhofer, O., Flachsland, C. and Lotze-Campen, H. (2008), 'Emissionen müssen etwas kosten'. *Welt-Sichten*, 5, 9–11.

Edenhofer, O., Flachsland, C., Lotze-Campen, H., Lotze-Campen, H., Wallacher, J. and Reder, M. (eds) (2010), *Global aber gerecht. Klimawandel bekämpfen, Entwicklung ermöglichen.* München: C. H. Beck.

Ekardt, F. (2008), 'Wie die Klimawende wirklich gelingt. Neuer Lebensstil, neue Weltordnung – Freiheit und Gerechtigkeit neu gedacht'. *Freiburger Universitätsblätter*, 180, 9–22.

Epiney, A. (2007), '"Gerechtigkeit" im Umweltvölkerrecht'. *Aus Politik und Zeitgeschichte*, 24, 31–38.

Faber, R. (2003), *Gott als Poet der Welt. Anliegen und Perspektiven der Prozesstheologie.* Darmstadt: Wissenschaftliche Buchgesellschaft.

Gardner, G. (2003), 'Engaging religion in the quest for a sustainable world', in Worldwatch Institute (ed.), *State of the World 2003.* New York: W. W. Norton & Company, pp. 152–175.

German Bishops' Commission for Society and Social Affairs and Commission for International Church Affairs (eds) (2007), *Climate Change – A Focal Point of Global, Intergenerational and Ecological Justice*, second edition. Bonn: Secretariat of the German Bishops' Conference.

Höhn, H.-J. (2010), *Zeit und Sinn. Religionsphilosophie postsäkular.* Paderborn: Schöningh.

Hünermann, P. (ed.) (2006), *Das Zweite Vatikanische Konzil und die Zeichen der Zeit heute. Anstöße zur weiteren Rezeption* (Festschrift für Kardinal Lehmann). Freiburg: Herder.

IPCC (Intergovernmental Panel on Climate Change) (2007), *Climate Change. The Physical Science Basis.* Contribution of Working Group I to the Fourth Assessment Report of the Intergovernmental Panel on Climate Change. Cambridge: Cambridge University Press.

Jonas, H. (1994), *Das Prinzip Verantwortung. Versuch einer Ethik für die technologische Zivilisation* (second edition). Frankfurt am Main: Suhrkamp.

Leggewie, C. and Welzer, H. (2009), *Das Ende der Welt, wie wir sie kannten. Klima, Zukunft und die Chancen der Demokratie.* Frankfurt am Main: Fischer.

Leist, A. (2007), 'Ökologische Gerechtigkeit als bessere Nachhaltigkeit'. *Aus Politik und Zeitgeschichte,* 24, 3–10.

Lienkamp, A. (2009), *Klimawandel und Gerechtigkeit. Eine Ethik der Nachhaltigkeit in christlicher Perspektive.* Paderborn: Schöningh.

Lübbe, H. (1998), 'Kontingenzerfahrung und Kontingenzbewältigung', in Graevenitz, G. and Marquard, O. (eds), *Kontingenz (Poetik und Hermeneutik 17).* München: Wilhelm Fink, pp. 35–47.

Luhmann, N. (2000), *Die Religion der Gesellschaft.* Frankfurt am Main: Suhrkamp.

Miegel, M. (2010), *Exit. Wohlstand ohne Wachstum.* Berlin: Propyläen.

Offe, C. (1989), 'Fessel und Bremse. Moralische und institutionelle Aspekte "intelligenter Selbstbeschränkung"', in Honneth, A., Mc Carthy, T., Offe, C., Wellmer, A. (eds), *Zwischenbetrachtungen. Im Prozeß der Aufklärung. Jürgen Habermas zum 60. Geburtstag.* Frankfurt am Main: Suhrkamp, pp. 739–774.

Ostheimer, J. and Vogt, M. (2008), 'Energie für die Armen. Entwicklungsstrategien angesichts des Klimawandels'. *Amos-international,* 1, 10–16.

Ott, K. (2010), 'Ethical foundations of climate change policies', in S. Bergmann and D. Gerten (eds), *Religion and Dangerous Environmental Change.* Münster: LIT, pp. 195–204.

Ott, K. and Döring, R. (2004), *Theorie und Praxis starker Nachhaltigkeit.* Marburg: Metropolis.

Oxfam International (2008), *Climate Wrongs and Human Rights* (Oxfam Briefing Paper 117). Oxford: Oxfam International.

Pauer-Studer, H. (2009), 'Global justice: problems of a cosmopolitan account', in L. Meyer (ed.), *Justice, Legitimacy, and Public International Law.* Cambridge: Cambridge University Press, pp. 207–231.

Petermann, P. (ed.) (2008), *Sichere Energie im 21. Jahrhundert.* Hamburg: Hoffmann und Campe.

Rahmstorf, S. and Schellnhuber, H.-J. (2007), *Der Klimawandel.* München: C. H. Beck.

Reis, O. (2003), *Nachhaltigkeit – Ethik – Theologie. Eine theologische Beobachtung der Nachhaltigkeitsdebatte.* Forum Religion & Sozialkultur, B 18. Münster: LIT.

Renn, O. (2008), *Risk Governance: Coping with Uncertainty in a Complex World (Risk, Society and Policy).* London: Earthscan.

Santarius, T. (2007), 'Klimawandel und globale Gerechtigkeit'. *Aus Politik und Zeitgeschichte,* 24, 18–24.

Schönwiese, C. (2008), 'Der Klimawandel in Vergangenheit und Zukunft – Wissensstand und offenen Fragen'. *Amos-international,* 1, 17–23.

Sloterdijk, P. (2009), 'Das 21. Jahrhundert beginnt mit dem Debakel vom 19. Dezember 2009' (interview with A. Kreye). *Süddeutsche Zeitung,* 21 December, p. 10.

UNDP [United Nations Development Programme] (2007), *Human Development Report 2007/2008. Fighting Climate Change: Human Solidarity in a Divided World.* New York: Palgrave Macmillan.

Vogt, M. (2009), *Prinzip Nachhaltigkeit. Ein Entwurf aus theologisch-ethischer Perspektive.* München: Oekom.

WBGU [Wissenschaftlicher Beirat der Bundesregierung Globale Umweltveränderungen] (2008), *Welt im Wandel. Sicherheitsrisiko Klimawandel.* Berlin: Springer.

Chapter 6

Climate Justice and the Intrinsic Value of Creation: The Christian Understanding of Creation and its Holistic Implications

Friedrich Lohmann

Introduction

The story of the relationship between ecology and Christian theology is quite complex. Even if there is currently broad agreement in (self-)criticizing the long-standing lack of ecological awareness in mainstream Christianity, there is no corresponding positive consensus on the theological grounds and the scope of the newly discovered Christian sensitivity towards nature. The 'turn to ecology' has brought about very different 'eco-theologies'.[1] One of the issues that is most contentious is anthropocentrism. Some of today's eco-theologians – as well as many non-Christian environmentalists – claim that the traditional idea of human superiority over the rest of nature is the main reason for the long history of human exploitation and destruction of nature (e.g. Moltmann, 1995, p. 45[2]); others maintain anthropocentrism and reject the idea of an intrinsic value of nature altogether (see Irrgang, 1992, p. 85[3]). Still others take an intermediate position by acknowledging the importance of nature while criticizing 'holistic, biocentric and pathocentric' approaches and distinguishing between the intrinsic value of nature and human dignity (Kehl, 2008, pp. 339–341). The latter position comes quite close to the position that I want to argue in support of in this chapter. I, too, think that from a Christian perspective, it is adequate to ascribe an intrinsic value to nature while, at the same time, preserving the notion of dignity as proper only to humans. I will, however, try to show that this position is not anthropocentric but holistic: it takes a 'systemic' approach, stating that the created world is a well-ordered structure, a wholeness in which everything is interconnected and in which human superiority is part of the system. Therefore this superiority is by no means a justification for selfish exploitation of nature but an obligation to serve the whole of creation in a responsible attitude of stewardship. If one wants to put a label on this Christian vision of nature, it is neither physiocentrism nor anthropocentrism but holism.

I am not the first to emphasize the idea of interconnectedness in the Christian notion of creation (see Altner, 1991, pp. 84–91; Welker, 1991; Bergmann, 1993). However, in the current age of climate change, it seems necessary to develop it a bit further, by profiling its Biblical and theological background against other, more influential accounts of the Christian narrative. In the current context, the reciprocal, 'holistic' interrelatedness and interdependence of humanity and nature, as well as human responsibility for the fate of nature, are more visible than ever. If, in the context of global warming, 'it is imperative to complement the existing technological and economically oriented problem solutions with alternative perspectives – narratives that integrate the entanglement of humans and their environment' (Bergmann and Gerten, 2010, p. 5), a fresh look at the Christian narrative and its holistic implications is justified.

In the first three sections of this chapter, my intention is to defend a Christian version of holism against traditional anthropocentrism. I will then argue that this version of holism must not be confused with physiocentrism. Following the idea of a hierarchical system, a specific task, specific privileges, specific responsibilities and a specific dignity of humanity can be re-established without falling into the traps of either anthropocentrism or physiocentrism.

Gods, Human Beings and the Rest of the World

In recent decades, the notion of human dignity has become one of the most prominent, widely acknowledged foundations for societal values. Despite its universal recognition, there are many different understandings of human dignity. The notion of human dignity that has dominated Christian theology over the centuries was shaped in the first centuries of the Christian era, when the Biblical narrative was moulded in a philosophical, mainly neo-Platonist ontology and anthropology by thinkers such as Ambrose or Augustine. The classical Western[4] Christian definition of human dignity comes from Augustine and is closely linked to the notion of the human as created in the image of God: 'The true honour of man is the image of and the similarity to God'.[5] 'Honour' here means the same as 'dignity' and is understood in the sense of a ruling lordship, as can be seen in the following reference, also from Augustine: 'The great dignity God has given to you can be concluded best from the fact that God who alone is your lord by nature has created other valuable things over which you are a lord too'.[6] Human lordship over the rest of creation is based on human participation in divine reason:

> There is no bigger privilege of man with regard to the other living beings than his participation in reason, his capacity to investigate the origins of things, and his willingness to search for the creator of his own species who has power over our life and death.[7]

Human dignity is thus defined by the human capacity to govern the rest of creation. It is shaped by the possession of reason, which is a gift of the creator to humankind alone, thus distinguishing between humanity and the rest of creation. At the same time, the possession of reason is thought to be the common characteristic of humans and God, and, therefore, the Biblical notion of man and woman created in the image of God (Gen. 1.26–27) is understood in the same way: it is the gift of reason that reflects the image of God, whereas the body unites them with the rest of creation. Leading a good life according to God's will means to live in the image of God, in other words, governing, ordering and dominating the body and its passions by means of reason. Sin, on the other hand, is understood as domination in the wrong way: fleshly and beastlike concupiscence captures reason, destroying the image of God and human dignity.

I will show in the next section that this understanding of human dignity, with its emphasis on reason and questions of dominion, is – in spite of its venerable supporters and its long-standing history – not an authentic rendering of the Biblical creation narrative and its implications on the relationship between (1) God and humanity, (2) mind and body, (3) reason and passions and (4) humanity and the rest of creation. But, first of all, I would like to give some evidence from classical Greek philosophers that illustrates some striking similarities to the Augustinean–Ambrosean picture referred to above.

It is commonplace for almost all ancient philosophers to maintain that the human soul is divided, with reason and passions as the two poles. Everything is a bit more complex, of course, but the essential point is that, within these two poles, only reason represents *true* human nature. It is therefore necessary that reason be assigned primacy in order to assure a good life, which in this Greek context means a life according to one's own nature. The most important virtue, then, is to live as much as possible according to one's (true) nature, which is identical to living under the rule of reason.

Let us begin with Plato, who is the most influential philosopher to make this claim. His *Politeia* ('The Republic') examines the question of true justice and answers it by going back to anthropological questions, such as the nature of the human soul. For Plato, the human soul has three parts, with reason being the main characteristic. Justice is fulfilled when the three parts are in a just, well-ordered relationship, which for Plato means that reason dominates the two beastlike parts (the passionate and vegetative part). 'Isn't it proper for the calculating part to rule, since it is wise and has forethought about all of the soul, and for the spirited part to be obedient to it and its ally?' (Plato, 1991, 441e). Not only human justice, but even human health is thus defined by following a nature-given order of ruling and obeying:

> To produce health is to establish the parts of the body in a relation of mastering, and being mastered by, one another that is according to nature, while to produce sickness is to establish a relation of ruling, and being ruled by, one another that is contrary to nature.
>
> (Plato, 1991, 444d)

In his dialogue *Phaedrus*, Plato has found a particularly telling imagery for this idea of ruling and obeying: he describes the human soul as a carriage that is pulled by two horses, one of godly origin, heading towards heaven, representing reason, and one of bad origin, heading downwards, representing the passions. The goal of human life is to reach heaven, which is possible by living a life according to the God-alike part of the human soul: reason (cf. Plato, 1986, 246a–249d).

Some centuries later, we find the same pattern of thought in a famous passage of the Stoic philosopher Seneca: 'What is best in man? Reason: with this he precedes the animals and follows the gods. Therefore perfect reason is man's peculiar good, the rest he shares with animals and plants.'[8] Thus, the well-known Stoic slogan 'to live in accordance to nature' means nothing other than to live according to (human) reason, to approach a perfect, godly life by dominating the more earthly, beastlike impulses of passion.

Ambrose, Augustine and all Christian theology building on them do not exactly follow in the footsteps of their Greek and Latin forebears. There is, for example, no real corresponding word in Greek philosophy for the Christian notion of sin. But there can be no doubt that the notion of human

dignity as put forward by the Western fathers of the Church is largely dependent on Plato's image of the human soul. No surprise, then, that Nicholas of
Cusa, man of the Church and philosopher in the fifteenth century, calls
the human being 'a second god' (quoted in Bergmann, 2005, p. 23). No
surprise, then, that Pico della Mirandola, a neo-Platonist philosopher at
the end of that century, re-establishes the connection between the specific
place of humankind in the world – between God and the rest of creation –
and the notion of dignity. In his *Oratio de hominis dignitate*, it is obvious that
humanity, by using its reasonable free will, is closer to God than to other
living beings, given that God himself introduces the first man to his special
ability, which is related to his place 'at the very centre of the world':

> We have given you, O Adam, no visage proper to yourself, nor endow-
> ment properly your own, in order that whatever place, whatever form,
> whatever gifts you may, with premeditation, select, these same you may
> have and possess through your own judgement and decision. The nature
> of all other creatures is defined and restricted within laws which We have
> laid down; you, by contrast, impeded by no such restrictions, may, by your
> own free will, to whose custody We have assigned you, trace for yourself
> the lineaments of your own nature. I have placed you at the very centre
> of the world, so that from that vantage point you may with greater ease
> glance round about you on all that the world contains. We have made you
> a creature neither of heaven nor of earth, neither mortal nor immortal,
> in order that you may, as the free and proud shaper of your own being,
> fashion yourself in the form you may prefer. It will be in your power to
> descend to the lower, brutish forms of life; you will be able, through your
> own decision, to rise again to the superior orders whose life is divine.
>
> (Pico della Mirandola, 1956)

Even if the good, masterful life for Pico's Adam is more a life of contem-
plation and knowledge than an active life of forming nature according
to his will, Pico and his philosophical and Christian predecessors have
opened the door widely for Descartes's idea of the human being as the
'*maître et possesseur de la nature*' (Descartes, 1973, p. 62). Human beings
are created in the image of God and best fulfil their destiny by exercising
their free, rational will, thus governing their own passions and the rest
of nature. The underlying world view is hierarchical and strictly ordered,
with heavenly creatures above all, 'brutish forms of life' on the bottom
and the human being just in between, participating in heavenly life by
means of reason and drawn downwards by lower passions. Humanity's

'true' nature, however, is Godlike, a divine companion entirely separate from the rest of nature.

The Place of Humanity According to the Biblical Evidence

It is a fact that the way that Christians have treated nature over the centuries is very much in line with the pattern of thought I have described in the preceding section. With regard to the *factual* influence of Christianity on the sad history of human domination and exploitation of the world, all those who (self-)criticize Western Christianity are entirely correct. It is, nevertheless, necessary to enlarge the picture: if we are justified in giving negative credit to Christianity, we should also see the negative influence of non-Christian, philosophical ideas (cf. Groh and Groh, 1991). And we should keep in mind the effects of human concupiscence on nature, concupiscence which was castigated by Augustine and other Christian theologians as the utmost manifestation of sin.

But, in saying this, I do not want to minimize the bad influence of the Christian tradition I have referred to. My question here is different: is the influential interpretation of human dignity and human lordship that was fostered by Augustine and others correct with regard to the Biblical notion of humankind and its relationship to God and the rest of creation?

There is one Biblical reference that is the source for all Christian justifications of human dominion over against the rest of creation – the so-called *dominium terrae* (Gen. 1.28) – where God addresses the first, freshly created human couple with the following words:

> God blessed them, and God said to them, 'Be fruitful and multiply, and fill the earth and subdue it; and have dominion over the fish of the sea and over the birds of the air and over every living thing that moves upon the earth'.[9]

At first sight, this seems to be a clear-cut authorization to selfishly exploit the rest of creation.[10] However, Biblical and theological scholarship in recent decades have increasingly insisted that this controversial commandment must be seen and interpreted in the context of (1) the subsequent chapter of Genesis, which gives a fairly different account of the creation, (2) the whole story in Genesis 1, and (3) the whole Biblical tradition, including the New Testament with its Christological revision of the notion of dominion. Let me briefly summarize the main points.

First, one of the most important differences between the two accounts of creation in Genesis 1 and 2 concerns the relationship between the first human being(s) and the surrounding world. Whereas Genesis 1 emphasizes the original chaos of the world, which demands a step-by-step ordering by God (cf. Jenson, 1992, pp. 216–217), and which humanity is to pursue, Genesis 2, with its notion of a peaceful garden, depicts the first man in a much friendlier atmosphere. His task, therefore, is not dominion but a much more conservative approach of 'tilling and keeping' (Gen. 2.15). He is seen as a gardener whose interventions are limited to what serves the whole of creation and not his own egoistic purposes.

In current theology, the *dominium terrae* of Gen. 1.28 is interpreted in the light of Genesis 2, stating that the 'dominion' of Gen. 1.28 is a dominion of unselfish ordering, without any notion of exploitation. This reading can be supported by the fact that it is only in Genesis 9 – the end of the Noah story, written by the same priestly school as Genesis 1 – that God speaks of 'fear and dread' among animals with regard to human dominion (Gen. 9.2), probably related to the permission to eat animals (Gen. 9.3), which is missing in Gen. 1.29. What happened in the time between the creation and Noah? Sin came into the world (Gen. 3; 6.5). For the priestly school, it is therefore a consequence of human sinfulness that tension has entered the relationship between humans and other creatures, necessitating the covenant concluded in Genesis 9. If one wants to know the *real* will of God at the time of creation, one has to go back to Genesis 1 (and 2) where the relationship is much more harmonious.

Second, we have seen that for Augustine, the honour of humanity – its creation as an image of God – is interpreted as a similarity between God and humankind in ruling. Gen. 1.28, the dominium terrae, is used as a source for understanding the preceding verse, which speaks of the image of God: 'So God created humankind in his image, in the image of God he created them; male and female he created them' (Gen. 1.27). Modern interpretations of Genesis 1 invert the scheme: they understand the dominion of Gen. 1.28 in the light of Gen. 1.27 and its notion of 'image of God'. Of course, this inversion only makes sense when there are hints that the 'image of God' can and must be understood other than by 'dominion'. And there are, indeed, two hints. The first is an observation one can make in Gen. 1.27 itself: the image of God is not represented by one single person, but by two – 'male and female'. Modern theology, having rediscovered Trinitarian thinking as a framework for the whole of theology (e.g. Schwöbel, 1995), sees here an allusion to the Trinity: God himself is not a single person, but a relationship, and therefore it is more than correct that God's 'image' on earth is represented by a relationship and not by a single person. Now, in the Trinity the relationship is not one of power or dominion, but is a relationship of love (it was, by the way, none other than Augustine who interpreted the Trinity in this way – unfortunately without using his conception of the divine Trinity as a hint for the interpretation of the relationship between the 'image of God' and nature). Therefore, the 'honour' of mankind to have been created to the image of God can no longer be understood in the way of ruling out other creatures, but more in the light of a Trinitarian love affair.

The other hint for a more 'democratic' interpretation of Gen. 1.27 can be found when looking at parallel patterns of thought in contemporary cultures of the Near East (Genesis 1 is thought to have been written in the sixth century BC). Actually, there is some evidence that the idea to describe a human being as an 'image of God' came to the fore first in ancient Egypt. There, it was the king who could claim to be an 'image of God'. Several significations are joined with this title, but it seems as if the idea of the king as a *representative* of God on earth had become more and more important in Egypt, and, in this context, the notion of the king as an *image* of God replaced the more ancient idea of the king as a *son* of God. An image is less close to its origin than a son. When speaking of the king as a (mere) image, the ancient Egyptians left the whole authority and dominion in God and transformed the former autocratic king into a (mere) representative of the God who alone dominated the world (cf. Ockinga, 1984, p. 137).[11] As an image of God, the king was clearly subordinate to God, and his task was to fulfil God's purpose, which is a *beneficent* lordship: 'As his image Re has instituted you, in order to save the shipwrecked (i.e. the weak, the one who has failed in life)' (Ockinga, 1984, p. 146).[12] According to Ockinga, this Egyptian parallel helps to explain Gen. 1.27. Of course, the Biblical text 'democratizes' the Egyptian idea: not only the king, but each member of the human species is created as an 'image of God' (cf. Schmidt, 1986, p. 206).[13] The idea of a representative, beneficent lordship can, however, be transposed in the egalitarian, Old Testament context: the dominion of Gen. 1.28 has to be seen as a *beneficent* way of exercising authority, exercised by all humanity as representative governors of the beneficent God (cf. Ockinga, 1984, p. 154; Schmidt, 1986, p. 207).[14] This is confirmed by recent Old Testament scholarship (cf. Groß, 2001).

Third, if one is ready to interpret the *dominium terrae* by means of the notion of the 'image of God' (and not the other way round, as Augustine did) and if one goes beyond the Old Testament context towards a specific *Christian* understanding of the 'image of God', a third point has to be made. In the New Testament, the way to speak of the 'image of God' is somehow backwards, in as far as it is again – as in the early Egyptian inscriptions – only one person who is honoured with this title: Jesus Christ who is at the same time seen as the son of God. 'He is the image of the invisible God, the firstborn of all creation' (Col. 1.15; cf. 2 Cor. 4.4, Heb. 1.3). However, this shift does not mean a return to an understanding of dominion as an authoritarian, egoistic hegemony. In Jesus Christ, the idea of a 'democratic' and beneficent leadership is intensified.

> But Jesus called them to him and said, 'You know that the rulers of the Gentiles lord it over them, and their great ones are tyrants over them. It will not be so among you; but whoever wishes to be great among you must be your servant, and whoever wishes to be first among you must be your slave; just as the Son of Man came not to be served but to serve, and to give his life a ransom for many.
>
> (Mt. 20.25–28)

Jesus Christ is paradigmatic for the Christian vision of leadership in as far as his leadership, his way of exercising authority, is entirely oriented towards the well-being of his subjects. He is 'the Lord as servant' (Barth, 1956). And particularly in becoming a servant, he is the image of God; he is the revelation of God himself. 'That Jesus Christ is very God is shown in His way into the far country in which He the Lord became a servant' (Barth, 1956, p. 157). Jesus Christ is the paradigmatic image of God; his dominion goes far beyond the human dominium terrae and includes nothing less than *everything* (cf. Col. 1.16–17) – but his dominion is built on peace and reconciliation:

> For in him all the fullness of God was pleased to dwell, and through him God was pleased to reconcile to himself all things, whether on earth or in heaven, by making peace through the blood of his cross.
>
> (Col. 1.19–20)

In the light of the New Testament, there is no reason to deny the existence of relationships in the world that are asymmetric and imply the notion of dominion. But Christ's dominion over the world is of a very special kind. Given that the New Testament writers connect Christ's enthronement with him being the image of God, and given that the same title is given to humanity in Gen. 1.27, it seems logical to understand the dominium terrae in Gen. 1.26, 28 in a similar way, as a contribution to a beneficent and peace-oriented common life on earth.

Fourth, still following the Biblical evidence, there is an important difference in the status of Jesus Christ and that of humanity, however. Both are entitled to be the image of God, but only Jesus Christ is called a son of God: 'And a voice came from heaven, "You are my Son, the Beloved; with you I am well pleased"' (Mk 1.11). Therefore, Christian theology has drawn a clear distinction between Jesus Christ and the rest of humanity. As was said in the Trinitarian creeds of the fourth century, Christ is the only begotten son of the father, being of the same substance as him. This was dogmatized over the preachings of Arius and his followers, who claimed Jesus to be at the very top of creation, but still a creature, clearly subordinate to God. Against Arius, the Trinitarian dogma stipulates that Jesus is begotten, not created. Therefore, he is God, the second person of the Trinity.

This debate and dogmatic decision leads us, hundreds of years later, to an important point in the understanding of creation.[15] Arius was right in stating that everything that is created is subordinate to God. He was not right in his claims regarding Jesus Christ, given Christ's non-created status. But he was right for every other member of the human species. Jesus Christ was and is the image of God by his very essence, while we fellow humans are *created* in the image of God. We are first of all creatures, and it is a divine gift, not an ontological feature, that we are images of God. Ontologically, as for the other creatures too, a clear-cut distinction separates us from God: 'God is in heaven, and you upon earth' (Eccl. 5.2).

Furthermore, it is only by entitlement that God gives us the right of dominion over the other parts of creation. A special word, the dominium terrae, was necessary for that. The human being is, then, a sort of *primus inter pares*, surely with a specific function and a specific dignity in the world, but still part of creation. If one envisions a line that is drawn in order to separate different levels in the order of being, the Biblical evidence speaks in favour of a line between God and the rest of creation, making humanity entirely a part of creation, without separating human body and reason, and therefore clearly opposing the Greek tradition briefly portrayed in the first section of this essay.

The Holistic Implications of the Christian Idea of Creation

If the position of mankind in the whole of creation is understood in the way developed in the preceding section, the dominium terrae of Gen. 1.28 can no longer be used as permission for the selfish exploitation of nature. Both Biblical stories of creation – Genesis 1 and 2 – suggest a well-ordered system of being in which human superiority over nature is largely relativized. It is superiority only in grade, and it has to be exercized in a fashion that is beneficial for all. This vision of created nature and of the human position within it has clear holistic implications.

Here and in the following I use the term 'holistic' in a similar way to Baird Callicott, one of the advocates of holism in the philosophy of nature. For him (and for me), holism is a *worldview* and is identical with a *systemic* paradigm, opposed both to a mechanical and an individualistic worldview (cf. Callicott, 1999, pp. 21, 68). The notion of worldview is important in order to avoid confusion with the well-known distinctions between anthropocentrism, biocentrism, pathocentrism and physiocentrism in environmental ethics. Of course, there are worldviews that are either anthropocentric, biocentric, pathocentric or physiocentric. But in my terminology, I like to restrict these terms to the question of the foundation of environmental *ethics*. Respect (or non-respect) for the environment can be justified on anthropo-, bio-, patho- or physiocentric grounds. However, this distinction with regard to ethics should not be confused with the notion of a comprehensive worldview, as is usually done when identifying a mechanical worldview with anthropocentrism and a systemic worldview with bio- or physiocentrism. As I will argue later, one can have a holistic worldview and still reject a physiocentric stance with regard to ethics. Therefore, I insist on 'holism' as a vision of the world without identifying it with physiocentrism in ethics. The identification of a holistic and a systemic approach is important in order to avoid an individualistic understanding of holism (which is characterized by an emphasis on the untouchable dignity of *each individual member* of the whole). Apparently, Aldo Leopold, the forebear of Callicott's land ethic, was not clear on that point (cf., also for the following, Callicott, 1999, pp. 68–69). What is important here is the openness of a systemic worldview – taken in my sense – to rather radical interventions, if they are necessary for the benefit (here I differ from Callicott, who only speaks of conservation)[16] of the whole.

The moral norm that follows from this holistic and systemic worldview is the following, slightly (but decisively) modifying Leopold and Callicott: An action is right when it tends to support the integrity, stability, and beauty of the whole of creation. It is wrong when it tends otherwise (cf. Callicott, 1999, p. 68).[17]

I take this norm to be an authentic ethical consequence of the worldview that is implied by the Biblical narrative of creation. The Christian idea of creation has holistic implications. Creation is seen as a whole, as a system, and it is the task of humanity to support the integrity, stability, and beauty of the whole of creation. Evidence for this can be found in both Biblical stories of creation. In Genesis 1, creation is understood as the opposite of chaos. God creates step by step, everything is well-ordered and – after six days of work – 'the heavens and the earth were finished, and all their multitude' (Gen. 2.1). The world in its created order is good, even 'very good' (Gen. 1.31). Everything (including the non-living) has its specific internal value within the whole of creation (cf. Jenson, 1992, pp. 216–217). In Genesis 2, the more human image of a garden is chosen. This garden, too, has a specific order; it is planted by God himself (not a wilderness), and man is put in the garden 'to till it and keep it' (Gen. 2.15). Man is the gardener, supposed to maintain the order intended by God. In both stories, the human being is entirely part of creation, part of the system.

Holism and Physiocentrism

But the notion of a well-ordered system does not imply that everything in the system is of *equal* value. The order of creation in Genesis 1 is clearly ascending, beginning with the non-living, adding first plants and then animals, finishing with the human being and the seventh day of rest. Animals are, rather late in the story, the first ones to receive a benediction (Gen. 1.22), humanity receives a benediction and the dominium terrae, and humanity is the only species to be called 'image of God'. The distinction is further emphasized by a small, yet important detail: God just 'says' the benediction of the animals, whereas the benediction of the male and female human being is said 'to them' (Gen. 1.28). This indicates a personal relationship between God and humanity, more personal at least than the relationship between God and the rest of creation. Additionally, there is the specific human notion of 'image of God' as it has already been interpreted above. In Genesis 2, the specific place of the human being is indicated by God giving him a specific command (Gen. 2.16–17) and purpose (gardener), and that the man names the animals (Gen. 2.19). The notion of a special place for humanity with particular responsibilities within the system of creation is further supported by the story of Noah (Genesis 6–9) which presupposes a suffering of other creatures because of human sin, an idea which is shared later, in the New Testament, by Paul (Rom. 8.18–23).

To put it boldly: both Biblical stories of creation imply a *hierarchical* system. There is a clear hierarchy between the non-living and plants (whose recreational ability is emphasized in Gen. 1.11–12), between plants and animals (only animals receive a benediction; only animals receive a name and are considered as possible partners for the human being) and between animals and humanity.

Therefore, in my view, the Biblical image of the created world is holistic and systemic, yet hierarchical. The first point marks an important caveat with respect to all traditional ideas about creation that take the non-human world to be just an instrument for human pleasure and exploitation; the second point indicates a difference regarding all bio- or physiocentric visions of the world. The difference can be explained when we consider the following descriptive (and – in fact – also normative) statement by Arne Naess: 'Human nature is such that, with sufficient comprehensive maturity, we cannot help but identify ourselves with all living beings, beautiful or ugly, big or small, sentient or not' (Naess, 2008, p. 81). Yes and no! Yes, we are creatures of God like the whole world around us and therefore definitely 'cannot help but identify ourselves' with all other creatures. No, even if our 'self' should not be confused 'with the narrow ego' (Naess, 2008, p. 81), it remains a *human* self with characteristic capacities and tasks, distinguished from the capacities and tasks of other members of the system.

In this point, I do not agree with *theological* supporters of physiocentrism, such as Jürgen Moltmann. Moltmann argues emphatically for a 'decentralized' ethics of creation that implies a claim for a charter of rights of nature, similar to the existing declarations of human rights (Moltmann, 1995, pp. 44–45). I agree with Moltmann (and Naess) that everything in creation has an intrinsic value and should thus be protected 'for its own sake' (Moltmann, 1995, p. 45) from human exploitation. But does this mean an *equal* standard of protection as the one guaranteed by the notion of human dignity? (cf. Moltmann, 1995, pp. 44–45).[18] This notion implies that absolutely *no* intrusion into physical and personal integrity is allowed without informed consent by the person whose dignity is involved – a concept that is rather difficult to implement regarding nature. Moltmann himself does not go that far: he allows, later in his paper, human intrusions into the integrity of nature; such intrusions must be justified, but they *are* justified if 'the interest in the intrusion is more important than the interest in an undiminished conservation of the rights of nature, and if the intrusion is not excessive' (Moltmann, 1995, p. 45[19]). Let us imagine someone comes up with such a claim in order to justify the intrusion into the integrity of *humans*, in order to justify, for example, torture or medical experiments. Even if, unfortunately, such claims are expressed time and again in public discourse, there can be no doubt that they are not acceptable from an ethical standpoint. I am quite sure that Moltmann agrees with me on this point. But if he does, he gets into trouble with his claim of *similar* ethical standards concerning human beings and nature. In fact, in admitting at least *some* justification for human intrusion into nature, Moltmann agrees with at least some sort of human superiority. And he is right to do so. I cannot imagine a society or even a single person to live entirely accordingly to a physiocentric worldview. He or she would be prompted to *live* in the way that Albert Schweitzer has only imagined: protection of each blade of grass and each insect that gets into one's way. Cooking a meal, using each sort of modern means of transportation or writing on paper in order to publish one's ideas would be strictly prohibited.

Here, a physiocentric worldview becomes contradictory in itself.[20] Speaking of an obligation to protect presupposes a certain hierarchy of the protector and the protected. Formulating an ethics with regard to our human conduct towards nature (and not the other way around) is not possible without at least some sort of idea of an advanced human responsibility. Therefore, I cannot agree with the idea of a 'decentralized' ethics. The task of environmental ethics is not to deny a specific, 'superior' responsibility of humanity but to discuss how this undeniable responsibility can be guided towards a behaviour that respects, as much as possible, the intrinsic value of creation. For the same reason, the idea of human superiority is unavoidable in ethics, and the task is, once again, not to deny it but to distinguish ethically 'good' and 'bad' ways of exercising human superiority. It is just not true that an anthropocentric conception of environmental ethics is necessarily equivalent to a destructive behaviour towards nature.[21] I do not employ the term 'anthropocentric' because it is too closely linked to the idea of a mere *extrinsic* value of nature, which means that nature has moral value only by its instrumental or aesthetic worth to humanity, and not in itself. But the 'anthropocentric' idea of a superior place of humanity in the world is, actually, the best way to engage the specific human responsibility that must be emphasized in all environmental questions, if this idea is embedded in a comprehensive holistic and systemic worldview. A 'decentralized' ethics could, on the other hand, even be abused in order to deny this enlarged responsibility.

If the environment is a system – and the systemic interferences between human conduct and the functioning of nature have never been as evident as in the current age of global warming – then it is a system that is marked by internal differences, by a hierarchy in which the human being has a central responsibility. It is, therefore, necessary to speak a bit more about the relationship between humanity and the rest of creation.

Humans as Stewards

I have already pointed out that the Biblical narrative is entirely conscious of this special human responsibility and its necessity. The notion of *imago Dei* and the image of the gardener, installed by God, give credence to this responsibility. The system of creation does not work autonomously, without 'tilling and keeping', without a representative of the creator on earth, who can – unfortunately – also work in a destructive way, as when human sinfulness negatively impacts the well-being of nature (Genesis 6–9 and Romans 8). The centrality of the human being within the system of creation echoes the centrality of God as the creator. Imago Dei implies, as I have argued above, a way of exercising beneficent dominion that is supposed to be an image of the dominion God exercises over the whole of creation.

We must, therefore, speak briefly about the relationship between God and creation, before coming back to the human–nature relationship. Physiocentric ethicists tend to put forward the immanence of God within nature, somehow replacing the classical idea of a transcendent, superior God. Moltmann, who can once again serve as an example, emphasizes the inhabitation of God within creation by the life-giving Spirit, and he finds the principle of life in reciprocal relationships, excluding unilateral dominion (Moltmann, 1995, p. 40).[22] Other contemporary eco-theologians go even further by explicitly speaking of a Biblical pantheism (see Butting, 2010).[23]

In my reading of Genesis 1, the chapter emphasizes much more the distance between God and creation than their togetherness. The world is created by the Word of God; it is not an emanation or a part of God. Following Old Testament scholar W. H. Schmidt, *all* talk about creation in the Old Testament intends to *distinguish* the creator and the result of creation, thereby setting up a vision of creation that is singular within the scope of contemporary near-east religions and mythologies (cf. Schmidt, 1986, p. 182).[24] Christian theology has followed this line and has taken a clear stance against pantheism – with good reason (cf. Lohmann, 2002). The idea that is pursued by this stance is precisely the one criticized by Moltmann: the idea that God, complementary to the inhabitation of the Spirit in the world, maintains sovereignty over the world. God's immanence is a special way of exercising dominion, far from the notion of a reciprocal relationship between God and creation.

If the human being is called an image of this God, and if this title is connected with the dominium terrae, humans are supposed to represent God on earth by exerting this dominion in God's place. I have already mentioned that this signifies a beneficial dominion, one that does not seek selfish purposes but the well-being of the whole world – a dominion of service, ideally represented by Jesus Christ as the true image of God.

It is here that the notion of stewardship comes to mind, which has received a lot of attention in recent discussions of environmental ethics (cf. Basney, 2000; Berry, 2006; Lincoln, 2006; Robinson and Chatraw, 2006; Van Dyke et al., 1996). Seen by many as 'key to a theology of nature' (Hall, 2006), others challenge it as 'an imperial concept that assumes an automatic superiority invested in those in charge' (Lovelock, 2006, p. 108). After the explanations I have given above, it should be understandable that the assumption of an 'automatic superiority' is not something that frightens me. I actually take the opposite stance: instead of challenging any notion of superiority, I take it as an unavoidable consequence of creation that the earth as a holistic system only works and flourishes if there is an order, including some sort of superiority. Once again, it is not superiority as such, but its abuse that must be challenged. The notion of stewardship, with its allusion to service, is definitely up to the challenge. The gardener of Genesis 2 is a good image for the proper exertion of stewardship, emphasizing the conservative attitude of keeping but indicating at the same time that the task of keeping order may mean a more intrusive approach for the benefit of the whole. Sometimes it may be necessary to cut down a tree. Following Moltmann, such intrusive conduct needs justification, but it is an integral part of human responsibility for the world.

Human Dignity and the 'Dignity of Creation'

Nature as the object of divine creation has an 'inherent value'.[25] Does this imply that we can talk of a specific 'dignity' of creation, similar to human dignity? At first sight, there should be no doubt that 'inherent value' equals 'dignity', given the fact that Immanuel Kant, in a famous passage of his philosophical work, defines dignity by the possession of an inherent value (Kant, 1964, p. 102).[26] Kant remains ambiguous, however, because he links this notion of intrinsic value exclusively to human autonomy, thereby following the long-standing tradition that identifies dignity with the possession of reason. For Kant, there is a condition for dignity: the possession of autonomous reason. Yet, to bind the existence of dignity to the fulfilment of a condition is a hidden contradiction to the idea of an *intrinsic* value, which can never be lost or revoked.

In any case, from a Christian standpoint, there is no reason to withhold the possession of 'intrinsic value' from everything that has been created by

God. There are no Biblical grounds for the long history of linking dignity with the possession of reason. Baranzke, who has written an important monograph on the notion of the 'dignity of creation' (Baranzke, 2002), therefore rightly identifies two different concepts of dignity in the history of Christian thought. She prefers the tradition that acknowledges the internal value of creation (she calls it the tradition of 'bonitas'). That is why she is not reticent about the concept of a 'dignity of creation'.

The problem with this concept is its inherent ethical implication. In the current human rights framework, the possession of human dignity implies a very high moral status, connected to an absolute protection of personal freedom and integrity. I have already stated above: whoever has dignity should be protected from all forms of non-consensual intrusion into his or her physical and personal integrity. Now, if we speak about the 'dignity of creation' in the same way as 'human dignity', we get into trouble with this clear-cut ethical implication of dignity. Such a perspective leads to one of two conclusions – both problematic. Either we must attribute to nature the same sensitive moral status as to fellow human beings, which is impractical (see above), incompatible with the idea of a hierarchical system of creation and senseless – a tree cannot 'consent' to being cut down. Or we must lessen the moral status implied by the possession of dignity, which would damage the whole ethical, juridical and political effort of recent decades spent bolstering 'human dignity' as a last resort of protection from all kinds of inter-human discrimination and atrocity.

Knoepffler, who clearly sees the dilemma produced by the idea of a 'dignity of creation', argues for a gradual understanding of dignity, depending on whether it is attributed to human beings, to sentient non-humans or to the rest of nature. For him, human dignity is not the same as the dignity of a dog, and the dignity of a dog is not the same as the dignity of a bacterium; all different grades of dignity are bound together by a common, albeit decreasing, obligation of respect (Knoepffler, 2010, p. 93).[27] But this gradual understanding implies a lessening in the sense of the second alternative given above: when we get used to speaking of the (rather small) 'dignity' of a bacterium, this will inevitably result in a loss of the moral requirement associated with the notion of human dignity.

Facing this inevitable dilemma with regard to the idea of a 'dignity of creation', I plead for a – somehow artificial, admittedly – distinction between 'dignity' and 'intrinsic value'. In the ethical discourse, we should speak of 'dignity', including the highest possible protection of integrity, only with regard to humans. The rest of creation is subject to respect and recognition; it has 'intrinsic value', but is open to human interventions, which are ethically justified whenever they serve 'to support the integrity, stability, and beauty of the whole of creation'.[28] Human dignity, according to the idea of imago Dei, is best realized with this kind of responsible service for the rest of creation.

Notes

[1] See Deane-Drummond (2008) for a very instructive overview. 'The turn to ecology' is the title of the preface (ibid., p. IX–XV). For the discussion in philosophy, see Krebs (1999) and Meyer (2003).

[2] '. . . anthropozentrischen, naturzerstörenden Charakter'.

[3] 'Ein Eigenrecht, ein Recht, das der Natur qua Natur zukommt, kann ihr aufgrund sittlicher Argumentation nicht zugesprochen werden. Von Natur aus kommen Teilen der Natur oder ihr selbst kein Selbstwert zu.' Irrgang refers explicitly to the ecological anthropocentrism of Alfons Auer (see e.g. Auer, 1984, p. 55: 'Die Natur kommt zu sich selbst nur im Menschen, nur in ihm erfüllt sich ihr Sinn.').

[4] In Eastern Orthodox theology, traditionally the presence of God within creation and the unity of creation is much more emphasized than in Western Christianity; see Bergmann (1993); Bergmann (2005); Zizioulas (2006, pp. 273–290); Deane-Drummond (2008, pp. 56–68).

[5] Augustine, *De trinitate* 12, 11, 16; quoted by Volp (2006, p. 235): 'Honor enim hominis verus est imago et similitudo Dei'.

[6] Augustine, *Contra epistulam fundamenti Manichaeorum* 37; quoted by Volp (2006, p. 237): 'Et hinc maxime adparet, quantam tibi tribuerit dignitatem, quod deus, qui solus tibi naturaliter dominator, fecit alia bona, quibus tu quoque dominareris'.

[7] Ambrose, *De officiis*; quoted by Volp (2006, p. 226): 'Nihil est enim magis quod homo ceteris animantibus praestet quam quod rationis est particeps, causas rerum requirit, generis sui auctorem inuestigandum putat, in cuius potestate uitae necisque nostrae potestas sit'.

[8] Seneca, *Letter* 76; quoted Long et al. (1987, p. 395, no. 63D).

[9] All Biblical quotations are from the New Revised Standard Version, 1989.

[10] Groh and Groh (1991, p. 65), give one example of such a use of Gen. 1.28 by a sixteenth-century scholar.

[11] 'Als Sohn Gottes im AR [Alten Reich] und MR [Mittleren Reich] besaß der König kraft seiner Geburt die Herrschaftsautorität, auch wenn diese im MR durch das direkte Eingreifen Gottes beschränkt wurde; als Abbild Gottes, d.h. als sein Repräsentant, bleibt die Herrschaftsautorität beim Gott, der König übt sie stellvertretend auf Erden aus.'

[12] Translation of an Egyptian inscription: 'Als sein Abbild hat Re dich eingesetzt, zur Rettung des Schiffbrüchigen (d.h. des Schwachen, im Leben Gescheiterten).'

[13] 'Der Titel wird nur noch vom Menschen, nie vom König gebraucht. Das Alte Testament hat verallgemeinert und jedermann – nicht nur den Angehörigen eines Volkes, sondern allen Menschen, auch Mann und Frau in gleicher Weise

(Gen 1, 27f) – zugesprochen, was einst im wesentlichen nur dem König zukam: als "Bild Gottes" Herrschaft auszuüben.'

[14] Ockinga: 'So wie die Herrschaft des ägyptischen Königs über die Menschen sollte die des Menschen über die Tiere eine positive, segnende Auswirkung haben'; Schmidt: 'Als Gottes Stellvertreter ist der Mensch Gottes Statthalter auf Erden; er übt seine Stellung als "Bild Gottes" in der Schöpfung aus'.

[15] Another interesting re-reading of fourth-century Trinitarian theology with regard to the notion of creation and ecological concerns has been undertaken by Sigurd Bergmann. After an investigation of Gregory of Nazianzus's theology, which focuses not on the second, but on the third person of the Trinity, Bergmann emphasizes the ecological implications of Gregory's thinking about the Holy Spirit: 'The Spirit's unique characteristic in Gregory's theology is its capacity to be with both the Father and the Son *as well as* with creation. As God's Spirit *in the midst of* creation, it leads God and creation ever closer together' (Bergmann, 2005, p. 171). There is Biblical evidence for this very special position of the Spirit, indwelling not only in the Father and the Son, but also in the whole of creation as a giver of life. But there is also evidence for a remaining distance between God, the creator, and the world as his creation. I'll come back to the idea of inhabitation later in this chapter.

[16] I speak explicitly of a *benefit* in order to mark here a point of difference with regard to Callicott, who allows such 'draconian' interventions only for the sake of the *conservation* of the whole or individual parts of it. In my view, a systemic worldview does not imply per se a conservative approach: changes and progress in nature occur, they can be implemented by human interventions and those changes and interventions are 'good' once they support – not only 'preserve' (Callicott, following Leopold) – 'the integrity, stability, and beauty of the biotic community' (Callicott, 1999, p. 68). From a Christian perspective, a romantic ecological conservatism must be questioned for not taking sufficiently into account the conflicts and diseases that are part of creation after the intrusion of sin.

[17] Quotation from Leopold's 'golden rule': 'A thing is right when it tends to preserve the integrity, stability, and beauty of the biotic community. It is wrong when it tends otherwise.'

[18] 'Der Schutz der Natur, der Arten von Pflanzen und Tieren sowie der Lebensbedingungen und der Gleichgewichte der Erde müssen aber einen der Würde des Menschen entsprechenden Rang in den Staatszielbestimmungen der Staaten und in den internationalen Vereinbarungen bekommen.'

[19] ' . . . wenn das Eingriffsinteresse schwerer wiegt als das Interesse an ungeschmälerter Wahrung der Rechte der Natur und wenn der Eingriff nicht übermäßig ist'.

[20] Let me briefly note another contradiction: isn't it a result of just another type of anthropocentric thinking to proclaim *rights* of nature? Who claims rights in nature? Only humans can do this. Physiocentrism, it seems to me, cannot avoid, at its very heart, anthropocentric thinking in applying categories from the *human* discourse to the non-human world.

[21] Against Moltmann (1995, p. 45): ' . . . anthropozentrischen, naturzerstörenden Charakter'.

[22] 'Nicht einseitige Herrschaft, sondern Wechselseitigkeit der Beziehungen ist das Prinzip des Lebens.'

[23] On p. 2 of her paper, Klara Butting takes the whole story of creation in Genesis 1 as a rendering of the *immanence* of God within the world, culminating on the seventh day of rest in a feast of God *within* the whole of creation. This is a very creative interpretation of the Biblical text: on the seventh day, God 'rested' – there is no feast mentioned – 'from all the work that he had done' (Gen. 2.2), therefore marking a clear distinction between God and the world as the result of the work of creation.

[24] 'Gewiß gibt es unter den vielfältigen Darstellungsweisen, in denen das Alte Testament von der Schöpfung redet, keine alleingültige; *denn sie wollen alle Schöpfer und Schöpfung gegenüberstellen*' (italics FL). This emphasis of the Biblical narrative on a separation between God and creation is neglected far too much by Welker (1991). See my criticism of Welker in Lohmann (2002).

[25] This notion of 'inherent value' is emphasized quite strongly by Arne Naess, among others: 'The flourishing of human and nonhuman life on earth has inherent value. The value of nonhuman life-forms is independent of the usefulness of the nonhuman world for human purposes' (Naess, 2008, p. 111). I agree entirely with this proposition. I also agree with the following: 'Humans have no right to reduce this richness and diversity [of life-forms] except to satisfy *vital* needs' (ibid.). I just claim that the last exception can be stated only in a framework that tacitly presupposes human superiority because it is nobody else than the human community who will decide when vital needs are at stake. Naess's conception shows once again the internal contradictions of a physiocentric approach.

[26] 'What is relative to universal human inclinations and needs has a *market price*; what, even without presupposing a need, accords with a certain taste – that is, with satisfaction in the mere purposeless play of our mental powers – has a *fancy price* (*Affektionspreis*); but that which constitutes the sole condition under which anything can be an end in itself has not merely a relative value – that is, a price – but has an intrinsic value – that is, *dignity*.'

[27] 'Natürlich verdient ein Hund eine andere Form der Achtung als ein Gerstenhalm oder ein Bakterium, aber eben keine Achtung wie ein Mensch. Er verdient diese größere Achtung, weil er nach allem, was wir naturwissenschaftlich wissen, komplexe Empfindungen und Präferenzen hat – von Empfindungen und Präferenzen eines Bakteriums zu sprechen, erscheint übertrieben und wirklichkeitsfremd. Das vollständige Instrumentalisierungsverbot gilt für nichtmenschliche Lebewesen also gerade nicht, es sei denn, Exemplare ihrer Gattung wären analog zu uns moral- und vernunftfähig.'

[28] See note 17. I thank Sigurd Bergmann and Dieter Gerten for their helpful commentaries to the first draft of this chapter.

References

Altner, G. (1991), *Naturvergessenheit: Grundlagen einer umfassenden Bioethik.* Darmstadt: Wissenschaftliche Buchgesellschaft.

Auer, A. (1984), *Umweltethik: Ein theologischer Beitrag zur ökologischen Diskussion.* Düsseldorf: Patmos.

Baranzke, H. (2002), *Würde der Kreatur? Die Idee der Würde im Horizont der Bioethik.* Würzburg: Königshausen & Neumann.

Barth, K. (1956), *Church Dogmatics*, Vol. IV/1. Edinburgh: T&T Clark.

Basney, L. (2000), *An Earth-Careful Way of Life: Christian Stewardship and the Environmental Crisis.* Vancouver: Regent College Publishing.

Bergmann, S. (1993), 'Die Welt als Ware oder Haushalt? Die Wegwahl der trinitarischen Kosmologie bei Gregor von Nazianz'. *Evangelische Theologie*, 53, 460–470.

— (2005), *Creation Set Free: The Spirit as Liberator of Nature.* Grand Rapids: Eerdmans.

Bergmann, S. and Gerten, D. (2010), 'Religion in climate and environmental change: towards a symphony of voices, memories and visions in a new polycentric field', in S. Bergmann and D. Gerten (eds), *Religion and Dangerous Environmental Change.* Münster: LIT, pp. 1–12.

Berry, R. J. (2006) (ed.), *Environmental Stewardship: Critical Perspectives – Past and Present.* London and New York: T&T Clark.

Butting, K. (2010), 'Schöpfung, Natur und Gottes Welteinwohnung'. *Junge Kirche*, 71, 1–4.

Callicott, J. B. (1999), *Beyond the Land Ethic: More Essays in Environmental Philosophy.* Albany: State University of New York Press.

Deane-Drummond, C. (2008), *Eco-Theology.* London: Darton, Longman & Todd Ltd.

Descartes, R. (1973), 'Discours de la méthode', in C. Adam and P. Tannery (eds), *Descartes – Œuvres*, Tome 6. Paris: Vrin.

Groh, R. and Groh, D. (1991), *Weltbild und Naturaneignung: Zur Kulturgeschichte der Natur.* Frankfurt am Main: Suhrkamp.

Groß, W. (2001), 'Gen 1,26.27; 9,6: Statue oder Ebenbild Gottes? Aufgabe und Würde des Menschen nach dem hebräischen und dem griechischen Wortlaut', in *Jahrbuch für Biblische Theologie 15: Menschenwürde.* Neukirchen-Vluyn: Neukirchener Verlag, pp. 11–38.

Hall, D. J. 'Stewardship as key to a theology of nature', in Berry, R. J. (2006) (ed.), *Environmental Stewardship: Critical Perspectives – Past and Present.* London and New York: T&T Clark, pp. 129–144.

Irrgang, B. (1992), *Christliche Umweltethik: Eine Einführung.* München: Reinhardt.

Jenson, P. P. (1992), *Graded Holiness: A Key to the Priestly Conception of the World.* Sheffield: JSOT Press.

Kant, I. (1964), *Groundwork of the Metaphysic of Morals.* New York: Harper & Row.

Kehl, M. (2008), *Und Gott sah, dass es gut war: Eine Theologie der Schöpfung* (second edition). Freiburg, Basel and Wien: Herder.

Knoepffler, N. (2010), *Angewandte Ethik: Ein systematischer Leitfaden.* Köln, Weimar and Wien: Böhlau.

Krebs, A. (1999), *Ethics of Nature: A Map.* Berlin and New York: Walter de Gruyter.

Lincoln, S. F. (2006), *Challenged Earth: An Overview of Humanity's Stewardship of Earth.* London: Imperial College Press.

Lohmann, F. (2002), 'Die Bedeutung der dogmatischen Rede von der "creatio ex nihilo"'. *Zeitschrift für Theologie und Kirche*, 99, 196–225.

Long, A. A. and Sedley, D. N. (1987), *The Hellenistic Philosophers. Vol. 1: Translations of the Principal Sources with Philosophical Commentary*. Cambridge: Cambridge University Press.

Lovelock, J. (2006), 'The fallible concept of stewardship of the earth', in Berry, R. J. (2006) (ed.), *Environmental Stewardship: Critical Perspectives – Past and Present*. London and New York: T&T Clark, pp. 106–111.

Meyer, K. (2003), *Der Wert der Natur: Begründungsvielfalt im Naturschutz*. Paderborn: Mentis.

Moltmann, J. (1995), 'Ökologie', in *Theologische Realenzyklopädie* XXV. Berlin and New York: Walter de Gruyter, pp. 36–46.

Naess, A. (2008), *The Ecology of Wisdom*, A. Drengson and B. Devall (eds). Berkeley: Counterpoint.

Ockinga, B. (1984), *Die Gottebenbildlichkeit im alten Ägypten und im Alten Testament*. Wiesbaden: Otto Harrassowitz.

Pico della Mirandola, G. (1956), *Oration on the Dignity of Man*. Chicago: Regnery Publishing.

Plato (1986), *Phaedrus* (with translation and commentary by C. J. Rowe). Warminster: Aris & Phillips.

— (1991), *The Republic* (translated, with notes, an interpretive essay and a new introduction by A. Bloom; second edition). New York: Basic Books.

Robinson, T. and Chatraw, J. (2006), *Saving God's Green Earth: Rediscovering the Church's Responsibility to Environmental Stewardship*. Norcross, GA: Ampelon Publishing.

Schmidt, W. H. (1986), *Alttestamentlicher Glaube in seiner Geschichte* (fifth edition). Neukirchen-Vluyn: Neukirchener Verlag.

Schwöbel, C. (1995), 'The renaissance of Trinitarian theology: reasons, problems and tasks', in C. Schwöbel (ed.), *Trinitarian Theology Today: Essays on Divine Being and Act*. Edinburgh: T&T Clark International, pp. 1–30.

Van Dyke, F., Mahan, D. C., Sheldon, J. K. and Brand, R. H. (1996), *Redeeming Creation: The Biblical Basis for Environmental Stewardship*. Downers Grove, IL: InterVarsity Press.

Volp, U. (2006), *Die Würde des Menschen: Ein Beitrag zur Anthropologie in der Alten Kirche*. Leiden: Brill.

Welker, M. (1991), 'What is creation? Rereading Genesis 1 and 2'. *Theology Today*, 48, 56–71.

Zizioulas, J. (2006), 'Priest of creation', in Berry, R. J. (ed.), *Environmental Stewardship: Critical Perspectives – Past and Present*. London and New York: T&T Clark, pp. 273–290.

Chapter 7

Evangelicals and Climate Change

Michael Roberts

Introduction

The 2001 edition of the *World Christian Encyclopedia* stated there were 2.1 billion Christians in the world, or 33 per cent of the total population. Of those Christians, more than a quarter are Evangelical or Pentecostal (Barrett, 2001; Mandryk, 2010). Hence, Evangelical (and Pentecostal and Charismatic) Christians number in excess of half a billion people today and represent at least 10 per cent of the world's population. In Sub-Saharan Africa, Latin America and the United States, they are the dominant religious group and are of considerable influence socially and politically. It is probably more precise to term many of these groups Neo-Pentecostals, but their Evangelical roots must not be forgotten, nor the fact that their beliefs are substantially the same as Evangelicals. Thus the views, or rather diversity of views, of such a large and disparate religious grouping on climate change are very important. Here I agree with Christopher Catherwood (2010) and make a relatively small distinction between Evangelical and Neo-Pentecostal.

If we consider only the mainstream Protestant, Catholic and Orthodox churches and statements from ecumenical bodies, it is easy to conclude that Christians – at least officially – are convinced both of anthropogenic climate change and the need for concerted action to mitigate the effects. However, Evangelicals and Pentecostals are divided both on the recognition of the reality of climate change and the need for action. As Evangelicals have much influence in the world today, their understanding of climate change needs to be understood.

Most Evangelical responses to climate change emanate from Britain and the United States, and that is inevitably the focus of this paper. Pro- and anti-views, regarding the existence of anthropogenic climate change, have filtered down to the 'average' churchgoer and have become a part of the fundamentalist/moderate divide. With the influence of American Evangelicals throughout the world, such a divide can be expected to spread. Simplistically, we can divide Evangelicals into pro- and anti-climate change groups, but this does not consider the numbers (probably the majority) who are either confused by the issues or simply indifferent.

American and British Evangelicalism have long been characterized by a strong environmentalist emphasis, seen especially in groups such as Au Sable in the United States and the John Ray Initiative in the United Kingdom. These have attracted several leading environmentalists, including American Cal de Wit and R. J. Berry and Sir John Houghton FRS in the United Kingdom. Houghton has been very influential and was the first Chairman of the IPCC in 1988. Climate change came to the fore in the agendas of these groups in the early 1990s, and several environmental initiatives were launched before 2000. Houghton himself convinced the National Association of Evangelicals (NAE) in the United States to take a stand on climate change in 2004. That caused a strong reaction from more right-wing American Evangelicals. This has resulted in statements from the Interfaith Stewardship Alliance (ISA) (mostly conservative Evangelicals and some Catholics) who responded with an *Open Letter* in 2006 that included the signatures of many leading Evangelicals. They have the support of Senator James Inhofe, a Republican from Oklahoma, who opposed climate change. The divisions and conflict are more apparent in the United States than in the United Kingdom, but the issue is making inroads in Britain. This paper does not investigate the influence of the debate on the rest of the world, but such influence is liable to increase if only because of the opposition to perceived liberal theological views.

This paper describes the history and present situation in the United States and United Kingdom but only surmises the situation in Africa and Latin America. With Evangelicals and Pentecostals coming to dominate the Christian presence in Africa, parts of Asia and Latin America, it is easy to forget the roots of these movements, which are in the Evangelical Revival that began in Britain and North America in the 1730s.[1] Evangelicals came to dominate churches in the United States and Britain in the nineteenth century and were at the forefront of the Protestant missionary enterprise throughout the world. Pentecostalism grew out of Evangelicalism in the early twentieth century and forms a distinct but often overlapping group with Evangelicals. Pentecostals and Evangelicals share a faith centred on Christ with a very high view of the Bible. In the late twentieth century, the number of Evangelicals and Pentecostals grew exponentially in Africa, Latin America and parts of Asia so that, today, these movements are much less of a European religious faith. Within the Western world, Evangelicals are also the most vibrant sector of Christianity and are the main Christian group not in decline but actually growing. They are increasingly becoming more politically and socially active in many parts of the world, and because their numbers exceed half a billion they are a significant force in regard to climate change. Indeed, as described below, the Evangelical response to climate change is very influential in the United States.

Evangelicals and Ethical Implications of Science

Many aspects of science, such as the environment, genetic modification, abortion and euthanasia, have ethical implications that are addressed by Evangelicals. With the prevalence of Creationism[2] among Evangelicals today, it is often assumed that Evangelicals take a literal view of the Bible and thus reject evolution and any historical science. That is only half the story. Perhaps the most visible Evangelicals today are Creationists – as exemplified in groups such as Answers in Genesis – but many Evangelical churches and most Evangelical scientists are not Creationists and accept standard evolutionary science.[3]

It is very easy to assume that the loudest voices from the Evangelicals are typical and to conclude that Evangelicals are in the forefront of *The Republican War on Science* (Mooney, 2005) and echo the opinions of Tom Bithell in *The Politically Incorrect Guide to Science* (Bithell, 2005) – denying the reality of global warming, having no concern for energy usage and regarding embryo stem cell research as murder. That simple scenario is true for *some* Evangelicals but not all. Evangelicals have been both at the forefront of environmental concern and also in denial of global warming. There is no one monolithic Evangelical attitude towards any of these issues.

First, many Evangelicals, whether lay members or hard-working pastors, are simply uninterested in these issues and accept the lifestyle of those around them. The reasons for this indifference may be apathy or simply that these issues are of less importance than spiritual matters.

Secondly, attitudes of Evangelicals will depend on their individual religious and theological orientation. Certain Evangelical theologies, such as forms of the Holiness Movement and Dispensationalism, are more otherworldly and put the emphasis on a Christian life as purely 'spiritual'. As a result, concerns over 'this' world, whether pertaining to the environment or science, are regarded as secondary – unless they impinge directly on personal morality. Over the last 150 years, both the Holiness and Dispensational movements have greatly influenced Anglo-Saxon Evangelicalism, especially in America, and consequently have been exported to the rest of the world. This has resulted in a greater concern for Evangelicalism and personal holiness than for creation care or social action. Hence, for most of the twentieth century, Evangelicals have been weak on social action. Part of this is a reaction against the Social Gospel movement of the early twentieth century.

Thirdly, many Evangelical Calvinists have long had a political and social side to their faith, as may be seen in Abraham Kuyper and other Dutch Calvinists. Their influence in the United States has been disproportionate to their numbers and is partly due to Calvin College. The influence of Calvinists has been both to the 'left', as in environmentalism, and to the 'right', as Calvinism has been a source of both the right-wing theonomy associated with Rousas Rushdoony and the support for Apartheid by the Dutch Reformed Churches in South Africa until 1991.

Fourthly, since the 1970s, a good proportion of American Evangelicals have been associated with the religious right in its various forms and look to such leaders as Jerry Falwell and Pat Robertson. In addition to supporting every kind of anti-evolutionism, these leaders are militantly pro-life and have a tendency to oppose environmentalism. Mooney's *The Republican War on Science* documents this and makes a persuasive case that Evangelicals who are more right-wing politically or conservative/creationist theologically have greatly influenced scientific decisions in President George W. Bush's Administration, whether over climate, stem cells or the teaching of evolution. Examples of this can be seen on the websites of AIG (Answers in Genesis), ARN (Access Research Network), ICR (Institute of Creation Research) and DI (Discovery Institute).

Evangelicals and the Environment

Though Evangelicals are often seen as a homogenous group, the movement has always been characterized by strong internal divisions. Attitudes to the environment and global warming are no exception. Although on both sides of the Atlantic and in Australia there are numbers of Evangelicals who are important players in the environmental movement, there is a body of Evangelicals, especially in the United States, that is not overly concerned for the environment and considers those who are to have rejected the Gospel for a potpourri of liberalism, leftism and New-Ageism. John McKeown (2006) delightfully refers to the 'Greens' and the 'Browns', respectively.

Concern for the environment generally gained momentum in the 1960s, partly due to a previous lack of awareness of large-scale environmental damage. During the nineteenth century the effect of contaminated water on human health and the air pollution that resulted from factory emissions became apparent and Christians such as William Buckland and Charles Kingsley were involved in bringing about environmental improvements. Reverend F. O. Morris, an anti-Darwinian Evangelical, campaigned to protect seabirds beginning in the 1860s, when sporting gentlemen were killing them off by the thousands. He helped found the Society for the Protection of Birds, which was given its royal charter in 1904, and has since been one of the foremost British conservation societies. The great passion of nineteenth-century naturalists was collecting and classifying flora and fauna. However, in the latter part of the nineteenth century there was a sea change among naturalists, including Darwin and some Evangelicals, and the gung-ho attitude to collecting gradually fell out of favour.

These humble beginnings and the rise of ecology as a science led to greater environmental awareness, but it was only in the 1960s that environmentalism took the Western world by storm, beginning with Rachel Carson's *Silent Spring*, which catalogued the devastating effects of pesticides on wildlife. In 1967 Lynn White published his classic paper (White, 1967) firmly placing the blame for all environmental ills on the Judaeo–Christian faith and especially Gen. 1.28 – the Biblical verse that gives mankind 'dominion' – which White argues has been interpreted in a rapacious sense by Western societies. 'Dominion', he argues, was taken to mean domination and exploitation, so that beginning with the Industrial Revolution, Western society went into technological overdrive. After Carson's book, there was little immediate response from the churches, except from a few concerned individuals, but Christians were beginning to respond to environmental matters. Nevertheless, well into the 1970s and beyond, the environment was of minor concern to most Christians, Evangelical or otherwise.[4] Since the 1980s it has been of considerable importance to Christians of all traditions (see Oelschlaeger, 1994, for an account).

The Greens

Though most seemed to ignore him, some Evangelicals responded critically to White. Francis Schaeffer in *Pollution and the Death of Man* (1970) was probably the earliest to defend Christianity against White. He had a great concern for the environment and this book was probably the first *popular* Evangelical book on the subject. His promise was not fulfilled partly because of his superficial scholarship and involvement in the religious right. In the same year Richard Wright (1970) published a response to Lynn White's article in *Bioscience*. Wright is a marine microbiologist with a PhD from Harvard who taught for three decades at the Evangelical Gordon College in Massachusetts; he is the author of the textbook *Environmental Science* (7th edition, 2000).

Beginning in the early 1970s, an increasing number of Evangelicals began to emphasize the idea that care for the environment was an important Christian concern. This paralleled the growth of Environmentalism both in general and within Christian churches. But it was only in the late 1980s that many Christians took the environment to heart.

In Britain, two of the earliest Christian environmentalists were Hugh Montefiore, the liberal Bishop of Birmingham, and Prof R. J. (Sam) Berry (b. 1934), who was an Evangelical and professor of genetics at University College in London from 1974 to 2000. Berry has had a distinguished career spanning half a century on genetics, evolutionary biology and, increasingly, environmentalism. Berry wrote what was probably the first publication in Britain on Christian environmentalism, his booklet *Ecology and Ethics* (1972), at a time when concern for the environment was very limited. Looking back more than 30 years later, it is almost unbelievable that this 32-page booklet was the *only* Christian offering on the environment. Since that time, Berry has been a significant environmentalist in Britain and beyond. Along with colleagues from Christians in Science, he has done much to galvanize Evangelical opinion in the wider world. In 1980 he contributed an article on ethics to the World Conservation Strategy (WCS) of the United Nations Environmental Programme, in which he stressed that humanity is inseparable from nature, a viewpoint that the WCS had overlooked. In fact, both society in general and the church tend to separate humanity from nature for different reasons. At this point Berry agreed with the 'Deep Greens' and New Agers – though for very different reasons. Since nature is created by God, Berry maintained that it should be 'cared for' rather than just seen as a 'resource base' for humans. A quarter of a century later, it is difficult to comprehend how novel Berry's approach was on this. Evangelicals still tend(ed) to see people as souls to be saved from a wicked world and the earth as the stage upon which salvation was played out. They did not much consider that humans belong to the earth and that Christ affirmed creation in his Incarnation. In the early 1980s, mainstream Christians did not think that the environment was an important element in the concern for social justice. Yet now in Britain, few Christians would dare deny the necessity of environmental awareness. The development of environmental concern in the United States has been similar, except that religious right Evangelicals tend to dismiss environmentalism as 'leftie' and damaging to the economy, although in the more recent years, some have emphasized 'stewardship'. This attitude has been amplified by the movement's opposition to evolution, because creationism tends to accentuate the difference between humans and the rest of the natural world, as well as reject any science that argues the earth has existed for longer than c. 10,000 years, be it geology or cosmology.

Other significant environmentalists are Sir John Houghton (b. 1931), Chairman of the Intergovernmental Panel of Climate Change (IPCC) from 1988 to 2002, and Sir Ghillean Prance (b. 1937), former director of the Royal Botanic Gardens, Kew. They and others formed the John Ray Initiative[5] (named after the seventeenth-century biologist) in the mid-1990s to encourage a greater awareness of the environment among Christians, based on an open Evangelical theology of creation. Today the number of British Evangelical environmentalists are almost too numerous to list. They have possibly seen more tangible results than their American counterparts.

Evangelical environmentalism in the United States also began in the early 1970s, partly as a result of the influence of David Moberg, author of *The Great Reversal* (1973), which called Evangelicals back to the social concern of their nineteenth-century forebears. This idea was also developed at the 1974 Lausanne conference, which defined a wider view of 'mission' than Evangelicalism commonly held. Part of the same process was the Chicago Declaration of Evangelical Social Concern in 1973, which led to the formation of Evangelicals for Social Action (ESA). Environmentalism grew slowly in the 1970s, and, in 1980, Loren Wilkinson published *Earth-Keeping*. The same year saw the establishment of the Au Sable Institute for Environmental Studies to provide courses for the national Christian Colleges Coalition. Most of the staff were scientists; led by biologist Calvin DeWitt, they helped develop theological engagement with environmental ethics. In 1992, the Theological Commission of the World Evangelical Fellowship (WEF) hosted a forum at Au Sable. As a result, the ESA formed the Evangelical Environmental Network (EEN), which, in turn, collaborated with Au Sable and Christianity Today to produce the 'Evangelical Declaration on the Care of Creation', which was signed by more than 200 American Evangelical leaders. (An exposition of the declaration was later published as *The Care of Creation*.) Significant American signers included Loren Wilkinson, Calvin de Witt (1991) and Richard Wright, all of whom have written profusely for many decades.

A public joint declaration on the environment by the EEN – 'An Evangelical Declaration on the Care of Creation' – was made in 1994.

It was one of the first fruits of the EEN. Both resulted as a reaction to the World Council of Churches consultations on the 'Justice, Peace and Integrity of Creation' (JPIC) at Seoul in March 1990 (and earlier JPIC meetings) and from issues raised by the 1992 WEF meeting at Au Sable. The EEN obtained support from several hundred Evangelical leaders throughout the world, including John Stott (a leading British Evangelical and an accomplished ornithologist), Prof O. T. O'Donovan of Oxford and many others. In doing so, the EEN was able to present *Care of Creation* to the Evangelical constituency in several parts of the world, forming the basis of action for environmentally concerned Evangelicals. *The Care of Creation* (Berry, 2000) contains significant essays by leading Evangelicals and summarizes many of their aims. Books by Evangelicals on the environment are now quite numerous, and authors include Tony Campolo and James Jones, Bishop of Liverpool.

Whereas Evangelicals have often been less concerned about social issues than other Protestants, they have been in the vanguard on the environment both in Britain and America, despite the carping criticism of more conservative Evangelicals.

In recent years, the Greens have built support for a narrower and tougher venture, on climate change, calling for US emissions targets. A turning point was the Oxford Climate Forum in 2002, organized by the John Ray Initiative, where climatologist Sir John Houghton played a key role in gaining support among (largely Republican) conservative Christians. Richard Cizik, Vice President of Government Affairs for the NAE attended, 'dragged there by Jim Ball' of the Evangelical Environment Network and coordinator of the 'What Would Jesus Drive' campaign. As a result, Cizik claims to have had a 'conversion' so dramatic that he likened it to an 'altar call'. Since then, he has tried to convince American Evangelicals that care for creation is a core Christian responsibility.

The result of this was the 'Evangelical Climate Initiative' in February 2006, an event widely reported on in the science journals *Nature* and *Science*, and in the US news media, producing headlines such as 'Evangelicals Go Green'[6] in *Time* in February 2006. This has literally made global warming the hotspot in American Evangelicalism.

The Browns

Whereas most Christians and many Evangelicals have developed environmental awareness over the last 40 years, numbers of Evangelicals have not. Many of these are associated with the religious right in the United

States and have a great suspicion of anything liberal or 'leftie'. Since 1990, Evangelicals who are opposed to the approach of Evangelical environmentalists have been gaining strength and have formed coalitions to express their understanding of environmental stewardship, culminating in the *Cornwall Declaration* produced in 2000.

An essential aspect of opposition to mainline environmentalism came from free-market economics, which was linked to the upholding of conservative theological principles, both Catholic and Evangelical, with the founding of the Acton Institute for the Study of Religion and Liberty in 1990 by Father Robert Sirico. The goal of the institute was to 'promote a society that embraces civil liberties and free-market economics'. The Acton Institute and Calvin Beisner opposed the *Evangelical Declaration on the Care of Creation*. In 2000, the Acton Institute established the Interfaith Council for Environmental Stewardship, whose founders included leading Evangelicals such as James Dobson (Focus on the Family) and James Kennedy (Coral Ridge Ministries) as well as conservative Roman Catholics and Jews. Their *Cornwall Declaration* was produced in 2000 and posted to 35,000 churches. This declaration ran counter to the *Evangelical Declaration*, but it was not overtly 'anti-environmental'. First, the declaration is anthropocentric and emphatic that humanity has dominion over the earth, and it offers the criticism that 'some unfounded or undue concerns include fears of destructive manmade global warming, overpopulation, and rampant species loss'. Then, in the section on beliefs, the fifth statement reads, 'By disobeying God's Law, humankind brought on itself moral and physical corruption as well as divine condemnation in the form of a curse on the earth. Since the fall into sin people have often ignored their Creator, harmed their neighbours, and defiled the good creation'. This, as we see, claims that the Fall of Adam had an effect on the whole of creation in that it was a *curse* and not just a *fall*. (The notion of a curse often includes the idea that the earth is only a few thousand years old, as no animal could have died before the Fall.) David Kenneth Larsen wrote that '"the Cornwall Declaration represented the first acknowledgment of the need for environmental care" by politically conservative leaders'.[7] That in itself may be very significant for the future. In 2005 ICES was relaunched as the ISA.

To understand the Browns and the ISA, it is best to focus on their leading theoretician, Calvin Beisner, who is an associate professor of social ethics at Knox Theological Seminary in Florida and has written three books on environmental stewardship: *Prospects for Growth: A Biblical View of Population, Resources, and the Future* (1990); *Man, Economy, and Environment in Biblical*

Perspective (1994) and *Where Garden Meets Wilderness: Evangelical Entry Into the Environmental Debate* (1997). Beisner is not a scientist and studied under the economist Julian Simon, who did not recognize the limited nature of natural resources and whose book *Resourceful Earth* (1984) advocated the 'cornucopia hypothesis' of unlimited economic growth.[8] Hence Beisner takes far more of a free-market approach to the environment rather than a scientific one, whether on climate, pollution or material resources.

Beisner supports his understanding of environmental stewardship with his interpretation of early Genesis. He argues that there are two different mandates in Genesis 1 and 2 and that the 'curse' of Genesis drastically changed the natural world. Richard Wright argued in 1995 that 'the presumed biblical support for this position [for the emerging Christian anti-environmentalism] is currently found primarily in Beisner's work' (Wright, 1995). Beisner rejected the commonly held idea that the meaning of subdue and rule in Gen. 1.28 and to till and keep in Genesis 2 are essentially the same. He argues from the Hebrew, as he did in *Where Garden Meets Wilderness,* that there are two contrasting cultural mandates: Gen. 2.15 is gentle, and Gen. 1.28 is harsh. One is appropriate for the garden, the other to the earth outside the garden – the wilderness. Thus the wilderness must be 'subdued' to become a 'garden', a view that includes the necessity of taming wild animals. As Beisner expressed it:

> The incremental transformation of wilderness into garden, bringing the whole earth under human dominion, taming the wild beasts, and building order out of chaos . . . while tender cultivation is suited to a garden, forceful subduing is suited to all of the earth that has not yet been transformed into the garden. In short, subduing and ruling the earth should metamorphose gradually into tilling and keeping the garden as the earth is progressively transformed into the garden.

Many reject this biblical interpretation, but it has serious implications in that it transforms Gen. 1.28 into a command to tame the wilderness, and – as McKeown put it – 'so the logical outcome of his reading of Genesis (though he mostly avoids it) is that it is a dereliction of duty to leave any wild area untransformed or any wild creature untamed' (McKeown, 2006). This interpretation is completely contrary to any understanding of protecting wildernesses and the ideal of national parks, for example.

Beisner also claims that 'there is a difference between the Fall and the Curse. The Fall is man's sin, and the Curse is God's response to man's sin. The Curse is on the earth'. He points out that 'most evangelical books on the environment never mention the Curse' but only the Fall and that 'the only degradation that the *Declaration* mentions occurring to the earth is all through human action', neglecting God's direct action against the earth by curse and flood. Beisner judged that this silence was motivated by the Greens' desire to identify environmental problems as human-caused, but the report of the 1992 WEF meeting (cf. above) indicates that the reason was their uncertainty about whether the earth's physical aspects were actually changed by the curse. In other words, were earthquakes, storms, predation, death and disease actually introduced after the Fall to be the curse? This is a basic premise of creationism.[9] In his contribution to the Pontifical Council for Justice and Peace in April 2007, Beisner wrote: 'According to both the Bible and sound science, the great pools of oil and veins of coal formed from sudden, simultaneous deposits of vast numbers of plants and animals in a great geological cataclysm – what Christians recognize as the Flood of Noah's time' (Beisner, 2007).[10] Most would not agree that this is sound science, as he rejects all geological time and claims that carbon fuels were formed in the few months of the Flood.

It is not possible to give a detailed discussion of Beisner's and the ISA's reasons for their positions on environmental issues, but it is difficult not to conclude that they are based on three contentious conclusions: (1) there are unlimited resources on the earth, (2) that the events and time scales reported in early Genesis are a historic reality (3) the Fall also entailed a curse on creation by God.

From the presentation to the US Senate on religious views of global warming (June 2007) discussed below, it is clear that Beisner has convinced a large proportion of religious conservatives, including many Southern Baptists, of the wisdom of his views. However, his whole approach has been savaged by two environmentally informed Evangelical scientists, Richard Wright and the environmental geologist Jeff Greenberg of Wheaton College in Chicago. In spite of their critiques, many Evangelicals and conservative Catholics have supported the Cornwall Declaration and, under the guise of good stewardship of the environment, reject many of the aims of most environmentalists, particularly those that are seen as 'junk science'. This has caused a rift among American Evangelicals.

Global Warming/Climate Change

As I write this, there is immense controversy over global warming, especially in the wake of the Copenhagen climate talks and leaked e-mails from the University of East Anglia. The causes of warming are a mixture of natural effects, including solar fluctuations, and a general warming of the climate due to human technology, especially the use of carbon fuels. Thus, the scientific consensus is that the global temperatures have been increasing since the 1960s and that the future will be dire if greenhouse gas emissions are not curtailed. However, the global warming hypothesis also has its critics, who are often either right-wing Republicans or from the religious right, many of whom are Evangelicals. Their critiques of the global warming hypothesis are often accompanied by charges of junk science. Yet, one of the ironies is that Evangelicals are well-represented on both sides of the global warming imbroglio.

Global warming was presented as a threat to the planet in the 1980s, hard on the heels of warnings of a nuclear winter. The basic thesis is that not only has the earth been warming since about 1820, but that it is now warming at a faster rate due to human activity and, above all, the emission of greenhouse gases. Suffice it to say that the hypothesis was initially questioned, but since the early 1990s few scientists have doubted the reality of the situation. It has been a concern of many throughout the world of all faiths and none. Even so, the US Republican Senator James Inhofe has called global warming 'the greatest hoax' and tried to ensure that the Bush Administration would regard it as such. According to Mooney (2005, p. 78f.), he has been fairly successful, and, as we will see, has the support of numbers of Evangelicals.

Green Evangelicals and Climate Change

The Evangelical interest in global warming is due to its causing polarization in the Evangelical community. Evangelical environmentalists have been proactive in taking up the cause and forceful in their attempts to persuade the large American Evangelical constituency of the rightness of their position. One of the leading scientists on global warming over the last decades has been Sir John Houghton, an Evangelical. After holding a post as professor of atmospheric physics at Oxford, Houghton was director general of the UK's Meteorological Office from 1983–1991 and then Chairman of the Royal Commission on Environmental Pollution (1992–1998) and Chairman or Co-Chairman of the IPCC from 1988 to 2002. He has published widely on the subject, including a popular book for Christians called *Global Warming* (Houghton, 1994). He has been involved in environmental efforts at the highest level on an international scale, including in the Kyoto Protocol.

Alongside his international and scientific activities, Houghton has striven to make Christians aware of environmental problems and global warming, and has spent much of his 'retirement' travelling the world, either for international environmental groups or for church groups. Without undervaluing the work of American Evangelical environmentalists, Houghton was probably instrumental in persuading many in the NAE of the dangers of global warming.

The Evangelical Climate Initiative of February 2006 has already been mentioned. It has divided the 30 million strong NAE with its statement that

> as Evangelical leaders, we recognize both our opportunity and our responsibility to offer a biblically based moral witness that can help shape public policy in the most powerful nation on earth and therefore contribute to the well-being of the entire world . . . Many of us have required considerable convincing before becoming persuaded that climate change is a real problem and that it ought to matter to us as Christians. But now we have seen and heard enough.

This aptly describes how many, including Richard Cizik, rejected the theory of global warming for many years. The statement made four claims:

1. Human-induced climate change is real.
2. The consequences of climate change will be significant and will affect the poor the hardest.
3. Christian moral convictions demand our response.
4. Governments, businesses, churches and individuals all have a role to play in addressing climate change – starting now.

Given the whole nature of American Evangelicalism, this was a remarkable turnabout, and now some two-thirds of Evangelicals accept that global warming is a fact and that they as *Christian* individuals have a responsibility. A reaction was inevitable; the ISA challenged the report, arguing that global warming will actually lead to increased agricultural productivity and that the poor would suffer most from attempts to *slow* climate change.

In Britain, many Evangelicals support action on climate change, including such organizations as the Evangelical Alliance,[11] Tear Fund,[12] The John Ray Initiative and Christian environmental groups. A good example of serious Evangelical thinking on climate change and other environmental issues can be found in the book produced under the auspices of the Faraday Institute, *Creation in Crisis, Christian Perspectives on Sustainability*

(White, 2009). Contributors include leading scientists, theologians and other academics. Most of the essays are on environmental sustainability, but the first three are on climate change. Sir John Houghton discusses climate and energy; James McCarthy from Harvard deals with the distortion and denial of climate change by the 'misinformation industry' and Donald Hay, an economist from Oxford, focuses on how we should respond to climate change. This book is a good example of how experts writing for the well-informed general public can also give a Christian, if not Evangelical, perspective on the environment.

At the end of 2010, the Rev Jim Ball of the Evangelical Environmental Network published *Global Warming and the Risen LORD: Christian Discipleship and Climate Change*. His commitment on climate change has been described earlier and the EEN website encourages people to be involved. The website describes the book as follows:[13]

> *Global Warming and the Risen LORD* moves beyond the old debates about climate change to a new conversation focusing on the tremendous opportunities there are and the biblical and spiritual resources we have been given to meet this threat. A major focus of the book is the deep biblical basis for our engagement with global warming. Filled with inspirational stories and sobering scientific research, Rev. Ball shows us that global warming is one of the major challenges of our time, but one that can be overcome by following the Risen LORD.

Ball sees global warming as one of the ethical challenges of the present day, which the church must engage in – not because it is a secular matter, but because of faith in the Risen Christ. Clearly, these green Evangelicals share the same view as others concerned about climate change, but they have a particular faith perspective. For those who share this concern for the environment, the opposition to climate change by some Evangelicals makes for sorry reading. It is to this that we now turn.

Brown Evangelicals and Climate Change

Since 2006, a number of American Evangelicals have opposed the junk science (in their view) of global warming. One of their chief spokesmen is Calvin Beisner, who gave oral testimony to the US Senate's Environment and Public Works Committee on 20 October 2006, despite having no relevant scientific training. In early 2007, James Dobson and others suggested the NAE stop its support of action to curb global warming. Additionally,

Evangelicals and other members of the Acton Institute and the ISA warned readers that 'scientific orthodoxies and politicized science, like those encountered in the global warming debate, make for dangerous waters, and Evangelicals who want to swim in them should look carefully for rocks and riptides and be well prepared before they dive in'. Beisner and the ISA have also had support from several leading anti-evolutionary groups, notably Answers in Genesis, the Institute of Creation Research (ICR), the Discovery Institute and the ARN. William Dembski, a champion of the Intelligent Design movement and a senior fellow with the Discovery Institute's Center for Science and Culture, often writes strident articles criticizing the validity of global warming in his blog, *Uncommon Descent.*

On 25 July 2006, the ISA released *An Open Letter to the Signers of 'Climate Change: An Evangelical Call to Action'* . . . *and Others Concerned About Global Warming,* a treatise that was highly critical of any action to address global warming, signed by more than 130 scholars, theologians, scientists, economists and other leaders. The signatories included James A. Borland, D. A. Carson, Guillermo Gonzalez, Wayne Grudem, James Kennedy, Michael Oard, Joseph A. Pipa, Robert L. Reymond and Jay W. Richards. Several of these are leading American Evangelical theologians.

As many of the signatories are creationist, the simplest interpretation is to conclude that there is a strong correlation between creationism and rejection of global warming and creation care. That was true until just a few years ago. Many of the signatories to *An Open Letter* are creationist, as are many signatories of *Evangelical Climate Initiative.* What has happened is that some 'creationists' have now made common cause over the environment with mainstream scientists.

This division of opinion among Evangelicals was clearly seen in the US Senate hearings on 'An Examination of the Views of Religious Organizations Regarding Global Warming' on Thursday, 7 June 2007.[14] Although this was clearly a purely American event, it actually reflects the worldwide issue of global warming from a religious perspective. Most contributions were from Christians, though there was also a Jewish submission (but no Muslim one). All shades of Christian opinion were presented. There was a contribution from the Roman Catholic Bishops appealing for action, which was shared by that of the Presiding Bishop of the Episcopal Church, and which included statements from several mainstream Protestant churches. The consensus of all these was that global warming was a reality and must be urgently addressed.

Four Evangelicals countered the statements made by one Catholic, one Protestant and one Jew. Three were essentially global warming deniers, and only one was convinced of its reality. This was the Rev Dr Jim Ball, president of the EEN, who essentially reiterated the concerns of the Evangelical Climate Initiative of 2006, in basic agreement with the mainstream churches. The three other Evangelicals – Russell Moore, Dean of Theology at Southern Baptist Theological Seminary,[15] David Barton and Dr James Tonkowich – all presented the case against global warming and largely based their presentations on Beisner's work. Moore included a new article by Beisner in his submission, and Senator Inhofe referred to him favourably.

The result of this was that the submissions to the US Senate hearing appeared to be evenly balanced between the opposing views, but instead reflected the partial shift by Evangelicals. In June 2007, President George Bush also warmed to global warming as he realized some of the arguments in favour of it. This must be seen as a step closer to a post-Kyoto policy. However, the world has moved on since then, especially after the election of Barack Obama. Many leading right-wing Republicans, especially those from the 'Tea Party' movement, are hostile to global warming and other environmental issues. It is highly significant that there is a close identity between right-wing Republicans and the most conservative, or fundamentalist, Evangelicals. As I edit this (August 2011), possible nominations are coming in for Republican candidates for the 2013 election, who are both conservative Evangelicals, anti-evolution and anti-climate change. Hence the Evangelical and creationist denial of climate change is important in the context of world politics.

Creationists and Climate Change

American Evangelicals have been highly influential in their opposition to climate change theory in the mid-2000s, and it is highly significant that most of these opponents were also creationist. In recent years, the main creationist organizations have become vociferous in their opposition to anthropogenic climate change. The leading organizations have produced DVDs and books, which are professionally produced and heavily supported by donors, for wide distribution.

The largest creationist organization is the American-based Answers in Genesis, which has an annual income of $23 million. It is headed by an Australian, Ken Ham, and has a creationist museum in Ohio. Its activities are worldwide and include organizing creationist meetings and publishing creationist materials, both in hard copy and on the web. In 2008, AIG produced a US$14.99 DVD entitled *Global Warming: A Scientific and Biblical Expose of Climate Change* in conjunction with Coral Ridge Ministries of Florida, one of the American Evangelical super-churches. The advertizing blurbs ask rhetorically:

> What is the truth about global warming? Are the ice caps melting? Will polar bears and penguins soon be found starving on small floating icebergs? Does the future survival of man hinge on an immediate reduction in carbon emissions?
>
> This 'politically incorrect' documentary is an exciting and important tool for all who face the rampant misinformation propagated by ecological alarmists. *Global Warming* addresses subjects that most others won't touch, including misinformation which is contained in Al Gore's *An Inconvenient Truth*.

To substantiate their case they list the contributors, who – despite their doctorates – are all Young Earth Creationists, except for Al Gore, who is the fall guy:

> Larry Vardiman, PhD, Institute for Creation Research
>
> Michael J. Oard, MS, National Weather Service (Retired)
>
> E. Calvin Beisner, PhD, Cornwall Alliance
>
> Jason Lisle, PhD, Answers in Genesis
>
> Al Gore (former vice president)
>
> Ken Chilton, PhD, Lindenwood University

In 2006, there was a major rift in Answers in Genesis. As a result, the Australian-based Creation Ministries International was formed. Despite the rancour of the split, both groups put forth the same ideas on creationism and climate change. A related website published an article by Russ Humphreys in August 2009[16] entitled 'God's global warming worked just fine; evidence from the pre-Flood world suggests that we need not fear global warming from carbon dioxide'. His rejection of global warming is a result of his Young Earth Creationist convictions. The introduction to his article reads:

> Governments today are trying to reduce carbon dioxide (CO_2) emissions into the air, because they fear that the greenhouse effect (which traps heat trying to leave the earth) of CO_2 will trigger a global climate catastrophe. They point to computer simulations suggesting that result. But the evidence suggests that about 6,000 years ago God created the world

with large amounts of carbon dioxide in the atmosphere. This lasted 1,656 years, from Creation until the Genesis Flood. The rocks and fossils laid down by that flood suggest that the result was very beneficial, with no climate catastrophe, as we shall see.

Few scientists accept such a scenario, but this is typical of creationist arguments. Humphreys first dispenses with six myths on both sides of the argument: CO_2 is a pollutant. CO_2 is not increasing. The earth is not warming. Global warming must mean hotter tropics. Melting icecaps will drown the continents. Global warming is making weather more violent. Having rejected such myths, Humphreys claimed that before Noah's Flood, the atmosphere contained much more CO_2 as evidenced by Ordovician Goethites, which to him date from the early months of the Flood. Further, he asserts that carboniferous ferns found at high latitudes demonstrated a warmer climate at that time. Of course, that is a geological truth, but Humphreys does not accept that the fossils date from 300 million years ago, arguing instead that they are from about 2400 BC. From such false science, Humphreys claims that the earth produced more plants at that time and concludes that rising CO_2 concentrations and global warming are *good* things, because they would result in increased food production. Humphreys concludes:

> So we should not fear 'global warming'. God created a world with *much* more carbon dioxide in the air – a lush green world. Such a world was indeed warmer on the average, equators being about the same as now, but poles much warmer. Scripture speaks of a future *'period of restoration of all things'* (*Acts 3:21*). It is ironic that our technology is pumping carbon buried by the Flood back into the earth's biosphere, perhaps in preparation for a time when the earth will again be like Eden – at least in terms of the climate.[17]

My third example is from Creation Research, headed by another Australian, John Mackay, a self-styled creation geologist. For the record, Creation Research and Creation Ministries International loathe each other. Much like the other creationist organizations, Creation Research concentrates on trying to provide scientific support for a young earth, and Mackay gives lecture tours in many parts of the world. As geological science his lectures are woeful, but he is convincing to his pious audiences. A brief look at the Creation Research website shows how the group considers climate change to be a myth, and Mackay has produced a DVD called *Climate Change & Creation – A Really Inconvenient Truth!* to confirm his view. The subtitle is an unsubtle reference to Gore. The content and substance of the video can be seen from the advertizing blurb:

> Join world leader on Creation Research, John Mackay, as he looks at God's world and God's word and shows you the evidence from rocks and records.
> What does Islam say about global warming?
> Is man causing global warming?
> Is it global warming, climate change, or tax revenue?
> What was the weather like at creation?
> What has been its history since then?
> What effect did Noah's flood have?
> What role does God have in weather?
> Does the Bible speak about future global warming?
> Does it matter if Polar Bears become extinct?

In an additional web article entitled 'Cooked data provides most heat for Global Warming', Mackay alleged that temperature data illustrated by the 'hockey stick' graph – which shows steep and rapid warming over the last half of the twentieth century – were 'cooked', especially by scientists at the University of East Anglia. His allegations go further than those circulating at the end of 2009:[18]

> The first graph below is based on historial (*sic!*) records in the UK and rep-resents one of the longest data bases (*sic!*) on observed temperature fluctua-tion on planet earth. Underneath this graph is the now infamous hockey sticky graph used by Al Gore etc which took the same sort of data and passed it (*sic!*) through computer filter designed to show temperatures had dramati-cally increased at the end of the 20th century for the first time in a thousand years. The graph below was compiled by the founder of the East Anglia cli-mate unit which under current leadship (*sic!*), has now become infamous by not only totally ingnoring (*sic!*) the historical data, but as climate gate shows, they have set out to alter all historical data to fit the climate change agenda.
> . . . The many graphs below showed major differences between recorded temperatures around the globe verses climate change temperatures.

Along with these allegations Mackay proceeded to allege the 'data cook-ing' of temperature records and graphs for New Zealand and the United States. His web article concluded with a graph of the 'Biblical History of Weather', showing how human longevity declined after the Flood because of the loss of the benign pre-Flood climate. (Mackay believes that the earth is only 6,000 years old and that the Flood occurred in about 2500 BC.)

I have discussed these two creationist responses to climate change at length as these kind of arguments, along with those from the Discovery Institute, are the ones that inform most Evangelicals in the Anglo-Saxon world and probably elsewhere. Creationists take great pains to show that their ideas are sound science; in fact, a recent web journal claims to provide that. The web journal is the *Answers Research Journal*, which AIG claims 'is a professional, peer-reviewed technical journal for the publication of inter-disciplinary scientific and other relevant research from the perspective of the recent Creation and the global Flood within a biblical framework'. A recent article entitled 'A proposed Bible Science Perspective on Global Warming'[19] attempts to provide a thought-out creationist case on global warming and concludes that warming is a good thing. The author is Rod J. Martin, who is described only as an independent researcher. The website provides no information about his qualifications, and I have not been able to ascertain the relevance of his credentials. However, the paper gives a good summary of how creationists view global warming. Surprisingly, Martin claims that the church has had little to say on climate change 'and has made scant use of Scripture to evaluate the alleged problem'. As well as describing scientific aspects of climate change, he proposes 'a biblical (young-earth Creationist) framework for evaluating the issue, and high-light basic scientific data related to the alleged claims'. In his view:

> The contention that man's activities are causing global warming, as described in the media and by its advocates, is a myth. There is no reason either biblically or scientifically to fear the exaggerated and misguided claims of catastrophe as a result of increasing levels of man-made carbon dioxide (CO_2).

Martin summarized his findings in a series of bullet points; the following are his findings concerning carbon dioxide:

O_2 and CO_2 in the atmosphere were created; they did not evolve.

Today's atmosphere likely contains significantly less CO_2 than before the Flood.

CO_2 is necessary for life, and was created prior to plants and animals.

CO_2 is not a pollutant.

Increasing levels of CO_2 are beneficial for plants.

Decreasing levels of CO_2 could be a serious problem.

Burning fossil fuels simply returns CO_2 to the air, from which it originated, in the pre-Flood atmosphere. Increasing CO_2 in the atmosphere
does not reverse a billion-year-old evolutionary trend and upset the delicate balance of nature.

The present levels of oxygen in the air are adequate without any unusual
efforts to plant trees or to further limit the forestry industry.

Plants were created as food for humans and animals. They are not necessary for storing carbon or for generating O_2.

Essentially, his argument is that there was more CO_2 in the atmosphere before
the flood (i.e. from 4000 BC to 2400 BC) and that the resultant plant growth
was deposited as either coal or oil during the Noachian Deluge. Thus, if we
burn more fossil fuels, CO_2 will increase in the atmosphere, which will be a
good thing. Not only will plants grow more and the earth be more luxuriant,
but it will be a return to the halcyon days before the Flood. I will end with
Martin's summation of the Creationist approach to climate change:

> The biblical history of the earth, contained in the first 11 chapters of the
> Book of Genesis, provides a useful and sufficient framework for evaluat-
> ing the current global warming issue. As we have seen, CO_2 is a natural
> atmospheric gas that is essential for man's existence. It is not a pollutant.
> The atmosphere is likely deficient in CO_2 compared with the original
> created atmosphere. Reducing CO_2 would definitely create problems,
> but increasing it will not. Burning fossil fuels merely returns CO_2 to its
> place of origin. Forests are to be used for man's benefit. They are not
> needed to produce O_2 and they have no intrinsic rights, but should be
> managed responsibly and effectively.

Peter Forster, Bishop of Chester

Standing against both the mainstream Evangelicals and the conservative Browns is the relatively lone voice of Peter Forster, Bishop of Chester.
Over the last few years, Forster has publicly stated and also argued in the
House of Lords that the issue of climate change is an 'open question'. In
2009, he became a trustee of the newly formed Global Warming Policy
Foundation (GWPF), an organization based in the United Kingdom that
promotes scepticism of policy measures envisaged by governments to mitigate anthropogenic global warming.

Peter Forster (b. 1950) originally trained as a chemist and has a PhD
in chemistry from the University of Edinburgh. He is probably the most

scientifically informed of the Anglican Bishops. Forster is an Evangelical of a moderate hue and takes a conservative line on many issues such as abortion and homosexuality.

In May 2008, the Bishop claimed in a debate in the House of Lords during the second reading of the energy bill that discussion about the causes of global warming was 'still open'. He claimed that 'climate science is a notoriously imprecise area, because the phenomena under investigation are so large', a fact 'that makes precision difficult to achieve'. He also claimed that there was no consensus among climate scientists that 'carbon dioxide levels are the key determinant'. Forster's views are in stark contrast to the majority of Anglican bishops, especially the Bishops of Blackburn, Durham and Liverpool (of which the latter two are also Evangelical), not to mention the scientific community.

Early in 2010, Forster backed a call made by the former Chancellor the Exchequer, Lord Lawson, for an independent inquiry into 'Climategate' (the affair in which e-mails were leaked from the Climate Research Unit [CRU] of the University of East Anglia). He told the Church of England Newspaper, 'I think an independent inquiry into the CRU emails would helpfully clear the air'. This was very soon after he had joined the GWPF and indicates his scepticism about climate change. As it happened, the inquiry cleared the CRU scientists of any wrongdoing. I do not know what Peter Forster's response was to this, although many sceptics regard the inquiry as a whitewash.

Bishop Forster presents a very different position from the majority of his fellow bishops, whether Evangelical or not. Almost at the same time he joined the GWPF, the Church of England launched a seven-year Church and Earth Climate Change Action Plan.[20] Among other things, this aimed to cut the Church's carbon footprint by 42 per cent by 2020. This plan was commissioned by the Archbishop of Canterbury and chaired by Richard Chartres, Bishop of London. It reflects the consensus of the Church of England and thus has support of many Evangelicals within the church, including at least two Evangelical bishops, James Jones of Liverpool and Tom Wright of Durham.

Conclusion

It is not possible to draw a neat and simple conclusion on Evangelical attitudes to climate change. McKeown's division into Browns and Greens is good, but is too simple. McKeown highlights the divide between the different Evangelical factions, but matters are more complex than his aptly polarized scenario shows. There are the influential activists on either side, personified by John Houghton for the theory of climate change and Calvin Beisner against it. These individuals have been highly active for the last 15 years, and at times it seems that there can be no resolution and that Evangelicals are simply divided.

However, certain things are clear. The more moderate Evangelicals are convinced of climate change and work positively with the wider church and – if they have scientific skills – in the scientific community. Those opposed are very vocal and dismissive of the 'junk science' and have made much of alleged 'fraud' by Chris Jones of the CRU. Despite the vindictiveness of these allegations, the conservatives or Browns have become more environmentally aware in the last decade, as groups such as the ISA have slowly shifted their position. The strongest examples of shifts in opinion are to be seen in those such as Richard Cizik, who rejected decades of environmental indifference almost overnight.

As I write on a cold and damp July evening (and revised it after the coldest December for decades), it is difficult to foresee the future and whether the political clout of the more conservative Evangelicals will inhibit efforts to address climate change. For most Evangelicals, climate change is a matter of indifference and they will probably reflect what they have been taught with varying levels of conviction. As Creation care is more widely espoused by Evangelicals, whether in the conservative or moderate form, environmental concerns are becoming of greater concern. According to a recent article in *Christianity Today*[21], environmental issues have hit the United States hard this year (2010). The editorial, entitled 'Let the sea resound', begins: 'The question is no longer, "Do you believe in global warming?" but, "What do you believe about the Gulf oil spill?" The BP spill has brought creation care closer to home. Whether global warming is a dire threat or not, human-made or not, we are all now more aware of our relationship to other parts of God's creation'. No one around the Gulf of Mexico has been able to avoid the effects of the spill, and it has become a primary concern of President Obama. The environmental record of America has never been good, but this spillage exceeds any previous catastrophe. Americans have been forced to see that the environment is fragile in a way they have never before perceived it. As the *Christianity Today* article says, 'There seems to be little doubt that the Gulf oil spill is the United States' environmental 9/11'. Tree huggers are objects of ridicule, but many have become 'sea huggers'. Perhaps American Evangelicals may become 'climate huggers'.[22] If that happens, the present bias against climate change in the United States will change, as American Evangelicals have considerable political influence, especially in the Republican Party. Most American Evangelicals support the Republicans and as long as they follow the creationist line of climate change, Republican politicians will do the same.

Over the next few decades, both the absolute numbers and proportion of Evangelicals and Neo-Pentecostals are set to rise, making them of greater significance, both socially and politically, in many parts of the world. I must emphasize that this will not only be in the United States, where they are so influential now, but in countries in Asia, Africa and Latin America (especially Brazil). Thus, their views on climate change and what should be done about it are of great significance for our planet.

Notes

[1] For historical surveys, see Noll (2004).
[2] Creationism is the view held by many Evangelicals and some Muslims that the earth is only a few thousand years old and that evolution has not occurred. It originated in the United States.
[3] These include members of the American Scientific Affiliation and Christians in Science.
[4] I am well aware that reports were published by the World Council of Churches and that there were individuals concerned about the environment, but on the ground in the churches there was little concern. This is what I found to be the case in the Church of England in the 70s and 80s.
[5] www.jri.org.
[6] www.time.com/time/nation/article/0,8599,1157612,00.htm.
[7] www.clas.ufl.edu/users/bron/PDF--Christianity/Larsen--Interfaith%20 Council%204%20Enviro%20Stewardship.pdf (accessed 15 August 2011)
[8] As I was formerly an exploration geologist and am well aware of the finitude of all mineral resources, I find that attitude bizarre as well as wrong.
[9] This cannot be stated too strongly.
[10] www.cornwallalliance.org/docs/climate-change-and-the-responsibility-of-civil-society.pdf
[11] www.eauk.org/public-affairs/pqprayerandcampaigns/upload/marchpq.pdf.
[12] www.tearfund.org/webdocs/website/Campaigning/Q%26A%20on%20climate%20change.pdf.
[13] www.creationcare.org/blog.php?blog=19.
[14] www.epw.senate.gov/public/index.cfm?FuseAction=Hearings.Hearing& Hearing_ID=e39940af-802a-23ad-4371-252edd78194f.
[15] The President of SBTS is Dr Albert Mohler, who is attempting to make the Southern Baptist Convention more conservative, more Calvinistic and more creationist.
[16] www.creation.com/global-warming-facts-and myths.
[17] I find it very difficult to describe this objectively as I consider these ideas not only daft but pernicious.
[18] www.creationresearch.net/items%20subjects/Climate%20Change/Cooked_ Data.htm. (Note: the spelling errors are from the website.) This web article

'disappeared' from the Creation Research website in the last few weeks of 2010.

[19] www.answersingenesis.org/articles/arj/v3/n1/bible-science-perspective-on-global-warming.

[20] www.cofe.anglican.org/news/pr10009.html.

[21] www.christianitytoday.com/ct/2010/august/7.45.html.

[22] The way this unfolds will most likely be recorded on the web and one should be able to follow it by putting words – like Beisner, Cizik and the various Evangelical environment groups – into a search engine.

References

Barrett, D. (ed.) (2001), *World Christian Encyclopedia*. New York: Oxford University Press.

Beisner, E. C. (1990), *Prospects for Growth: A Biblical View of Population, Resources, and the Future*. Westchester: Crossway.

— (1994), *Man, Economy, and Environment in Biblical Perspective*. Moscow: Canon Press.

— (1997), *Where Garden Meets Wilderness: Evangelical Entry Into the Environmental Debate*. Grand Rapids: Eerdmans.

Berry, R. J. (1972), *Ecology and Ethics*. London: Inter-Varsity Press.

— (ed.) (2000), *The Care of Creation*. Downers Grove: Inter-Varsity Press.

Bithell, T. (2005), *The Politically Incorrect Guide to Science*. Washington: Regnery.

Catherwood, C. (2010), *Thy Kingdom Come*. Roper-Penberthy Publishing.

De Witt, C. (1991), *The Environment and the Christian*. Grand Rapids: Baker.

Houghton, J. T. (1994), *Global Warming*. Oxford: Lion.

Mandryk, J. (2010), *Operation World*. Colorado Springs: Biblica.

McKeown, J. (2006), 'The Use of Genesis in Debates about Environmental Stewardship among Conservative Christians in the USA'(Paper given at the Conference 'Critical Perspectives on Religion and the Environment'). Birmingham, 18–19 September 2006.

Moberg, D. (1973), *The Great Reversal*. London: Scripture Union.

Mooney, C. (2005), *The Republican War on Science*. New York: Basic Books.

Noll, M. (2004), *The Rise of Evangelicalism*. Leicester: Inter-Varsity Press.

Oelschlaeger, M. (1994), *Caring for Creation*. New Haven: Yale University Press.

Schaeffer, F. (1970), *Pollution and the Death of Man*. London: Hodder.

Simon, J. (1984), *Resourceful Earth*. Boston and Oxford: Blackwell.

White, L. (1967), 'The historical roots of our ecologic crisis'. *Science*, 155, 1203–1207.

White, R. (2009), *Creation in Crisis: Christian Perspectives on Sustainability*. London: SPCK Publishing.

Wilkinson, L. (1980/1990), *Earth-keeping*. Grand Rapids: Eerdmans.

Wright, R. (1970), 'Responsibility for the ecological crisis'. *Bioscience*, 20, 851–853.

— (1995), 'Tearing down the green: environmental backlash in the evangelical sub-culture'. *Perspectives on Science and Christian Faith*, 47, 80–91.

Chapter 8

Religious Climate Activism in the United States

Laurel Kearns

This is one problem which if we don't resolve it, no one is going to survive.
— Archbishop Desmond Tutu[1]

Introduction

These are strong words coming from an unlikely environmentalist, one of the leaders of the successful anti-apartheid movement in South Africa, yet they reflect the growing sense of urgency about climate change heard from religious, political and scientific voices around the globe. Despite this chorus, many world governmental leaders are seemingly incapable of transcending national interests in order to work for a planetary common good. Further, even with very strong scientific consensus and weekly headlines confirming that global climate change – or, as US journalist Thomas Friedman calls it, 'global weirding' – is happening faster than expected, politicians in the United States are far from legislatively acting on climate change at the federal level. This is despite what seemed to be promises during President Obama's election campaign that climate change would be a top priority of his administration. This elicited great hope from secular and religious activists, such that a leading Evangelical leader and author declared in an inaugural week blog: 'I feel an extraordinary happiness'. Brian McLaren, one of the leaders of the Emergent Church movement – a loose coalition of a variety of postmodern, decentralized, progressive Evangelicals seeking to be a different church from traditional Evangelicalism and mainline Protestantism – went on to express the breadth of that optimism in the United States: 'Younger people can understand it to a great degree, but I think many folks my age (52) and older – Euro American, African

American, Latino American, Native American, Asian American – share a sense of joy that is especially hard to explain'. In his litany of what he is now happy about, he proclaimed: 'I'm happy for the endangered species, for the coral reefs, for the rainforests, the mountains, in hopes that in the coming years, we'll turn a corner from a consumptive, extractive, destructive economy towards not just a sustainable economy but a truly regenerative one'.[2] Three years later, religious climate activists are nowhere near as optimistic. So what happened, other than the economic downturn?

Indeed, in 2011, some aspects of the politics of US (in)action on climate change must appear puzzling from afar. In order to understand the current political craziness in the United States in the face of global scientific, political and religious calls for action on climate change, one needs to understand the complex dynamics of religious environmentalism in the country. After briefly exploring the history of such activism, this chapter goes on to examine the frames that influence religious discourse on environmental issues in general, and global warming/climate change in particular, and how these have shaped and promoted the seeming current success of the religious climate denial movement in the United States.

History

Despite the headlines in US newspapers that still seem to be surprised by the extent of religious environmental activism in America, Christian-based environmentalism is not all that new. As of 2010, some religious groups in the United States had been active on environmental issues since the 1980s, and their roots go back even farther. In 1939, Walter Lowdermilk, an early soil conservationist, penned an 11th Commandment about environmental stewardship (for which a US Eastern Orthodox ecology group named itself in 1980).[3] Lutheran theologian Joseph Sittler, who was a pioneer for eco-theology and first began writing on topics related to his 'theology of the Earth' in the 1950s, led a World Council of Churches (WCC) programme 'Faith – Man – Nature' starting in 1963.[4] Ironically, Evangelical author Francis Schaeffer, a progenitor of the religious right in the United States (an often anti-environmental ideological group), wrote a now influential book on green Evangelicalism, *Pollution and the Death of Man* (1970), demonstrating early the future tensions that would emerge in US Evangelicalism.[5] The same year, the National Association of Evangelicals (NAE) passed a resolution stating: 'Today those who thoughtlessly destroy a God-ordained balance of nature are guilty of sin against

God's creation'.[6] Also in the 1970s, John Cobb and Rosemary Radford Ruether, key eco-theologians for decades to come, began writing on environmental concerns, and mainline US Protestant denominations issued a variety of statements, followed by the establishment of denominational offices and staff working on the issue in the 1980s. The 1980s saw the creation of the influential National Council of Churches Eco-Justice Working Group, as well as internationally known 'centres of practice' such as the Evangelical Au Sable Institute founded under the biologist Dr. Calvin DeWitt in Michigan and the liberal Catholic Genesis Farm under Sister Miriam MacGillis in New Jersey.

These US-based activities were paralleled on a more global level. The WCC held various conferences, such as the 1979 'Faith, Science and Man' conference at MIT, that led to the theme of a 'Just, Participatory and Sustainable Society' that incorporated concern over the limits of and threats to the earth's capacity to sustain current and future human life with concern for social equity. This vision expanded through the WCC theme of 'Justice, Peace and the Integrity of Creation' (1983–1991). Leaders of world religions, called by the World Wide Fund for Nature (WWF), met in Assisi, Italy in the mid-1980s to issue statements of concern. In 1995, the Alliance of Religions and Conservation was formed, which now consists of eleven faiths.[7] Pope John Paul II called for environmental concern to be a priority for Catholics in his 1990 World Day of Peace speech and in subsequent pronouncements. Pope Benedict XVI (see Markus Vogt's chapter in this book) has echoed this sentiment in more recent statements. Following his election in 1991, the Orthodox Christian 'green' Ecumenical Patriarch Bartholomew made the environment a central concern, declaring that the wanton destruction of nature was a sin. He still convenes annual 'floating' conferences of religious leaders to address various water-related issues (in 2006, for example, the meeting 'site' was the Amazon River).[8] Many now well-known US groups such as GreenFaith, Earth Ministry and the National Religious Partnership for the Environment (NRPE) were all started in the early 1990s. The constituent groups of the NRPE[9] mailed education and resource packets to tens of thousands of congregations as one of their first tasks.

In order to understand this growing movement, I identified in the 1990s three emerging 'ideal types' or ethics that tried to capture the spectrum of Christian environmentalism in the United States in the 1990s – Christian stewardship, eco-justice and creation spirituality (Kearns, 1996). Others have found this typology useful in understanding responses to globalization, activity in Finland or environmental ethics (Beyer, 1994; Pesonen,

2004; Jenkins 2008). Whereas these still name dominant clusters or emphases – ranging from the more Bible-oriented stance of stewardship to the more liberal post-Christian creation spirituality – the spectrum has broadened, and in many ways there is far less clear separation, as well as more division within each type. For example, with increased awareness of climate change, concerns for justice are now a central aspect of any of these religious positions, and thus the designation of only one strand as eco-justice can be misleading. The arena of eco-justice is complicated in the tensions between the broader, all-creation ethic of eco-justice and the specific anthropocentric liberation focus of much of the environmental justice movement. Additionally, the Evangelical activism that I previously labelled simply 'Christian stewardship' is now more divided (as this chapter later explores), so that I differentiate between creation-care Evangelicals (my previous Christian stewardship position) and those who advocate a wise-use[10] environmental stewardship but are 'climate sceptics'. I would also add that these positions could be used to describe foci – stewardship, justice and spirituality – in other faiths (such as Judaism and Islam), as well as the interfaith efforts in which they participate (GreenFaith, Interfaith Power and Light, or Faith in Place), because religious environmentalism on the whole is a very interfaith movement. Concern for a shared planet home seems to enable the overcoming of religious differences. There is now a rich chorus of religious environmental voices.

The Religious Climate is Changing

Although the WCC first started focusing on climate change in 1988, and the NRPE chose it as a central focus in the mid-1990s, it is in the twenty-first century that much of religious environmentalism, at the public advocacy level, has centred on climate change.[11] That work, described in part below, manifests the interfaith cooperation mentioned above, despite the controversial political, scientific, ethical and economic issues associated with climate change. What enables that work?

Using the Jewish–Christian coalition of the NRPE as an example, there seem to be four main areas in which arguments in this domain are grounded: theology/scripture, justice, scientific authority and economics. These provide a clear authoritative stance for religious groups, who often face opposition from their constituency over concern that linking ecological concern and religious faith entails worshipping the creation and not the creator, thus 'paganism'. These sources of authority also can help move the discussion beyond these debates, particularly references to scripture and justice, to overcome arguments that the environment is less important than issues of religious persecution, poverty and evangelization. Of course, they can also be the ground for religious anti-environmentalism.

- First, activists and theologians believe there is a strong Biblical foundation in the *scriptural* authority of the Hebrew Scriptures/Christian Old Testament (Robb, 2010). By linking concern over global warming to the divine assertion of the integrity and worth of all creation in the very beginning of their shared Scriptures – Genesis 1: 'In the beginning . . . God said that it was good', or the divine care for all of creation seen in Noahic covenant in Gen. 9.12, each group in the NRPE could claim a clear and unambiguous authority, a Biblical mandate, to speak on the issue.[12]

- Second, the effects of global warming have clear unjust consequences[13] and invoke a shared ethic of justice, based in both scriptures, of protecting the 'least of those' who will be the most affected – the poor, the more-than-human world and the future generations who will 'inherit the earth'. For instance, Rabbi Warren Stone, representing North American Jewish organizations, articulated why scores of religious groups would be present at the failed 2009 climate change talks in Copenhagen. 'We are called by our religious traditions to serve as a bold voice for justice. Climate change will have a dramatic impact on hundreds of millions of the poorest people on our planet, especially those who live in coastal areas'.[14]

- Third, despite the headlines, there is an unusually strong scientific consensus on climate change that allows groups to appeal to *scientific* authority while at the same time turning a scientific issue into a moral issue (Northcott, 2007).

- Finally, practical strategies such as energy conservation and identifying alternative sources of energy can be 'sold' through an ethic of economic cost saving, thus 'making sense' to actors whose everyday decision-making and thinking is more premised upon market economics than most care to admit. For example, as the pitch for the US Environmental Protection Agency's Energy Star congregations program on its website states: 'Most congregations can cut energy costs by up to 30% by investing strategically in efficient equipment'.[15] From looking at the EPA winners, it is clear that this appeal can override theological objections.

In other words, climate change is an example of how an environmental topic can be presented with scriptural, scientific and moral authority, and – as we shall see – both challenge and still appeal to aspects of the dominant cultural economic ethos. It is a topic that can be approached in various ways, with a variety of strategies of action that are 'acceptable' to diverse constituents, as this book and Gerten and Bergmann (2010) support by multiple claims to authority.

Stemming from the NRPE campaign, the Interfaith Climate Change Network (ICCN) 2002 action alert on faith and fuel economy illustrates the creativity of climate change activists: 'Have you heard the one about the rabbi, the priest, the pastor and the Toyota Prius? No, it's not a joke. And neither is global warming'. Perhaps, to more accurately capture the four constituent groups of the NRPE, it should have read 'a rabbi, pastor, priest and preacher'. This particular action alert encouraged individuals to bring their faith to bear on deliberations in the 2002 US Congress on increasing fuel efficiency. It was also related to the concurrent visit (driven by Catholic nuns in a fleet of hybrid cars)by Jewish, Catholic and Protestant leaders to carmakers in Detroit (McMorris, 2003). The website goes on to ask:

If God is With Me All the Time, Does that Include the Auto Dealership?

As people of faith, we use religious convictions to determine the movies we see, music we listen to, and activities we participate in. If we bring God to the movies, why do we leave God behind at the Auto Mall? There is no reason to drive gas-guzzling, climate-changing cars when there are options that give us freedom and reduce the impact on our environment.

Because it's not just about vehicles, it's about values.[16]

The message is clear – climate change is about values, not just religious values, but economic ones as well.

The results of that interfaith campaign, and the related 'What would Jesus Drive?' campaign by the Evangelical Environmental Network (EEN), made the headlines all over the globe. Its success helped build momentum for the 2006 Evangelical Climate Initiative's (ECI) Call to Action on Climate Change statement, signed by over 110 Evangelical leaders, including mega-church (over 5,000 members) pastors Joel Hunter and Rick Warren, the heads of key Evangelical seminaries and several writers for the widely circulated Evangelical Christian magazine *Christianity Today*.[17] Indeed, Evangelical Christians increasingly grabbed the headlines in their climate change initiative to the point that the decade plus of mainline and Catholic efforts were largely ignored. For some analysts of conservative Christianity, global warming and the environment have become key issues that are cracking the perceived monolithic Republican voting block of white Evangelicals (Gushee, 2008), estimated to be near 100 million strong in the United States. Certainly, the younger generation is resisting the platform defined by the old guard of the religious right (Smith and Johnson, 2010), such power figures as Focus on The Family's Tony Perkins and James Dobson, or the now deceased Jerry Falwell.[18] So threatened were Dobson, Perkins and others over the ECI that, even though they are not members of the NAE, they sought unsuccessfully in 2006 to have the head, so to speak, of Richard Cizik, Vice President of Governmental Affairs of the NAE, who was the lead spokesperson for the ECI (converted, he says, to the cause by Sir John Houghton of the IPCC). They succeeded in having his signature removed from the Call to Action and forced his resignation in 2008.[19]

Other groups were also very active. The Interfaith Power and Light (IPL) movement, which began in California in 1998, linked up with the ICCN state campaigns that came out of the collaboration of the National Council of Churches and the Coalition on Jewish Life as part of their work in the NRPE coalition. There are now IPL affiliates in 37 states, which, according to the group, have reached over 10,000 congregations. These IPL groups facilitated the showing of former Vice President Al Gore's movie *An Inconvenient Truth* to over 4,000 congregations (followed by members of the audience pledging to take action on climate change). GreenFaith and Earth Ministry, both started in 1992, also participated in showing the film in their states. GreenFaith has a long history of activism on renewable energy and climate change, including helping over 700 congregations become energy-efficient through energy audits and CF lightbulb distributions, as well as 24 with solar panels. The Catholic Coalition on Climate Change (CCCC), launched in 2006, also came out of the work of the NRPE. Showing a similar creativity to the 'What Would Jesus Drive?' Campaign, the CCCC asked, 'Who's Under Your Carbon Footprint?'

Headlines in 2008 announced that even the Southern Baptists (the largest Protestant denomination in the United States) were now at odds in their response to global warming, with the then current and two past presidents of the Southern Baptist Convention (SBC) joining 63 other SBC leaders in signing 'A Southern Baptist Declaration on the Environment and Climate Change'. In addition to calling for more preaching on the environment, the declaration admitted that 'our cautious response to these issues in the face of mounting evidence may be seen by the world as uncaring, reckless

and ill-informed' and urged Baptists to keep an open mind about considering environmental policy.[20] These are significant admissions coming
from the heart and soul of the Christian right (although admittedly from
its more moderate to progressive side), since the official convention statement, issued in the previous summer of 2007, urged 'Southern Baptists to
proceed cautiously in the human-induced global warming debate in light
of conflicting scientific research' and resolved '(t)hat we consider proposals
to regulate CO_2 and other greenhouse gas emissions based on a maximum
acceptable global temperature goal to be very dangerous'.[21] Thus, perhaps
most significant, is that the 2008 Baptist declaration says that lack of scientific unanimity should not preclude 'prudent action' and 'serious consideration to responsible policies that effectively address' global warming.
Indeed, it seemed, the religious climate on climate change was changing.

Because of this level of activity, when I first presented this chapter at
the 2008 workshop, 'Religion in Dramatic Global Change', in Trondheim,
Norway, I was optimistic. The 2008 US presidential election was around the
corner, offering two candidates who advocated action on climate change.
I had concluded my paper, 'My reporting on religion and climate change
in the U.S will hopefully soon be changing also, after the election of a
president who campaigned on the need to address climate change swiftly
and as a priority'. The ECI was citing a 2006 Ellison Research poll stating
that 70 per cent of Evangelicals believe global warming will have an impact
on future generations, and 64 per cent of Evangelicals polled think that
climate change was serious enough to warrant immediate action, even if
there was a high economic cost.[22] Even more attention grabbing was that
'89% believe the U.S. should take steps to reduce global warming regardless of whether other major nations are also taking similar steps'.[23] And
shortly after I returned from Norway, another survey, the Oxfam Climate
Change & Poverty Survey, reported in March 2009 that nearly seven in
ten Americans – with solid majorities of every religious group, including 71 per cent of Catholics and nearly two-thirds (64 per cent) of white
Evangelicals – believe there is solid evidence that the average temperature
on earth has been increasing over the last few decades. Of those, 60 per
cent say that the rise in temperatures is mostly due to human activity, while
only 29 per cent say that climate change is mostly caused by natural patterns in the earth's environment.[24]

Yet there was other polling that was not so clear. The Pew Center
reported that 'white Evangelical Protestants are the most likely to say there
is *no solid evidence* the earth is warming (31%)'. In fact, they were 'the least
likely to believe that humans have contributed to heating up the planet

(34 per cent), compared to black Protestants who were the most likely of the religions to believe global warming is occurring (85 per cent), although only 39 per cent say global warming is a result of human activity'.[25] The Barna research group, favoured by conservative Christians, reported in a 2008 survey widely hailed by Evangelical climate sceptics that only 27 per cent of Evangelicals firmly believe global warming is happening, while roughly two-thirds of Evangelicals are concerned that global warming has been hyped up by the media (65 per cent), that current warming is part of a cyclical climate change and not caused primarily by human activity (62 per cent), and that proposed solutions would hurt the poor, especially in other countries (60 per cent).[26] These statistics provided a glimpse of what was coming.

2010 – A Sudden Change?

Religious groups across the globe had been very active leading up to the 2009 Copenhagen talks with a symbolic number of 350 (the goal for reduction of CO_2 ppm in the atmosphere) actions and candlelight vigils scattered across the globe, marches with tens of thousands of participants and hundreds of groups attending the Copenhagen meeting itself. However, little came out of Copenhagen. Emboldened by the failure of the Copenhagen climate talks, and the overblown hint of conspiracy in leaked Climategate e-mails from scientists at the University of East Anglia, climate scepticism became an unofficial Republican Party orthodoxy in the 2010 US elections as Republicans were carried into office in Washington and state houses around the country on a wave of corporate-funded campaigns.[27] The Republican victories have ensured that no positive action on climate change is likely to happen during the Obama administration. Additional attacks on the Environmental Protection Agency are even trying to make sure that it has no regulatory power to enforce Clean Air laws concerning emissions that are already on the books. Climate deniers also launched a big publicity campaign in 2010 promoting a ten-video series (30 minute each) entitled 'Resisting the Green Dragon' that invokes the conspiracy theories that lurked on the right-wing fringes of Christian paranoia, implying that environmentalism is power hungry, with a 'lust for political power that extends to the highest levels'. Dr James Tonkowich of the Cornwall Alliance asserts in the trailer for the series that environmental 'fearmongering' is about obtaining power, for 'whoever controls the environmental regulations, controls the economy, controls the population'. Other speakers, such as chief Cornwall strategist Dr Calvin Beisner, warn of an impending global government (often connected to the Antichrist) or that environmentalists want to greatly reduce the population. This campaign has gained major publicity through high-profile conservative media figures Rush Limbaugh and Glen Beck. It contains all the usual arguments in the conservative Christian dismissal of the need for Christians to respond to environmental concerns: the central focus of Christianity should be on salvation and saving souls; environmentalists worship creation and not the Creator; any religious environmentalism is pantheism and 'New Age'. The series even goes so far as to suggest that the movie *Avatar* was designed to 'lure' children towards this 'pantheism'. In short, the campaign demonizes the 'green dragon' of the 'religious and political environmental movement', calling it the 'greatest threat to society'.[28] Like other Cornwall campaigns, funded in part by those with oil and mining interests (Kearns, 2007), it is wise to look for the money behind the funding for the video series in order to fully understand the underlying ideology (Feng, 2010).

The picture that seemed bright and hopeful for climate change activists in 2008 now looks much bleaker, as hard-won ground has been rapidly lost. For those who thought the US religious scene was hard to fathom, it may seem even crazier now. But for anyone following the complex greening of Evangelicalism, it is not a surprise, as we will see below.

In addition to knowing the history, Matthew Nisbet's (2009) work on how environmental issues are framed in public discourse is also helpful, for, as he comments, '(t)here is no such thing as unframed information'. He further explains that 'frames are interpretive storylines that set a specific train of thought in motion, communicating why an issue might be a problem, who or what might be responsible for it, and what should be done about it'. Thus, frames provide a shorthand for believers, citizens, journalists, policymakers and others who count on the reader or listener making associations that can be left unsaid. This has been crucial in the success of religious climate change deniers.

Nisbet's (2009) article presents seven main frames that have been used in science-related policy debates. Within each frame, of course, there are variations, and frames themselves are neutral, but they may be presented in a way that is favourable, neutral or opposed. These frames help us understand religious discourse about climate change. For example, the religious grounding in theology and scripture just reviewed clearly fits Nisbet's 'morality and ethics' frame as a clear source for authority, which his article argues is needed in scientific debates but often overlooked. The concern for justice, however, besides fitting into the ethics frame, can also be seen in the frame of 'social progress'. Religious grounding in the authority of science invokes the frames of 'scientific certainty/uncertainty' or a 'Pandora's Box of catastrophes', and these have become increasingly central in religious discourse. Three other frames, 'economic competitiveness', 'public accountability and governance' and 'conflict and strategy' between battling elites or ideologues, are also helpful in understanding the world of religious activism on climate change.

In the next section I will give a sense of the very significant amount of religiously based, highly funded 'anti-global warming' activism in the United States that also is presented under the guise of religious, often Evangelical, environmentalism (there is Jewish involvement also). Perhaps the strength and energy of this movement can be taken as an indication of the success and perceived threat of the success of the previously described campaigns to combat global climate change. Or perhaps it is an indication of how much is perceived to be at stake, mainly in economic terms.

Evangelical Climate Sceptics

The group behind the 'Resisting the Green Dragon' series is the Cornwall Alliance, which stems from a gathering of conservative religious leaders who issued the Cornwall Declaration in 2000 in response to the earlier 1994 Evangelical Declaration on the Care of Creation (Berry, 2000).[29] The two represent contrasting viewpoints within Evangelical environmentalism. The Cornwall Declaration, after declaring that 'the moral necessity of ecological stewardship has become increasingly clear', spends much of the declaration invoking the frame of scientific uncertainty, referring to 'some unfounded or undue concerns includ(ing) fears of destructive manmade global warming, overpopulation, and rampant species loss' (Acton Institute, 2007, pp. xi–xv). The Evangelical Declaration, in contrast, asserts the 'degradations of creation can be summed up as (1) land degradation; (2) deforestation; (3) species extinction; (4) water degradation; (5) global toxification; (6) the alteration of atmosphere; and (7) human and cultural degradation'.

The ECI[30] is also clear about the scientific certainty of its claims. After admitting that 'many of us have required considerable convincing before becoming persuaded that climate change is a real problem and that it ought to matter to us as Christians,' the ECI states, 'but now we have seen and heard enough'. The first claim of the call is that 'Human Induced Climate Change is Real'. It then goes on to list the reasons for this certainty, grounded in the work of the IPCC, mentioning Sir John Houghton in particular, a 'devout Christian' who was chair of the IPCC from 1998 to 2002 (ECI, 2006, pp. 3–4.)

The Cornwall Declaration goes on to affirm private property ownership and market economies, arguing that free-market forces can resolve environmental problems, invoking Nisbet's (2009) economic competitiveness frame:

> A clean environment is a costly good; consequently, growing affluence, technological innovation, and the application of human and material capital are integral to environmental improvement. The tendency among some to oppose economic progress in the name of environmental stewardship is often sadly self-defeating.

In contrast, the Evangelical Declaration's promotes 'lifestyle choices that express humility, forbearance, self-restraint, and frugality' and 'godly, just, and sustainable choices'. The ECI Call to Action recognizes how powerful the economic competitiveness frame can be, stating in the opening preamble that the ECI seeks to respond to climate change 'in a way that creates jobs, cleans up our environment, and enhances national security by reducing our dependence on foreign oil, thereby creating a safe and healthy future for our children'.

The Cornwall Declaration prioritizes the needs of humans over nature, and denounces the environmental movement for embracing faulty science and a gloom-and-doom approach, invoking the frames of uncertainty and a 'Pandora's box of catastrophes'. In contrast, the Evangelical Declaration encourages Christians to become ecologically aware caretakers of creation. Other key differences, worthy of exploration elsewhere, revolve around the place and privileges of humans relative to nature, issues of Biblical interpretation, the definition of stewardship, the meaning of God's sovereignty and the centrality of Evangelism. These disagreements reflect more than internal Christian conflict; the Cornwall Declaration reinforced the 'wise-use' emphases on the continuing improvement of the environment through human technology, the abundance of resources put here for human utility, and opposition to a view of nature as an idyllic, harmonious state that must be preserved. The economic framing remains dominant.

These emphases reflect the climate sceptic playbook, according to Nisbet (2009), who reports that

> during the 1990s, based on focus groups and polling, top Republican consultant Frank Luntz helped shape the climate sceptic playbook,

recommending in a strategy memo to lobbyists and Republican members of Congress that the issue be framed as scientifically uncertain, using opinions of contrarian scientists as evidence.

Luntz also wrote that the 'emotional home run' would be an emphasis on the dire economic consequences of action, impacts that would result in an 'unfair burden' on Americans if other countries such as China and India did not participate in international agreements.[31] These frames have been well played, aided by the American media's practice of presenting two sides to every issue, 'thus "by giving equal weight to contrarian views on climate science, journalists presented the false impression that there is limited expert agreement on the causes of climate change"' (Nisbet, 2009).

The climate sceptics have played the scientific uncertainty frame carefully, making sure to mention thousands of scientists that have signed a petition to challenge the consensus on global warming or by running full-page ads in the *New York Times*. The press has picked this up and reported with little investigation into the credentials of the scientists. My own limited investigation, and the larger investigations of groups such as the Union of Concerned Scientists, indicate that the vast majority of signers, if they are even scientists, are in non-related fields, teach high-school biology, work for extractive industries and so on. This illustrates one of the contradictions present in the religious climate sceptic movement: despite a general suspicion or distrust of science, played up through creationism if anyone invokes evolution, science is still used to support the frame of uncertainty, indicating that science still has some authority for sceptics. Another way to emphasize the scientific uncertainty frame has been to refer to the 'religion' or 'theology' of global warming, as if the science was something one could choose to believe or not believe, a point that creationists also like to make.[32] Finally, religious climate sceptics like to invoke the 'theory' of global warming, just like there is a theory of evolution, implying that theories are hypotheses rather than explanations of scientifically observed facts, as in the theory of gravity (Kearns, 2007). Thus, the scientific uncertainty frame evokes a large and defining discourse in conservative Christianity, allowing followers to fill in the blanks about the authority of science.

When it became clear that merely emphasizing the uncertainty wasn't enough, as religious climate change activists invoked the justice frame of morality and the ethics of the precautionary principle in response to emphases on uncertainty, the sceptics' emphasis again turned to economic framing, as Luntz suggested.

Cornwall's responses to the ECI Call to Action, the 'We Get It!' campaign, links the frame of economic competitiveness with several other frames – moral ethics, social progress, conflict/elitism – and reveals another part of the climate denial playbook – the question of who is looking out the most for the poor, a central stated concern of Christians. The second claim of the ECI Call to Action is that 'the consequences of climate change will be significant, and will hit the poor the hardest', ending with the concern that 'millions of people could die in this century because of climate change, most of them our poorest global neighbours, and concluding with the invocation that "Jesus said: 'Love your neighbour as yourself' – Mark 12:31"'. The motto and argument for Cornwall's We Get It! campaign – 'Caring for the environment and the poor – Biblically' – aims directly at this argument, making the linkage succinctly:

> Efforts to cut greenhouse gases hurt the poor. By making energy less affordable and accessible, mandatory emissions reductions would drive up the costs of consumer products, stifle economic growth, cost jobs, and impose especially harmful effects on the Earth's poorest people.[33]

On the front page of the website, the campaign urges people to sign the declaration because 'millions of people around the world are threatened by extreme environmental politics'. The signers include Senator James Inhofe, long an outspoken leader in denying climate change.

The emphasis on economics ranges from arguments that environmentalism is a cover for socialism to claims that the economic costs of curtailing climate change will be too high and thus undermine our whole economic system, furthering the current economic decline. The video series 'Resisting the Green Dragon' contains segments entitled 'Going Green Impoverishes You, Your Church, and Your Society' and 'Ravaging the World's Poor'. The threat to capitalism and the US economic system has been a very powerful frame, a new outlet for the opposition to communism. Protecting capitalism from 'socialist' environmentalism is linked with the trope that capitalism promotes democracy and thus protecting it is an issue of freedom and liberty, as clearly seen in Calvin Beisner's (the driving force behind Cornwall) segment of the video series: 'Threats to Liberty and the Move Toward a Global Government'. For many, capitalism is the economic expression of Christianity (Beisner, 1989). This almost religious belief in the sanctity of the free market (ruled by the invisible hand of God) (Hawken, 1994) presents environmentalism as a threatening religion. The influence of the invocation of threats to the economic system reveals one strong reason for the growth of religious climate scepticism during an economic downturn.

Religious climate sceptics and deniers have succeeded because they engage all the frames of climate debates in such a way that listeners do not need to know anything about the actual environmental issues because more familiar tropes of economic competitiveness, liberty and concern for the poor come across louder. Scientists, liberals, people of colour, environmentalists, gays, pro-choice women and social justice Christians all get lumped into what the 'Resisting the Green Dragon' series calls 'The Green Face of the Pro-Death Agenda'. When communism 'died' as a rallying call, environmentalists were the target, until 9/11 and the demonization of Islam. Now that such demonization has become less acceptable in American culture, and the economic downturn continues to cloud the futures of many, religious and political conservatives have once again resurrected environmentalism as the cause of all evils.

Conclusion

Using Matthew Nisbet's frames of environmental discourse illuminates the complex world of green and not-so-green Evangelicalism, and the many dimensions of climate change, not just within that Christian subculture but in the larger society. Focusing on the world of green Evangelicalism is important for understanding the larger political currents of climate change scepticism and denial in the United States and the hurdles faced by any religious group advocating action to counter climate change. Even as the issue of climate change has created deep fissures within Evangelicalism, it has also created fissures within green Evangelicalism. Some 'true' green Evangelicals have started to shy away from it as too political for their liking, leading to former EEN staff members establishing a new group – FLOURISH – that proclaims, 'We think that environmental "issues" are primarily heart issues, not political issues'.[34] Further, the complexity of green Evangelicalism illustrates that just because a group is religious and claims to be environmental does not mean it holds the same positions as other groups making the same claim. This can be very confusing to the larger public, primed by the headlines to welcome the voice of green Evangelicals. But focusing on green Evangelicalism also obscures the tremendous success of other religious groups in the United States and globally.

For example, the Environmental Protection Agency has designated almost 50 congregations as Energy Star award winners and lists almost 1500 congregations as part of its Energy Star network.[35]

GreenFaith – which focuses broadly on stewardship, justice and spirituality – has now gone national, certifying green congregations around the country and educating many in ministry who want to focus their efforts on greening their faiths. Christian and Jewish seminaries have started to green their curriculum, worship, community life, practices and institutional habits through the Green Seminary Initiative so that they can better train religious leaders for tomorrow. The environmental justice movement, primarily focused on the unjust environmental burdens born by people of colour and the poor, has brought many black and Hispanic churches into the movement. In a similar fashion, campaigns to end mountaintop removal for easy access to coal in the Appalachian region of the eastern United States have brought many poor rural whites into the environmental and climate justice movements. The documentary film 'Renewal' tells the stories of eight different US faith groups concerned about the environment, including a Mississippi black Pentecostal church concerned with environmental justice after Hurricane Katrina and mountaintop removal, as well as Islamic and Buddhist environmental groups. The film demonstrates the wide range of places where conversations about religion and ecology are taking place. Part of what it documents is the growing place of food and agricultural issues for the religious environmental movement. This emphasis is reflected in the exponential growth of Hazon, a Jewish environmental organization that funds its focus on food through organized bike rides and has committed to trying to reduce Jewish consumption of meat by 50 per cent. In other words, the landscape of religious environmentalism in the United States has grown varied and rich.

The same is true at a more international level. The work of the Forum on Religion and Ecology and the Earth Charter – both more connected to a creation spirituality inspired by the work of 'geologian' Thomas Berry that spans religious traditions – continues to expand, illuminating the common story of evolution and of sharing one planet. The Alliance of Religions and Conservation, also inspired by the work of Berry, had a meeting at Windsor Castle in 2009. There, 200 representatives of nine faith traditions from all over the globe – Bahai, Buddhism, Christianity, Daoism, Hinduism, Islam, Judaism, Shintoism and Sikhism – gathered as a lead-up to the Copenhagen climate talks. Leaders of these faiths, as well as 19 secular environmental organizations in partnership with them, announced major initiatives to mitigate climate change. GreenFaith and the IPL were among those present. The Grand Mufti of Egypt announced a seven-year plan by Muslims to print the Koran (over 15 million copies/year) on recycled paper and to green the Hajj. Another announced project included turning to solar power for 26,000 Daoist temples in China. Leaders of the Shinto religion in Japan, in partnership with the Church of Sweden, presented the development of a religious forestry standard for such replanting efforts and the management of the millions of acres of forested land owned by various faiths.[36] Many faith traditions are involved in reforestation, such as Buddhist efforts towards reforestation in Mongolia and China, or the planting of millions of trees by Christians and the Green Belt Movement in Tanzania, Kenya and other places in Africa threatened with climate change and desertification. While Christian climate sceptics try to derail the successes of secular and religious environmentalists in the United States, there are those of many faiths around the globe who forge ahead in the fight against climate change and its related injustices.

Notes

[1] www.christianaid.org.uk/images/CA-campaigns-toolkit-May2010.pdf, accessed 13 September 2011. Time for Justice is a toolkit distributed by the APRODEV's Time for Climate Justice campaign. APRODEV is the association of the 17 major development and humanitarian aid organizations in Europe which work closely together with the World Council of Churches. Among its members are Church of Sweden, Diakonia, Norwegian Church Aid, DanChurch Aid, Finn Church Aid, ICCO, EED, Brot für die Welt, Bread for All and Christian Aid.

[2] 'Inauguration Week Meditation', www.brianmclaren.net/archives/blog/inaugural-week-meditation-so-hap.html. Accessed 23 January 2009.

[3] Walter Lowdermilk is credited with the first formulation of an Eleventh Commandment. In a speech on Radio Jerusalem in June 1939 entitled 'The Eleventh Commandment', he defined it as: 'Thou shalt inherit the holy earth as a faithful steward, conserving its resources and productivity from generation to generation. Thou shalt safeguard thy fields from soil erosion, thy living waters from drying up, thy forests from desolation, and protect the hills from overgrazing by thy herds, that thy descendents may have abundance forever. If any shall fail in this stewardship of the land, thy fruitful fields shall become sterile stony ground and wasting gullies, and thy descendants shall decrease and live in poverty or perish from off the face of the earth' (quoted in Nash, 1989, pp. 97–98).

[4] For more information, see the website created about his contributions at www.josephsittler.org/topics/environment.html.

[5] Schaeffer (1970, p. 24) wrote: 'the hippies of the 1960s did understand something . . . they were right in the fact that the plastic culture – modern man, the mechanistic worldview in university textbooks and in practice, the total threat of the machine, the establishment technology, the bourgeois upper middle class – is poor in its sensitivity to nature . . . As a utopian group, the counterculture understands something very real, both as to the culture as a culture, but also as

to the poverty of modern man's concept of nature and the way the machine is eating up nature on every side'.

6 www.nae.net/resolutions/131-ecology-1970.

7 www.arcworld.org/about.asp?pageID=2. Accessed 18 March 2011.

8 www.patriarchate.org/patriarch/the-green-patriach. Accessed 18 March 2011.

9 The United States Council of Catholic Bishops, the National Council of Churches Eco-Justice Working Group, the Evangelical Environmental Network and the Coalition on the Environment and Jewish Life.

10 For more on the wise use movement, see Kearns (2010).

11 At the local level, religious environmentalism in the United States covers the range I outlined above – stewardship of resources and species, justice for those in degraded environments and cultivating a spirituality attuned to the presence of the divine in creation or nature – in addition to energy conservation and climate change education.

12 See for example, the Evangelical Declaration of Care for the Creation for such scriptural uses (Berry, 2000).

13 'Who dies first? Who is sacrificed first?', Lutheran theologian Christoph Stückelberger's (2009) haunting chapter title, conveys the centrality of justice issues in religious responses to climate change.

14 www.insights.uca.org.au/news/2009/US-religious-groups-urge-strong-action_08-12-09.htm. Accessed 8 March 2011.

15 www.energystar.gov/index.cfm?c=small_business.sb_congregations. Accessed 20 March 2011.

16 'If God Is With Me All the Time, Does that Include the Auto Mall?' available at www.gbgm-umc.org/NCNYEnvironmentalJustice/transportation.htm. Accessed 18 March 2011.

17 The ECI first introduced its Climate Change: An Evangelical Call to Action in February 2006 with a national media campaign, and in March 2007, ECI released a list of its concerns titled: Principles for Federal Policy on Climate Change. http://christiansandclimate.org/learn/call-to-action/. Accessed 17 January 2011.

18 Analysts estimate that about 30 per cent of young white Evangelicals voted for Obama in 2008. Of course, the number for black and Hispanic Evangelicals was much higher, regardless of age.

19 Interim president Leith Anderson commented, somewhat ironically, that the NAE would listen to its constituency on the subject, highlighting the fact that the majority of the signers were not members of the NAE. Cizik later resigned over remarks he made on a radio program Fresh Air, which airs on stations affiliated with the National Public Radio in the United States. On Cizik, also see Michael Robert's chapter in the present book.

20 www.baptistcreationcare.org/node/1. Accessed 1 March 2011.

21 www.sbc.net/resolutions/amResolution.asp?ID=1171. Accessed 1 March 2011.

22 Ellison Research (2006), 'Nationwide Study Shows Concerns of Evangelical Christians over Global Warming'. www.evangelicalclimateinitiative.org/pub/polling_report.pdf. Accessed 5 June 2007.

23 http://christiansandclimate.org/learn/polling/. Accessed 3 March 2011

[24] www.publicreligion.org/research/published/?id=198. 'Poll – Climate Change and Global Poverty Key Religious Groups Want Government to Address Climate Change and Its Impact on World's Poor', Oxfam Climate Change & Poverty Survey March 20–27, 2009.

[25] http://pewresearch.org/pubs/1194/global-warming-belief-by-religion.

[26] www.barna.org/barna-update/article/13-culture/23-evangelicals-go-qgreenq-with-caution. Accessed 15 March 2011.

[27] A November 2010 Pew Research Center poll reported that: 'A 53%-majority of Republicans say there is no solid evidence the earth is warming. Among Tea Party Republicans, fully 70% say there is no evidence. Disbelief in global warming in the GOP is a recent occurrence. Just a few years ago, in 2007, a 62%-majority of Republicans said there is solid evidence of global warming, while less than a third (31%) said there is no solid evidence.' See http://pewresearch.org/databank/dailynumber/?NumberID=1126, accessed 20 March 2011'.

[28] www.resistingthegreendragon.com/. Accessed 23 March 2010.

[29] All quotes are from the web-posted versions of these two documents, available at www.cornwallalliance.org/articles/read/the-cornwall-declaration-on-environmental-stewardship/ and www.creationcare.org/blank.php?id=39.

[30] http://christiansandclimate.org/learn/call-to-action/. Accessed 18 March 2011.

[31] For an example, see www.we-get-it.org. Accessed 18 March 2011.

[32] Climate sceptics are not the only ones to talk about belief in global warming, as this headline from the *Telegraph* exclaims: 'Climate change belief given same legal status as religion'. www.telegraph.co.uk/earth/earthnews/6494213/Climate-change-belief-given-same-legal-status-as-religion.html. Accessed 26 March 2011.

[33] www.we-get-it.org/information/. Accessed 25 March 2011.

[34] www.flourishonline.org/get-involved/. Accessed 25 March 2011.

[35] www.energystar.gov/index.cfm?c=small_business.sb_congregations. Accessed 26 March 2011.

[36] www.windsor2009.org/. Accessed 23 March 2011.

References

Acton Institute (2007), 'The Cornwall Declaration on Environmental Stewardship', in M. Barkey (ed.), *Environmental Stewardship in the Judeo–Christian Tradition*. Grand Rapids: Acton Institute, pp. xi–xv.

Beisner, E. C. (1989), 'Christian economics: a system whose time has come?', in R. N. Mateer (ed.), *Christian Perspectives on Economics*. Lynchburg, VA: CEBA.

Bergmann, S. and Gerten, D. (2010), *Religion and Dangerous Environmental Change: Transdisciplinary Perspectives on the Ethics of Climate and Sustainability*. Münster: LIT.

Berry, R. J. (2000), 'Evangelical declaration of creation care', in R. J. Berry (ed.), *The Care of Creation: Focusing Concern and Action*. Downers Grove, IL: InterVarsity Press, pp. 17–22.

Beyer, P. (1994), *Religion and Globalization*. London: Sage Publications.

Evangelical Climate Initiative (2006), 'Climate change: an evangelical call to action'. Available from www.christiansandclimate.org/learn/call-to-action/. Accessed 23 March 2011.

Feng, L. (2010), 'Exclusive: the oily operators behind the religious climate change denial front group, Cornwall Alliance'. Available from www.wonkroom.think-progress.org/2010/06/15/cornwall-alliance-frontgroup/. Accessed 24 March 2011.

Gushee, D. P. (2008), *The Future of Faith in American Politics: The Public Witness of the Evangelical Center*. Waco, TX: Baylor University Press.

Hawken, P. (1994), *The Ecology of Commerce: A Declaration of Sustainability*. New York: HarperBusiness.

Jenkins, W. (2008), *Ecologies of Grace: Environmental Ethics and Christian Theology*. New York: Oxford University Press.

Kearns, L. (1996), 'Saving the creation: christian environmentalism in the United States'. *Sociology of Religion*, 57, 55–70.

— (2007), 'Cooking the truth: faith, science, the market, and global warming', in L. Kearns and C. Keller (eds), *EcoSpirit: Religions and Philosophies for the Earth*. New York: Fordham Press, pp. 97–124.

— (2010), 'Wise use movement', in W. Jenkins (ed.), *Berkshire Encyclopedia of Sustainability: The Spirit of Sustainability*, Vol. 1, 435–436.

McMorris, C. M. (2003), 'What would Jesus drive?' *Religion in the News*, 6, 1.

Nash, R. (1989), *The Rights of Nature: A History of Environmental Ethics*. Madison: University of Wisconsin Press.

Nisbet, M. C. (2009), 'Communicating climate change: why frames matter for public engagement'. *Environment* (March/April). Available from www.environmentmagazine.org/Archives/Back%20Issues/March-April%202009/Nisbet-full.html. Accessed 14 January 2010.

Northcott, M. S. (2007), *A Moral Climate: The Ethics of Global Warming*. London: Darton, Longman & Todd Ltd.

Pesonen, H. (2004), *Vihertyvä Kirkko: Suomen Evankelishluterilainen Kirkko ympäristö-toimijana*. Helsinki: Vammalan Kirjapino Oy.

Robb, C. (2010), *Wind, Sun, Soil, Spirit: Biblical Ethics and Climate Change*. Minneapolis: Fortress Press.

Schaeffer, F. A. (1970), *Pollution and the Death of Man: The Christian View of Ecology*. Carol Stream: Tyndale House Publishers.

Smith, B. G. and Johnson, B. (2010), 'The liberalization of young Evangelicals: a research note', *Journal for the Scientific Study of Religion*, 49, 351–360.

Stueckelberger, C. (2009), 'Who dies first? Who is sacrificed first? Ethical aspects of climate justice', in K. Bloomquist (ed.), *God, Creation and Climate Change: Spiritual and Ethical Perspectives*. Geneva: Lutheran University Press, pp. 47–62.

Chapter 9

The Future of Faith: Climate Change and the Fate of Religions

Martin Schönfeld

Introduction: Standing Lynn White on his Head

As climate change worsens, world civilization finds itself in an increasingly unpalatable environment. How will this intensifying process affect religious worldviews and practices? Specifically, what will happen to different belief system as more bad weather puts ever harder pressure on civilization?

This inquiry is not a theological study. Religion is examined here as an empirical phenomenon, as a web of ideas in an environmental context. It is not a scholarly study, either, which concerns sources and records. Our questions point beyond present materials to future possibilities. Such an inquiry can only be a philosophical investigation, in the free-spirited sense of a pursuit of open questions. Clear reasoning, critical thinking and common sense are obvious tools. Less obvious, but just as needed, is another, more specific tool: conceptual *gestalts*.

Gestalts are patterns of information. One problem with such patterns is that they seem to be made up. They appear as interpretations projected on the data. Another is that they seem to be perilously close to clichés, stereotypes or cartoons. A related problem is that they can be pernicious; it is only a short step from working with a pattern to pandering to a prejudice. Particular over religion, history teaches us caution about the use of conceptual gestalts.

And yet, for an inquiry that aims to shed light on future events by extrapolating from the present, there is no way around the use of patterns, imagined or not. While it is true that a gestalt is at least in part a cognitive projection, this does not make it arbitrary, because it is also a synthesis of facts. But there is something strange about this synthesis, since a *gestalt* is not a straightforward summation of the facts (if it were that, it would remain a mere collection of details, lacking coherence). The particular synthesis of facts that amounts to a gestalt is a whole.

Sums are static; wholes are dynamic. Sums are aggregates of parts, but wholes represent interplays; they are the way parts work together in a sum. The interplays are mind independent, and happen in virtue of the facts participating in something larger. In that sense, wholes are objective. At the same time they are elusive, and what one believes to have identified as an actual interplay may well be an imagined structure unwittingly projected on the interactive aggregate. To the extent a gestalt is the result of a cognitive, structural projection on complex arrays of facts is the sense that a whole is subjective. Ideally (but not always), the subjective projection is a mirror of the objective interplay. A gestalt fits the facts if nothing can or should be added, altered or taken away; it fits, in short, if it works. And it works by revealing something about the phenomenon at hand, clarifying it.

Gestalts are vulnerable to abuse. But it is important to distinguish between use and misuse. Cartoons or caricatures are not always pernicious. A good cartoon compresses information instead of distorting it. Such compression can be revealing. It can also be provocative. Thus, conceptual cartoons must be drawn with care and are always subject to revision. If philosophy wants to contribute to big questions today, in the age of information overload, compression is of the essence, and there is no way around heuristic cartoons, however unsettling they may be.

One trivial reason for pursuing the question of the future of faith is that everything is more or less interconnected. Nature, culture and religion affect one another. We can understand nature as the planetary biosphere. Culture and its artefacts take place in the human sphere. Religion, roughly, can be defined as a sum of spiritual beliefs. Nature is distinct from culture, but culture shapes nature just as nature shapes culture. Religion differs from culture, but religion alters culture just as culture alters religion. The interplay of the three spheres is complex but not opaque. Their spatial arrangement guides how they modify each other. Like frames within frames, they progressively enfold one another, with the smaller nesting in the larger. Reminiscent of Russian dolls, religion nestles inside culture, and culture nestles inside nature.

The simile puts religion inside culture, almost as if religion occupied a central space within culture. Belief systems occupy a crucial cultural place by means of the power of their ideas. Religious ideas impact cultural identity, both historically and collectively. They influence ethical values and cognitive outlooks that make a culture into what it is. Faith is not required; socialization is all that is needed – growing up in a given family, circle of friends, neighbourhood or region suffices to leave a mark on mentality. It is difficult to overestimate the cultural power of religious ideas.

Similarly, culture can be said to be inside nature. This is not even a metaphor; it is a literal description of their physical relation. Over time, culture arose in nature; civilization has emerged in the biosphere. And in space, culture is placed in nature; civilization expands in the biosphere across the earth's surface. In dynamic terms, nature encloses culture as well; current carbon economies are open loops, with resource inputs from biosphere to civilization and emission outputs from civilization to the biosphere.

Historically, causal pulses may well have travelled from the interior to the exterior, from the religious centre through the cultural rim to the natural environment. Features of such a pulse were first claimed by Lynn White in 'The historical roots of the ecological crisis' (1967). The contentions of this essay spawned considerable controversy, attracted enormous criticism and have often been contested. White argues that Christianity's victory over paganism was a crucial event; it drained nature of sanctity, placed the divine in the supernatural and created via natural theology the impetus to scrutinize nature, a scrutiny that triggered the scientific revolution and allowed the rise of technology. As White puts it:

> Since both *science* and *technology* are blessed words in our contemporary vocabulary, some may be happy at the notions, first, that, viewed historically, modern science is an extrapolation of natural theology and second, that modern technology is at least partly to be explained as an occidental, voluntarist realisation of the Christian dogma of man's transcendence of and rightful mastery over nature. But, as we now recognise, somewhat over a century ago science and technology – hitherto quite separate activities – joined to give mankind powers which, to judge by many of the ecological effects, are out of control. If so, Christianity bears a huge burden of guilt.

On the one hand, White overstates his point. Blaming Christianity for environmental decline is akin to blaming parents for the deeds of children. This may be correct as long as offspring remains in parental custody, but it makes little sense when children come of age. Science and technology no longer answered to religious authority when they joined forces in the Industrial Revolution and spawned the ecological crisis.

Then there is the sheer density of White's narrative. History spanning 20 centuries is compressed into five pages. While such compression smacks of hubris, there is another side to it. As a cartoon of the historical record, White's perspective is anathema to serious scholarship. Arguably, one could say that White's sweeping generalizations do not live up to the scholarly rigor of historiography. At the same time, this compression suggests a gestalt, which is philosophically interesting. And one can also argue that it is a good cartoon, capturing a striking feature of the Abrahamitic religions.

Abrahamitic religions (Judaism, Christianity and Islam) represent a dualistic conception of reality. There is one God, and then there is nature. This one God is the creator of nature, and nature is the creation of God. Creator and creation are as distinct as an author and a book, or a composer and a song. Despite all the exceptions, qualifications and objections that scholars, historians and theologians have levelled against White's cartoon, his narrative compression points to a fundamental difference between the Abrahamitic religions and their indigenous counterparts. The former suggest a metaphysical dualism bifurcating divine and natural; the latter suggest a holism blending the two. Since the divine is of value, the Abrahamitic religions drain nature of value by conceiving of the divine as supernatural. Here, the transcendent is outside nature. Not so in the indigenous religions: there, the transcendent is immanent – the divine suffuses and dwells in nature. This is a cartoon, but a good one.

What about the other way then? Does causation also travel from nature back to religion? We know that causal pulses from nature impinge on culture, and even more so through environmental decline. We also know that causal pulses from culture impinge on religion, particularly in times of hardship. Considering that Western religions are partly (indirectly, complicatedly) responsible for this decline, and thus for the hardship, the backwards-travelling pulses are boomerangs of self-incurred consequences. How does this boomerang impact religion? Or rather, how *will* it impact them? Will there be winners? Will there be losers? How influential will climate change and its impacts be relative to other developments governing the dynamics of religions? Could the impact also trigger spiritual evolution?

White's study was about the past. Our questions are about the future. The pursuit of such questions cannot sift through empirical evidence and resort to historical analysis. It must rely on rational synthesis and conjectural extrapolation instead. This requires the construction of a considerable philosophical groundwork. Synthesis and speculation are fraught with perils, and to avoid going astray in uncharted territory we need to move slowly and cautiously by means of a series of preliminary steps.

A basic issue that needs to be addressed so as to avoid the charge of begging a question is whether and how climate change is 'bad'. The first step would accordingly be to pin down what 'bad' is. But if climate change were bad, one would expect that it would consequently be recognized as a peril. If so, one should think civilization would deal with it, mitigate its impacts and deflect the causal pulse. And if civilization did that, religion would not be impacted. So the next step would be to show why religion is likely to be impacted anyway, and why a timely response of civilization is quite improbable. Nonetheless, scientists tell us that considerable uncertainties blur climate change scenarios. If the scenarios are uncertain, predicting eventual impacts on religion seems rather dubious. Thus the third step would be to clarify that the uncertainties are not about whether climate change will be bad, only how bad it might be. It needs to be shown that the causal pulse is bound to arrive. But if it did arrive, it would impact civilization. What makes one sure that this impact would also be felt by religion? The fourth step would be to show how civilization and religion are linked, and how the latter is vulnerable to pressures absorbed by the former. If all these assumptions can be made, then the prospect of the climate-driven fate of religion will come into view. But since 'fate' has speculative meanings, the final preliminary step would be to show how fate makes sense in rational terms.

Now the path is clear to chart the climate-driven future of faith. Faith comes in two kinds, and the first takes the form of what one calls 'religion' in the West. Thus, what is the likely fate of monotheism in view of climate change? The second kind of faith refers to non-monotheistic, indigenous religions elsewhere. How will climate change affect them? And which creeds, overall and in the long run, will prevail?

Spinoza, Kant or What's Bad about Climate Change

Climate change is an emerging reality the likes of which civilization has not yet experienced. Global warming driven by human-made greenhouse gas emissions is an enormous biospherical shift. This shift has positive aspects, such as greater agricultural productivity in the far north, as well as regional beneficiaries, such as the northward movement and increased productivity of the boreal forest biome of North Asia. But on the whole, the shift is bad.

Now, 'bad' is a fuzzy term. What is bad for animals is not always bad for people, and what is bad for people is not always bad for business. Still, we can sharpen the meaning of 'bad' to a keener notion. Two viewpoints are particularly helpful: Spinoza's and Kant's. Spinoza defines the 'bad' as anything that prevents us from flourishing.[1] Bad in this sense is whatever impedes human development. Kant defines 'bad' as what is unsustainable.[2] Bad, in this second sense, includes actions that cannot be done by everyone, for if everyone did them, it would lead to a situation in which nobody could do these things.

Spinoza and Kant supply complementary perspectives. Together, they yield the conceptual equivalent of binocular vision, elucidating the bad in depth. Their views are two sides of the same coin. One side points to content, another to form. The content of what is bad is that *it stands in the way* – the bad is an impediment to flourishing that would otherwise unfold. In this sense climate change is bad just like a disease or an accident would be. For civil progress, climate change is a self-imposed handicap.

Specifically, climate change is bad in that it generates burdens and imposes constraints. It creates adverse conditions for human development. It makes life harder. Human development is a qualitative ideal, but also a measurable trait with quantifiable elements. Literacy, safety, health, longevity, well-being and economic stability are such elements. They lend themselves to empirical sampling, statistical analysis and comparative ranking. They are criteria for gauging how societies are faring and whether civilization is evolving. By impeding development, climate change is a regressive causal pulse. This anti-evolutionary aspect is the content-related, material or Spinozist part of the meaning of 'bad'.

Apart from this, anthropogenic climate change is bad in that *it will not last* – the actions that cause it are short-lived in any case. They cannot last because our civilization will either end them before climate change runs away from us, or because climate change will run away from us, ending any civilization that does such actions. Imagine, for example, that greenhouse gas emissions continue year after year at levels reached in the first decade of the new millennium. Atmospheric greenhouse gas concentrations would keep rising. Extrapolate this trend far enough and a catastrophe unfolds for chemical reasons alone. The consequence would be a blighted planetary surface, with parched and dusty lands, and sour and empty seas. Such a blighted world (the joint result of climate change, overpopulation and economic growth) would fail to sustain civilization at present consumption and population levels. A dieback would happen – with the result that survivors would not be capable of producing emissions at the levels that had led to dieback in the first place. Emissions would fall. Thus anthropogenic climate change is self-reducing.

This line of reasoning evokes Kant's categorical imperative. In this formal sense, climate change is bad as the global expression of unsustainable conduct. It cannot go on because it produces a situation that precludes further such conduct. Good actions, formally, are actions whose maxims can become and consistently serve as laws to all. Good actions can be universalized – they are capable of ongoing replication via a stable process. The form of the good is universalizability, and one aspect of this form is that it is sustainable – individual actions can be emulated.

Anthropogenic greenhouse gas emissions are not universalizable; actions that lead to global warming are unsustainable in the most basic sense. They are not merely unsustainable in undermining the biospherical basis of existence. Their destructiveness to biological diversity, agricultural productivity and such is coincidental. Their formal essence, instead, is that they are self-destructive. Their collective enactment injects a self-reducing pulse into a matrix of done practices.

Materially, anthropogenic climate change is bad because it is anti-evolutionary. It obstructs the flourishing of the species. A species may persist for eons. A habitat might also last for a long time. Climate can keep changing. But a species imposing climate change on its own habitat does something that will result in the undoing of its doing.

The Existential Blind Spot of Climate Change

A closer look reveals uncertainties over the climatic future, which means, among other things, that a window of opportunity is still open. It is getting smaller year after year, but – for the time being – trends are still fluid and their eventual course depends largely on what we shall do. Whether humankind will rise to the challenge remains to be seen. At present, conflicting perspectives create inertia. Science is at odds with the market, and politicians are split. Civilization has not yet decided how to proceed.

There is a range of possible reactions to climate change. They shade from bright to dark or from lofty visions to scary spectres. If the global village prioritizes mitigation, that is, if governments heed science, rein in corporations, push towards post-carbon economies and post-consumerist culture, and also curb population growth, warming will likely peak at a temperature rise of two degrees. This is the best scenario. Realizing it requires three things: acting sensibly, evolving sustainably and procreating minimally. If this cannot be done, temperatures will soar to four degrees and beyond.

Odds are we will not meet these conditions. A flaw in human cognition hampers the pursuit of future-oriented strategies. We are not well equipped to handle perils of the sort climate change presents. Our species is geared to responding to tangible threats. We react to clear and present dangers. Exposure to a direct menace triggers a fight-or-flight response – pupils dilate, heart rate increases, muscle tone tightens and adrenaline floods the brain. Thus hyper-alert and clear-minded, we are ready to face the threat down or run as fast as we can. The threat-response mechanism served our ancestors well, but for the generation forced to deal with climate change, this ancestral gift is a curse because climate change is subtle. It intrudes into our life-world on multiple levels, affecting biodiversity, agriculture and geomorphology, but its signs are delicate, distant or both. As intrusions go, they seem minor; as threats, they feel slight; as stimuli, they are too faint to trigger self-interested responses.

In cognitive terms, at least for the primary perpetrators in the developed nations, such as the United States, climate change is not a bear leaping from the underbrush in front of us but a more distant predator seen with binoculars on a safari, an entertaining sight that gives tourists vicarious goosebumps. Impacts of climate change are visible already – but they are more conspicuous in faraway lands, in flooded Pakistan, in parched Darfur or in the wilting Amazon. Impacts affecting the perpetrators are still on the level of deniability – it gets hotter and drier in summer, and colder and snowier in winter, but the scenery is not changing yet, and the harvests are not yet failing. Climate change hits humans in a cognitive blind spot. The subtlety of the threat is the chance to nip it in the bud but invites our failure to do so in time.

Consider biodiversity. The present extinction of non-human life is an event even bigger in scope than the end of the dinosaurs. It marks the transition from a green world to an urban world. Climate change makes it worse. Global warming hurts climax communities, such as coral reefs and equatorial jungles, and imperils entire phyla, such as amphibians and lizards. Animals and plants had already been dying in outsize numbers for two centuries, but now they are dying faster.

Still, we cannot really feel this acceleration. Extinctions become noticeable only when they are over. Endangered biomes and species still occupy space. Extinction events take time, and even when accelerated by global warming, they play out at speeds far too slow to impinge on our senses. Just as we are ill equipped to react to dangers spatially distant, we have trouble cognizing catastrophes that unfold in slow motion. So the shift from the Holocene to the Anthropocene that is the mark of our generation remains inconspicuous. The invidious phenomenology of perils too subtle to be seen hits home again.

Similar empirical ambiguities blur climatic intrusions into culture. The humanitarian catastrophe in Darfur is the breakdown of the age-old cooperation of two groups, herders and farmers, who used to share the same land. The cooperation collapsed when the carrying capacity of the land kept shrinking. The land turns to desert because the monsoon that waters the northeast African coast is now erratic. But media coverage is never about causation and only about events or sensations. Thus first-world observers see bad things happening, and they may donate to charities that promise to help, but they fail to connect their carbon lifestyle to the beginning of the chain that ends with the misery in the news.

A further cognitive problem is the tenuous link between trends and events. The causal relationship between overall processes (climate change) and concrete events (meteorological spikes) cannot be established rigorously; only the likely frequency of events can. As a cultural result, such probabilistic peculiarities are used to make excuses and to defend inaction. Once again the climatic intrusion is too large to grasp. The American Disenlightenment illustrates this – even in a society as open and literate as that of the United States, climate denial remains a mainstream position as late as 2010.[3]

As long as climate change remains subtle, distant and odd, we can fight it – but chances are we will not. And when climate change intrudes in ruder ways, we will want to fight it, but chances are we will not be able to. Evolution has left our species maladapted to meet threats of such kind. Thus, we can expect that things will go from bad to worse.

Uncertainties and the Bottleneck

There are uncertainties over the physical course of climate change independent of human action. These uncertainties reflect the limits of knowledge of the magnitude of events set in motion and generally about how the earth system ultimately works. Physically, global warming means that large bodies, such as the oceans, ice caps or permafrost soils, are absorbing thermal energy – they have been set into 'thermal motion'. Masses in terms of bulk point to inertia, just as masses in motion point to momentum. The inertial force of the masses in question expresses itself as a resistance to change, which is why they did not heat up right after annual global mean temperatures started to go up, doing so only after a delay.

The warming of the poles, the seas or the permafrost is like a train that starts moving and gains speed. (The same would occur in reverse.) Air capture technology for scrubbing carbon dioxide was invented in 2010; initial reports suggest that mass production is feasible. If the scrubbers were now put to work in such numbers that their uptake would reduce atmospheric carbon dioxide concentrations, then global warming would still continue as a physical result of the accumulated 'thermal momentum' acquired. Just as climate change is like an accelerating train, its mitigation is like pulling the brakes; trains moving at speed cannot stop right away.

The unknown length of the expected brake path points to a deeper uncertainty about the earth system. Most climatologists conceive of this system like a machine, which acts in a linear and orderly fashion. In a best-case scenario, with scrubbers switched on right away, the climate train could not instantly come to a stop but would immediately slow down. Climate change would keep 'sliding' on its pre-set track – more droughts, floods, heat waves, rising seas and failing harvests would occur – but, eventually, freak weathers would disappear, destabilization would be halted and the system would return to its former self. However, data in the geological and paleontological record tell a different story and point to a worse scenario. The record indicates that past shifts of the earth system were turbulent. Over time, climate behaves in some ways like the physiology of an organism. Things tend to stay in balance, but the system can tip from one state to another if it absorbs too much pressure. Here the railroad simile fails – unless one wishes to imagine a Daliesque train melting while sliding, naturally derailing and inexorably crashing. Even after pulling the brakes, accumulated momentum can have fatal consequences. Another simile would be more apt: climate as a nicely set up row of dominoes. Someone flicks the first stone, which falls, hits the next stone and sets off a cascade. If this were the make-up of the earth system, even optimal mitigation might not help much. CO_2 scrubbing, at this point, would be as futile as setting up fallen dominoes. The causal cascade of irrevocably melting polar ice, permafrost methane release and marine acidification will just run on, speed up and pull away.

For the purpose of determining the badness of climate change in the context of such uncertainties, and for gauging the likely pressure this would exert on civilization – and thus on religion – the climate debate between the mechanists and the geophysiologists might not matter all that much. Climate change is bound to spell difficulties either way. It will be bad; so much is certain. But how bad will it get?

This question points to the economic context of climate change. Free markets are structurally flawed. The global economic system cannot flourish while staying the same. Free trade works best when markets are expanding, and business is happiest when booming. The system is stable when growing. This means that the prosperity of civilization rests on an economic design analogous to cancer. Even with leaps of efficiency, ever greater exploitation of resources, ever larger commodity consumption, ever higher levels of emissions and greater amounts of waste are required. Economic growth collides with the biospheric limits. Signs of this clash are resource depletion, habitat destruction and biodiversity loss. The thirst for oil collides with absorption limits of the carbon cycle, and the expression of that clash is climate change. Growth plus oil contributed to conditions that yielded a fourfold increase of human numbers from 1900 to 2000. Demographic expansion is expected to peak by 2050 at six times the population of 1900. All these will be children deserving of a future, and persons aspiring to a convenient and carefree lifestyle. But, on one planet, with resources close to depletion and no land left to settle, the trends of economic growth, carbon growth and population growth are hitting a wall of environmental limits.

Civilization is forced to change its ways, but at the worst of times. Humankind must evolve towards post-consumerist stability and mitigate the consequences of a century of anthropogenic greenhouse gas emissions just when other problems emerge and multiply, and just when additional human growth will make it ever more difficult to embark on civil evolution. The context of climate change, in sum, is a looming bottleneck of murderously tight proportions.

Climate change is the consequence of a design flaw in the modern structure of world civilization. The adversity of this consequence forces us to adapt and evolve. Cultures can survive and prosper only if they are capable of fitting themselves to the new constraints. The bottleneck leaves us little choice. In light of all we know, nothing appears more certain than a far-reaching transformation of civilization this century. In the worst case, we face dieback. In the best case, we celebrate a sustainability revolution. In all cases, climate change is bound to impact civilization as a self-incurred evolutionary pressure.

There is thus little reason for optimism. The structure of human cognition makes it unlikely that civilization can react to climate change in time. The scientific uncertainties about the earth system merely concern the choice of whether the transition to a harsh world happens slowly or suddenly. Either way the pressure on culture will not relent. The species is being drawn towards a bottleneck. Thus we can expect things to go from worse to catastrophic.

The Fragility of Hope

Religion is an element of culture, and the question is how environmental pressures affect religion. This requires a closer look at the cultural function of religion. We will have a clearer idea how creeds will be faring in this harsher world as soon as we understand what it is that belief systems are actually doing. Generally, religion relates to all aspects of existence. Faith is a holistic experience that is not tied to one particular dimension of *dasein*. Meaning arises by engaging with the puzzle of existence in three ways. 'What can we know?', 'What should we do?' and 'What may we hope?' are the three ultimate questions. Being human arises in this triangle of knowing, doing and hoping. Perhaps we can define the essence of religion as a bond to something larger, which demands faith. This essence concerns all three sides.

Knowing differs from doing. Knowledge is theory, doing is practice and theory ends where practice begins. The opposites arise along a continuum, which connects them. Knowing informs doing, as when a plan spawns an action, and doing informs knowing, as when actions yield experience.

Doing and hoping are similarly related; they differ yet connect. Doing is activity per se, while hoping waits for something to happen and is accordingly passive. Hope arises in the context of inaction just as action supplants hopeful passivity. Hope informs doing; without hope there would be neither reason nor orientation for action. And doing informs hoping in turn: a failed deed discourages and deflates hope just as a successful action inspires and raises hopes.

Key to the function of religion in culture is the relation of hoping and knowing. Limits of knowledge about the primordial and the transcendent are not really a problem. The power of faith, which shapes cultural profiles and personal identities, is not vulnerable to epistemic concerns. Religion, after all, is not a falsifiable edifice of knowledge. It is a cluster of beliefs, and knowledge is not required for faith.

In this manner, religious doctrines emerge primarily as narratives of hope. And yet, while hope and knowledge are distinct, their relation is not only analogous to the other two relations considered but also involves a peculiarity of its own. Knowledge ends where hope begins, and hope falters where knowledge starts.

Consider, for instance, the relation of knowing and hoping in an existential boundary experience – what Jaspers calls *Grenzerfahrung* – as when caught in the trials one suffers with loved ones fallen ill. Suppose there is an ominous medical report. As long as the findings remain ambiguous, hope grows that things may not be all that bad. Should additional tests dash this hope, another hope may arise (say, that the thing now known as bad can be cured), pushed further out by the new knowledge. Hope and knowledge inform one another, obviously, but in contrast to the relations involving doing, a feature of this polarity-pair is the *proximity* of hope to knowledge. Hope arises in the field of the unknown, but doesn't thrive in the field's centre. Instead, hope thrives at the edge of its own field, just at the boundary to knowledge. Hope doesn't grow stronger the further it ranges away from knowledge. On the contrary, all hope seeks certainty, thus aspiring to a trait that belongs to knowledge. The power of hope is inversely proportional to its distance from knowledge, and it is strongest right at the boundary it shares with knowing.

The proximity of hoping and knowing means that faith is not perfectly free from verified information. Narratives of hope remain meaningful and persuasive as long as they manage to accommodate facts. They remain credible only if they can be made to fit what is known. Religious belief systems involve characteristic conceptions of nature. This is a fulcrum for climate pressure to find leverage over faith.

Another fulcrum lies in the sphere of doing, specifically the values that inform lifestyle, law and policy. Some values are now counterproductive, undermining efforts to prepare for the bottleneck. As climate change and environmental decline worsen, the ensuing pressures serve as a critical tribunal for values. This tribunal is both forward- and backward-looking. Values are to be examined on their responsibility for the problem and their potential to contribute to solutions. Belief systems that future generations will blame as culprits for the crisis are bound to lose appeal. Here climate pressure finds leverage too.

The persistence of religions depends on their capacity to deal with pressure. The degree of 'evolutionary fitness', and thus the likely fate of a faith, can be gauged along the aspects of dasein. Over hope, the question is whether the faith still inspires. Over knowledge, the question is whether the faith agrees with the facts. Over practice, the question is whether the faith contains the values now needed.

Gauging Faith, Charting Fate

Religions, like memeplexes, live through their core ideas. There are innumerable parts that add up to the structured sum of a belief system, but there are few traits that make these parts work together as the dynamic whole that is faith. The knowledge scholars unearth about a belief system contrasts with the simplicity of faith that prompts worshipers to pray. Data in the latter are fraction of the former, but it is the latter that shapes social and historic realities. Core ideas allow a memeplex to replicate and spread. Whatever else a belief system may contain – tenets and rituals, clerical issues and theological puzzles – is coincidental. They are the catch but not the net. Core ideas are the memetic strands that give a creed vibrancy and coherence. Such strands serve as the covenant of the faithful with what they hold sacred. They bind details together and turn a belief system into a lived reality.

This description applies not only to religions, but also to science. Both involve information that takes spiritual adepts or doctoral students years to absorb, but at bottom there are few ideas that hold all else together. General relativity is a complicated theory, but its core is just eight equations and two ideas ('spacetime tells mass to move' and 'mass tells spacetime to curve'). A memeplex can be a spiritual creed or a scientific theory. Either way, its fitness turns on the force and resilience of its core ideas. Concentrating on the power of core ideas allows us to gauge faith as a whole and to examine its fate.

In analytic chemistry, 'environmental fate' denotes what happens to pollutants in space over time. A compound's fate partly depends on how strong its molecular bonds are – a well-balanced, tightly organized molecule, such as DDT, is resilient to multiple types of exposure. Dust a field with it, and it will not sublimate in the open air. Let the sun shine down on it, and the rays will not break it down. Let rain fall on it, and it will wash unchanged into the nearest waterway. Let fish absorb it, and it will settle down in their tissue. Let birds eat the fish, and it will invade their metabolism where it impairs calcium build-up. A final act of DDT's fate is that bird eggs have shells so thin that the breeding hen crushes her offspring.

The environmental fate of a substance is a trajectory across places and over time. On one day it is here, on the next day there. Fate is observable – the locations of the compound can be charted as marks on a coordinate grid. And it is quantifiable – the concentration along its locations can be measured with mass spectrometers and gas chromatographs. What then is fate? In analytic-environmental chemistry, it's where a substance goes and what happens to it on its path from the source outward into the world.

Forecasting, in meteorology, is the art of predicting tomorrow's weather through today's conditions. Here fate is not just a trajectory of location, context and composition, but also a thrust of powers accumulating and discharging. Discharge mirrors accumulation. Thus thunderheads build up to a storm until pent-up energy unleashes in gales and squalls. Chemistry shows the structural dimension of fate. Meteorology supplies the dynamic dimension: energy thrusting as a momentum in space–time.

As a momentum in space–time, fate emerges as a groove of consequences. The more actions happen in one vein, the plainer a trail is left, the deeper a groove is dug and the greater the odds are of innocent events being pulled in. Like a river carving its own bed, the energy of actions bundles into a pulse of fate herding happenings along. Structure and dynamics thus meet over action, rounding off the concept.

Incessant human activity, mainly anthropogenic carbon emissions plus forest cover reduction, blazes a trail of consequences that mass into one relentless climatic pulse. The Assessment Reports of the Intergovernmental Panel of Climate Change show that the climatic pulse can be studied. The steady downward correction of the forecast to ever grimmer outlooks, from AR 1 (1991) to AR 4 (2007), illustrate a last aspect, namely, that fate – like any other scientific topic – is subject to review and revision.

Human actions braid biospheric storylines that entail climatic outcomes. Thus fate is what we make, but with this qualification: self-made fate acquires inertial mass, which makes it hard to change and gives consequences unsettling inexorability. It is this inexorability that makes prediction possible, not only about unfolding climatic futures but also about likely corresponding behaviour of belief systems.

The Climatic Fate of Monotheism

As a constant of civilizations, faith is here to stay. Spirituality and religiosity are anthropological fixtures; they seem to be as old as civilization. But religions appear to have certain lifespans that can be reckoned in centuries and millennia. The youngest of the world religions are the three Abrahamitic religions. Unless climatic pressures grow so overwhelming that they trigger a cultural collapse and introduce a genuine discontinuity, we can expect the world religions in the so-called West to remain core elements of civilization for the foreseeable future. Yet climate change puts the Abrahamitic religions on the defensive. Lynn White's accusations, while overstated, will likely linger as the lasting charge that it was the impact of these creeds on world civilization that ultimately drained nature of sanctity, with the biospheric and climatic consequences visible now.

And even apart from the issue of a destructive causal pulse travelling from monotheism via culture into nature, spawning the ecological crisis, monotheism will be affected simply in virtue of being part of civilization.

Monotheism will feel the pinch like any other part of culture. Faith is subject to pressure because the people who hold the faith and turn it into a cultural element are exposed to that pressure. A historical constant about pressure, people and faith is that the intensity of faith is proportional to the pressure suffered by the people. Religious zeal varies with the circumstances and intensifies through adversity.

Miserable conditions radicalize people. Those who are economically disenfranchised and politically marginalized flock to militant creeds. When everything else has been taken from you, the sole thing you have left to build on is faith. Fundamentalism is an expression of discontent, and – as irrational as its zeal may appear – the underlying misery is neither arbitrary nor subjective. Every time droughts and floods destroy harvests, or cold snaps and heat waves kill livestock (or, soon enough, marine acidification devastates fisheries), poverty deepens, despair spreads and faith grow desperate.

One could liken the dynamics between religion and environments (and, by extension, climate) to a class and a teacher. When times are good, the kids have fun, the lesson is engaging and the teacher is nice. Tests given in such gentle climes tend to lead to a Gaussian distribution of grades, a staggered set of performance curving like a gentle swell, flattening out at the extremes and bulging in a wide centre. There will be a few stragglers and a few bright lights, but most kids will be somewhere in the middle.

The faithful in a benevolent environment – as in a society prosperous, peaceful and just – tend to be moderates. Why should they not be? There is little cause for discontent and small reason for resistance. Zeal takes too much energy. Fundamentalist fervour is not worth the effort as long as the faithful feel happy and safe, and as long as they realize their aspirations freely and do not fear for their children's future. A benevolent environment keeps moderates in the majority and radicals at the margins.

Climate change takes matters to another level. In the classroom analogy, climate change speeds up the pace of learning. The lesson gets hard. Some students will be angry and scared, or sullen and resentful. Others will buckle down, take a breath and get to work. The middle ground will erode. The bulge of mediocrity caves in under the pressures, and the Gaussian distribution shifts to a bipolar distribution. The gentle swell gets choppy and crests twice. Now there will be more stragglers, who are falling behind and turn their back on the barrage of information. There will also be more superior students who persist and keep up with the hard lessons.

Climate change will produce deteriorating environmental situations and thus harsher social conditions. Angry and self-pitying creeds will serve as a cognitive umbrella to the dazed and confused. Jihadists may attract more Muslims, Zionism more Jews and rightist Evangelicals more Christians. Militant hardliners will rise in the Catholic Church. Just like the slackers who cannot maintain a stepped-up pace in school, fundamentalists of all three monotheistic stripes will increasingly cultivate a cynical attitude to the sciences. Creationists will celebrate their aggressive contempt for climatology. Like the slackers in school, fundamentalists will be stooges for bullies, join forces with corporate powers and be goaded into serving those who exploit them most. Ever more fractious, destructive and apocalyptic, fundamentalists will oppose mitigation attempts and resist the civil evolution to a sustainable world.

There is also another side. While some groups will cultivate resentment and anger, becoming part of the problem, the problem will motivate others to rise to the occasion. Visionary theologians and priests who wish to better the faith will hold fundamentalism in check. Many worshippers will surf the data wave and react constructively. The sought-for reconciliation between articles of faith and scientific findings will make segments of the three faiths spiritual. The faithful rising to the occasion will strive for ecumenical convergence and create spiritual evolution.

First signs of this monotheist polarization are already visible in Christianity, especially in Protestantism (see also Michael Roberts' and Laurel Kearns' chapters in this book). This polarization, interestingly, also affects cultural geographies. On the one hand, in Europe, Canada and the Pacific Northwest of the United States, the mainstreaming of 'Creation Care' and 'Stewardship Theology' is an ongoing process in churches, parishes and schools.

On the other hand, there is an equally visible, if not more conspicuous countertrend, which particularly affects American culture in particular, especially in the Midwest, the South and Alaska. This trend is visible in the radicalization of the Southern Baptist Convention, the largest Christian denomination in the United States. It is also visible in the radicalization of the Republican Party – manifest in the unprecedented rollback of environmental legislation during the Bush era and the unanimous denial of climate change among all Republican governor and senate candidates prior to the 2010 midterm elections. In the United States, politicians of both parties like to profess their faith, but there is a significant difference. Democrats do not have to be Christians, but Christianity is an indispensable part of Republicans' political identity – the brasher, the better. Only in the Republican Party will fundamentalists rise all the way to the top, as the careers of former president G. W. Bush and former vice-presidential candidate Palin illustrate.

This polarization, with European and Canadian Christians evolving and American Christians regressing, is a sign of things to come. Considering the ubiquitous rise of climate pressure, it is likely that such polarization will not stop with Christianity. The fate of the Abrahamitic religions in general, in the perilous times ahead, may well be a growing inner divide. In Judaism, Islam and Christianity, apocalyptic regression may become ever more visible in the decades to come, but so may ecosophical progression. Fundamentalism will make creeds more paranoid, parochial and local, just as green renewals of faith point to the opposite, contributing to a transnational, cosmopolitan and ecumenical convergence. A tug of war is brewing, between nature-hating fundamentalism and tree-hugging spiritualism. This may spawn schisms in the great religions. Whatever happens, due to climate and social pressures suffered, due to the faster pace of learning in an increasingly threatening classroom, a bipolar transformation of the three monotheisms can be expected. There is hope that the enlightened fringe will eventually take over the mainstream. But until that happens, there is a substantial risk that the monotheist centre will not hold.

The Climatic Fate of Paganism

Non-monotheistic religions, non-Abrahamitic or indigenous faiths, are not necessarily as diverse as it may appear to the anthropologist or the religious scholar. An older term for these creeds is paganism. In theology and religious studies this term is obsolete, but it remains philosophically useful. Its etymological root, *paganus*, refers to people living in the countryside, a rural population that dwells close to the land. In this manner paganism captures a feature shared by all indigenous faiths, namely, that the land itself is imbued with spiritual value – that mountains, rivers and groves can be sacred. Paganism, so understood, would consequently also include Buddhism, Daoism, Shinto and Hinduism.

Seen from a metaphysical point of view, there is one basic distinction between the two types of faith. This metaphysical distinction is a conceptual gestalt, and, as such, is the very opposite of a scholarly differentiation. The gestalt of monotheism is that God and nature are distinct. The divine is not only creative but also transcendent and supernatural. God is creator, nature is creation, and creator and creation are to one another like an author and a book, or a composer and a song. They are logically and ontologically different. Nature is not God.[4]

The metaphysics of paganism, however, conceives of the divine as being transcendent and immanent. Gods and spirits are transcendent in being different from tangible and visible nature, and yet they are immanent in that they dwell in nature. Divinity is part of nature, just as nature is part of divinity. Nature is both creative and created, and the logico-ontological difference between creator and creation plays out along a continuum of self-organizing forces on the one end and receptive matter on the other.

This metaphysics gives paganism a competitive advantage over the monotheistic narrative, at least in theory. For the pagan, the rightful place of humans is within nature, and the right thing to do is to live in harmony with the natural environment. Nature, after all, is sacred and thus deserving of respect and care. Human attempts at subjugating and exploiting nature rile the spirits and anger the gods. Nothing good can come to a civilization setting itself wilfully at odds with its natural environment. Nature will fight back – and the reason it is capable of doing so is because it is essentially active. In the pagan mind, nature is not a machine (the metaphorical clockwork) of lawfully moving and individually inert parts; nature is a living whole, a sentient web of interwoven power points. Should humans go against nature's way, nature will simply right the balance again, swiftly, powerfully and ruthlessly.

Since humans have done just that and global civilization is now facing the biospherical consequences, monotheistic religions are now forced to revise their narratives to make sense of the emerging reality. Monotheism assumed that nature, in virtue of being purely a creation, is passive and malleable. It also assumed that man, in virtue of being made in the image of God, is entitled to lord over earth. And it assumed that the right thing to do – for a Christian, a Jew or a Muslim – is to multiply one's numbers, domesticate the earth and live a busy life. Climate change is the outcome of such assumptions.

The pagan, by contrast, can simply say, 'I told you so'. However, paganism suffers from another peril. With the exception of Hinduism, Buddhism, Daoism and Shinto, pagan belief systems are creeds of native cultures threatened by globalization, resource exploitation and climate change. Whether these are Indians in the Amazon, Inuit in Siberia or Polynesians on low-lying atolls, their unique faiths and rituals may soon be a thing of the past. Details may well be lost. But there is a countervailing trend, which preserves core ideas of these creeds. The increasing availability of communicative devices can connect indigenous cultures everywhere. A result of this interconnectivity is the collective recognition of family resemblances across pagan faiths. Names and rites differ from native culture to native culture, but religious ideas and values are rather similar. They are so similar, in fact, that it is possible to map out a quintessence of indigenous belief systems, such as the world-view of the fictitious Na'vi in the 2009 film *Avatar*. This cultural 'flattening' of world civilization is an unexpected ally of paganism. The biospherical crisis reinforces values and ideas of native narratives. One cannot foretell how the cultural consequences of climate change will play out. But if there is any merit to the metaphysical gestalts suggested here, it would appear that indigenous creeds are poised to come back.

Notes

[1] Spinoza does not use the Aristotelian term εὐδαιμονία. Flourishing, for Spinoza, is a goal of *dasein* attained through an existential evolution from servitude to freedom, or from a state of being at the mercy of one's immediate passions to a state of being capable of appreciating the bigger picture. Ethically, flourishing is the evolution from the constraints of greed and fear to freedom and serenity. Cognitively, flourishing is the evolution from a parochial perspective to a holistic and cosmic viewpoint. In its optimal sense, it is *summa mentis acquiescentia*, the highest contentment of the mind (*Ethica* V 27), which consists in the ability to perceive reality *sub specie aeternitate* (V 25), i.e. the cognition of God (V 30), which amounts to gladness (*laetitia*, V 32). Gladness is tied to any realization of virtues. Virtue (*virtus*) is a *potentia* or potentiality (IV d 7). The opposite, sadness (*tristitia*, III 13), relates to the vices, anything that restricts one's ability to act, that holds one back and that impedes development. Things that impede us in this way are evil (*malum*; IV d 2).

[2] The term 'sustainability' (*Nachhaltigkeit*) does not come from Kant, but the idea can be traced to his conception of the categorical imperative – the idea that a good action is such that its intention or maxim, when realized, can be adopted as a general law (*allgemeines Gesetz*; cf. *Grundlegung zur Metaphysik der Sitten*, section 1, Academy Edition IV 402–403). A feature of the good is whatever is universalizable ('*solle ein allgemeines Gesetz werden*'; IV 402.18).

[3] For the term 'American Disenlightenment', see Phillips (2006). Phillips defines 'disenlightenment' as the mindset of a society that precipitates its decline. This state of mind in an era of decline is characterized by a concern over cultural and economic decay, a growing religious fervour, a rising commitment to faith as opposed to reason, a popular anticipation of a millennial time frame, and (if the nation happens to be an empire) strategic and military overreach as well as high debt levels (Phillips, p. 220). For the connection of the American Disenlightenment to anthropogenic climate change, cf. Schönfeld (2010).

[4] The metaphysical gestalt must be separated from the historical development of monotheism, which is far blurrier, more complex and more contradictory, as this gestalt suggests. For a survey of classic and medieval alternatives, see Bergmann (2005), esp. chapters 2–4.

References

Bergmann, S. (2005), *Creation Set Free: The Spirit as Liberator of Nature*. Grand Rapids: Eerdmans.

Phillips, K. (2006), *American Theocracy*. New York: Penguin.

Schönfeld, M. (2010), 'Amerigenic climate change: an indictment of normalcy'. *Human Ecology Review*, 17, 117–124.

White, L. (1967), 'The historical roots of the ecological crisis'. *Science*, 155, 1203–1207.

Part 3

Regional and Indigenous Belief Systems in Climate and Environmental Change: Case Studies

Chapter 10

Climate and Cosmology: Exploring Sakha Belief and the Local Effects of Unprecedented Change in North-Eastern Siberia, Russia[1]

Susan Crate

Introduction

Although I have worked with Viliui Sakha communities of north-eastern Siberia since 1991 and contemporary global climate change has been affecting their ecosystem for at least that long, it was only in 2003, with the telling of the bull of winter story that I began attending to how global climate change is affecting not only their physical but also their cultural and cosmological worlds.

> The bull of winter is a legendary Sakha creature whose presence explains the turning from the frigid winter to the warming spring. The legend tells that the bull of winter, who keeps the cold in winter, loses his first horn at the end of January as the cold begins to let go to warmth, then his second horn melts off at the end of February and finally, by the end of March, he loses his head as spring is sure to have arrived.
>
> (male Sakha elder, b. 1935)[2]

For centuries, Viliui Sakha have used *Jyl Oghuha* to explain the extreme 100°C annual temperature range of their subarctic habitat.[3] They personify winter, the most challenging season for them, in the form of a white bull with blue spots, huge horns and frosty breath. In early December the *Jyl Oghuha* arrives from the Arctic Ocean to hold temperatures at their lowest (-60° to -65° C; -76° to -85°F) for December and January. Although I had heard the story before, the 2003 telling had this unexpected ending: *'It seems that now with the warming, perhaps the bull of winter will no longer be'*. This novel ending began my contemplations on how global climate change – to date largely heralded as an issue affecting our physical world – was also having effects on peoples' cosmological worlds. My further investigations into the cosmological implications of global climate change continue to be inspired by my own personal encounters with Viliui Sakha (Crate and Nuttall, 2009) and by other social scientists who have made this a priority in their work, for example, the work of archaeologist Arlene Rosen (2007, p. 10),

> If rainfall is a divine gift, then solving the problems related to drought must involve dealings with the supernatural in the form of pleasing the deity responsible. Failure to adjust to environmental stress is as much a social and cosmological problem as an environmental one.

Since my 2003 awakening, I have been working with Viliui Sakha communities on a project that specifically looks at how inhabitants perceive and understand the local effects of global climate change (Crate, 2008a). In the process of this work we have found that the effect most urgent to local communities is that of increasing water on the land. This issue is problematic for local communities on many fronts but first and foremost in that it threatens Viliui Sakha's ability to continue their historically based subsistence practice of horse and cattle breeding. In previous publications I have argued that, because of cows' centrality to Sakha belief and sacred cosmology, cows and the sacred practices that accompany them are also essential to maintaining the social cohesion of rural village communities in a period of continued socio-economic and moral decline (Crate, 2008b). I will now further that argument to say that the main local effect of global climate change – increasing water on the land – threatens Viliui Sakha's ability to continue keeping cows and, therefore, their ability to maintain the social cohesion so central to their communities' adaptive resilience. For these reasons it is essential, if we are interested in gaining a comprehensive understanding of how place-based peoples are adapting and will be able to continue to adapt, to develop means and methods to investigate the cultural and cosmological, as well as the physical, implications of global climate change.

As a preliminary means to these ends, this chapter focuses on how global climate change is unprecedentedly affecting native agropastoralist Sakha communities, on both the physical and cosmological levels. I begin with some orientation to the field research, with background on local ecology, the culture, Viliui Sakha's historically based animistic belief system, and my research trajectory of the past 20 years. I next describe how contemporary differences affect both Sakha's physical world and their cosmology. I show how belief and cosmology shape a local people's perceptions of and responses to climate change – using the example of the increased abundance of water, one of the most prominent changes. I conclude by arguing for methodologies that capture these cultural and cosmological elements in order to inform interdisciplinary projects and policy efforts.

Orientation to the Case Study

Key to my investigation of the cosmological effects of global climate change is my in-depth ethnographic knowledge of Viliui Sakha based on long-term research and relationships with these communities. Since 1991, I have worked and conducted research with Viliui Sakha communities, analysing their summer *yhyakh* festival as a form of post-Soviet ethnic revival (Crate, 2006a), directing two environmental education and environmental policy projects focused on the physical and cultural effects of Soviet and post-Soviet diamond-mining activities (Crate, 2002a), researching their post-Soviet food production practices (Crate, 2002b; 2003; 2006b; 2008c), investigating local understandings of sustainable futures (Crate, 2006c; 2006d) and – my current project – focusing on climate change (Crate and Nuttall, 2009). I take time to mention the long-term relationship with these communities and my fluency in both Russian and the Sakha language because I believe both are crucial to a researcher's insight and awareness of how global climate change is affecting a people beyond the physical level.

Viliui Sakha, a Turkic-speaking native agropastoralist group, inhabit the Viliui River regions of the north-western Sakha Republic in north-eastern Siberia, Russia. They practice horse and cattle breeding, a southern subsistence brought to the north by Sakha's Turkic ancestors who migrated from Central Asia to southern Siberia around 900, then migrated northward, along the Lena River, to their present homeland beginning in the 1200s. They inhabit a subarctic region, characterized by continuous permafrost with annual temperature fluctuations of 100° Celsius from -60°C (-76°F) in winter to +40°C (104°F) in summer.[4] Sakha adapted a horse and cattle breeding subsistence to the northern subarctic climate by keeping their cows in barns nine months of the year and harvesting winter fodder for their herds in the brief summer. Russian colonization began in the Viliui regions in the mid-1600s. The resulting annexation of indigenous lands, taking of resources and demand for *iasak* or fur tribute from all

local inhabitants further burdened native inhabitants who already practiced an labour-intensive subsistence.

However, the last century of Soviet and now post-Soviet regimes have
presented far greater challenges for Viliui Sakha. Sovietization involved
both regional industrial exploitation and the transformation of kin-based
household-level production systems first into collectives and then into
agro-industrial state farms by the mid-1950s. Collectivization changed settlement patterns from extensive to concentrated and can be seen in the
landscape to this day. The mapping of contemporary elder birthplaces
shows a scattering of homesteads across the landscape which now are aban-
doned for life in the village centres (Crate, 2002b). Collectivization also
brought changes in subsistence practices, from an indigenous, time-tested
and ecologically based subsistence to an agro-industrial production system. Other effects of collectivization and state farm consolidation include
(1) the loss of indigenous ecological knowledge; (2) the loss of use of vast
areas of land, rendered too distant from farm centres; (3) dependence on
modern transportation to reach necessary resources; (4) environmental
stress in populated areas due to the concentration of wastes; (5) the radial
depletion of adjacent resources and (6) the dissolution of family/clan interdependence to redirect labour to the state farm, whose sole objective was
producing meat and milk for the diamond industry.

Soviet industrialization for Viliui Sakha meant diamond mining, which –
like all Soviet-period industrial practices – was not confined by environmental laws and regulations (Peterson, 1993, p. 175). This resulted in
contaminated water and air: local drinking water with heavy metals and
phenols, and local air with nuclear fallout (Crate, 2002a). Because large
amounts of electric energy were needed for the mining industry, the government built the Viliui GES (hydroelectric station), the reservoir of which
flooded 356,000 acres of prime fields and woodlands containing haying,
pasturing and hunting areas, as well as economically valuable timberlands.
The government imported workers from western parts of the USSR – mostly
from Ukraine, Byelorussia and European Russia – to supply the manpower.
This increased the overall population of the Viliui regions and diversified
their ethnic make-up.

In the early 1990s, with the collapse of the Soviet Union, the majority
of local and regional state farm directors in the Viliui regions agreed to
disband their farms. Overnight, village populations went from conditions
of near-full employment and ample larders to unemployment and empty
shelves. In response, Viliui Sakha communities reinstated household-level
food production via a system termed 'cows-and-kin', focused on keeping

cows and exchanging labour and products with kin (Crate, 2003; 2006b). A typical cows-and-kin arrangement involves the interdependence of an elderly parental household that keeps cows and performs all daily tasks with one or several young households, usually the elders' children, who receive all their needed meat and milk products in exchange for performing the labour-intensive work of harvesting annual forage for the herd. Cows-and-kin, in some ways a return to pre-Soviet subsistence, represents a unique adaptation, which is historically founded, environmentally sustainable, culturally resilient and offers a sound mode of household-level food production for contemporary rural Viliui Sakha.

To this day, Viliui Sakha households continue to rely heavily upon subsistence production, supplementing a mainstay diet of meat and milk products with gardens and greenhouses, forage (hunting, fishing and gathering) and other domesticates including horses, pigs and chickens. Village households depend on a mixed cash economy with most of their cash originating from state transfer payments in the form of state subsidies and pensions. Monetary resources are freely shared, most often elder pensions are shared freely with young kin households. Since the 1991 fall of the Soviet Union, inhabitants have access to Western media sources and a wider array of consumer goods.

Viliui Sakha Cosmology and Worldview

Like many native peoples, Viliui Sakha's historically based animistic belief system recognizes all aspects of the natural world as sentient (Jochelson, 1933, p. 103–106; Seroshevski, 1993, p. 593–655; Gogolev, 1994; Maak, 1994, p. 280–297). Concomitantly, Viliui Sakha's adaptation to the subarctic ecosystem is highly dependent on maintaining proper relationships with the spirit world, entailing an intricate web of plant, animal, human and spirit relationships (Crate, 2006b, p. 290). According to this belief, the world is divided into three realms: the *khallaan* (upper), *orto* (middle) and *allaraa* (lower). *Khallaan*, or upper world, is home to the *aiyy* (gods), organized in a nine-tiered pantheon, each level a home to one or more deity protectors. *Urung Aiyy Toion*, creator of the entire universe, inhabits the highest tier. The deities below are manifestations of that essential power. The next most highly regarded are *Juhugey*, who send horses to people of the middle world (Pekarski, 1959, p. 854), and *Aan Alakhchyn*, the deity of spring and fertility. *Allaraa Doidu*, the lower world, is an impassable swamp, inhabited by steel plants and *abaahy* (evil spirits), who represent the source of all existing and potential evil. Abaahy are in constant pursuit of middle world inhabitants.

Orto Doidu, the middle world, is home to earthly beings and *ichchi* (spirit keepers of nature). Sakha believe that all things animate and inanimate – including trees, rocks and even words – have ichchi. Ichchi can be both bad and good. Trees, rocks, water, words and all things animate and inanimate are sentient. All people have the ability and responsibility to appease these various deities in the context of their daily interactions and ritual cycles. Sakha rely on the ichchi and aiyy for protection from the abaahy by performing daily and annual rituals.

Oiuun (shaman), individuals possessing supernatural powers, also play a central role in these interactions at certain times (Alekseev, 1975; Crate, 2006b). Sakha call upon the oiuun, their human mediator of the spirit world and a person born with or indoctrinated into possessing supernatural powers. Sakha have both *urung* (white) and *khara* (black) *oiuun*. The *urung oiuun's* main role is as the benevolent priest who mediates the sky world deities during the yhyakh festival (summer festival honouring the upper world deities and asking those deities to again bring a bounteous summer). The khara oiuun can travel throughout the three worlds and utilize the powers of good and evil. They combat illness and bad fate for humans. The khara oiuun know which abaahy are the troubling source, and their souls travel between the three worlds to fight it by their 'spirit horse'. The khara oiuun personifies the horse's rhythmic canter by a *dungur* (shaman drum) and by speaking and singing prayers (Alekseev, 1975, p. 162). Reaching the lower world, the oiuun chases the particular abaahy away, healing the ailing person. In the past, the khara oiuun annually conducted a fall blood sacrifice of horse or cattle to the abaahy, a ritual event no longer practiced (Troshanski, 1902, p. 130).

Sakha believe that the horse was the first creation of *Urung Ayii Toion* (Great Lord Master), the highest god of Sakhas' sky pantheon. 'In the beginning, god made the horse and from it came the half-man half-horse and from there humans were born' (Seroshevski, 1993, p. 253). The horse was Sakhas' most prized domestic animal and their major source of transportation, food and clothing materials (Vinokurova, 2002). Sakha intricately decorated their riding horses far beyond any utilitarian need, out of their spiritual respect for the animal. The horse accompanied them on all their tasks involving subsistence and was their closest friend. Sakha fulfilled many rituals and traditions to honour their horses. 'Colts and horses were, at one time, our gods', and only a second-rate spirit did they give a cow; always the rope and pieces of hair used for sacrifice must be from a horse, usually from the mane (Seroshevski, 1993, p. 252). Undoubtedly, these horse culture beliefs and traditions were based in Sakhas' Tatar-Mongol origins.

Up until the nineteenth century, Sakha kept twice as many horses as cattle. Since the late 1800s, the opposite has been true (Seroshevski, 1993, p. 250; Maak, 1994, p. 332). Sakha used a local cattle, the *Bos taurus* Sakha (Yakut) breed. It could live outside to temperatures of -50°C, finding the majority of its fodder under the snow, and it grazed opportunistically, like a modern goat, utilizing a variety of grasses and other plant materials. It was known to graze in surrounding forestlands and swamps, and to swim across water to reach pasture. The Polish ethnographer Seroshevski, writing in 1896 about Sakha culture and environment, referred several times to the adaptive qualities of Sakha cattle, 'Sakha cattle can stand bad weather, hunger, cold, eat everything (twigs of birch, aspen, willow, cane, and fodder under the snow), eat very little, fatten quickly, and survive for a long time off their own fat reserves' (1993, pp. 144–149). Sakha also used bulls extensively for transportation, farm work and hunting (Maak, 1994, p. 331).

Although much of Sakha's cosmology and accompanying practices were stifled in the Soviet period, my two decades of work and life with Viliui Sakha have shown me that many continue to practice to this day. Since the fall of the Soviet Union, this belief has re-emerged and is being revived. Both these dynamics can be observed on a village level. I have illustrated this previously in my research on Viliui Sakha sacred cow beliefs (Crate, 2008b). In my research, I have witnessed how such sacred Sakha cow practices appear to make a difference in levels of food production, in the in situ continuation of ancestral Sakha customs, and in harmonic relationships both between cows and humans and intra- and inter-personal household relationships. I remember with great clarity the contrasting practices of contemporary cow-keepers while conducting household-level research on post-Soviet food production. Some took the utmost care of their herd while others threw rocks at and cursed theirs. In addition to noticing different ways of being with cows, I also started seeing signs of sacred belief, most notably the *salama*, a horse hair rope decorated with cloth and birch bark figures. I began asking questions about the various practices of contemporary cow-keepers. I was told by many that cows are people with every human attribute except language.

In response, I researched the roots of this belief. In the Sakha worldview, *Urung Aiyy Toion* created humans equal to horses, and the cow came from the water (Seroshevski, 1993, p. 253). 'The cow came from the water . . . and that is why Sakha call a pregnant cow "Water-filled cow" "Water-filled with the calf; becomes a cow and calf"' (Pekarski, 1959, p. 2999). The most important god and spirit-keeper for cows is: '*Suge-Toion-Khara-Begi-Toion*: the god of live-stock, that gives colts, calves and children' (Pekarski, 1959, p. 2378). To the ancient Sakha, the one who gives them all – horse/colts, cows/calves and humans/children – is *Suge-Toion-Khara-Begi-Toion*. Other important gods and spirit-keepers include Iyeksit, the god-protector of humans, horses and cows. *Mangkhal Toion* is the livestock's common God – he multiplies the herds in the middle world. *Mangkhalin Toion* created the herds. *Inakhsit Khoton* and *Mangan Mangkhalin* own all calves (Pekarski, 1959, p. 1525). *Mylaadai Khoton* is the creator of cows – she helps the cows to multiply (Pekarski, 1959, p. 1655). *Yhyn Kyuaar Khotyn* is also a god of herds and the wife of *Mangkhalin Toion* (Pekarski, 1959, p. 1197). There is also note that 'in the cow belief, the cow festival is the 11th (24th by the old calendar) of February' (Pekarski, 1959, p. 2552; Jochelson, 1933, p. 101). The cows' middle world spirit/care-taker is *Inakhsyt*, the spirit-protector of the horned herds and the one who gives calves. *Inakhsyt toion* and *Inakhsyt khotyn* mean literally 'sir and madam-geniuses of the horned herds' (Pekarski, 1959, pp. 3798, 3799).[5]

How do these beliefs manifest in contemporary practice? The most ubiq-uitous visual sign of a household that practices the sacred Sakha cow ways is the presence of *salama*. I had seen many salama before – hanging in trees and strung between posts at the annual yhyakh festivals. They were always prominently displayed, and I knew from my research on the festival that they symbolized the pathway for the gods to descend from the upper world and be present at the event. But in 2000, while I was helping with the milking for a household, I noticed for the first time a salama hanging, very much out of the reach of human eyes, between the cobweb-filled rafters in a *khoton* (cow barn). Over our cups of steaming tea I asked my host about what I saw hanging from the khoton rafters. She explained that it was salama (a sacrificial gift to hon-our the sky deity-protectors and that serves as their pathway from the sky into the khoton) and that it is necessary to hang a new one every year when the cows are close to calving to ensure their protection, fertility and good health (Figure 10.1). The horse hair string symbolizes power and strength. The *yaghyya* (miniature birch bark bucket) tied to one end is to place *aladye* (small pancakes) in, to keep the gods satiated. We returned to our tea-drinking and I thought of how amazing it was that this sacred practice continued after the blatant oppression of ethnic rituals during the Soviet period. Next my mind flooded with all I knew about the other issues of historical change, survival and adaptation that Sakha have persevered (Crate, 2006b, p. xvii).

Of course it would be naïve of me to purport that all contemporary Sakha believe and/or live by the worldview, myths, stories and proverbs of their ancestors. It would also be naïve to argue that they no longer have any ties

FIGURE 10.1 *Salama* hanging in a household *khoton*. Notice the four new ropes, which were added to the existing *salama* in spring for the four expected calves. © S. Crate

to their ancestral worldview, myths, stories and proverbs. I claim the middle ground – that Viliui Sakha, like most human inhabitants, frame their world – in this case in their perceptions and responses to the local effects of global climate change – with understandings based upon an ancestral past and a contemporary lived experience. Researchers have substantiated the extent that 'tradition', as a broader category for worldview, myths, stories and proverbs is both retained from one generation to the next and reinvented (Glassie, 1975; Hobsbawm and Ranger, 1983). These groundings provide a basis to explore the ways that a culture, in this instance Viliui Sakha, could be perceiving issues due to global climate change. They may also offer the raw materials to move forward to create means and methods for more comprehensive and effective research.

The Local Effects and Human Perceptions of Global Climate Change

The data that follow are results of a climate research project, involving a four-village, three-year collaborative effort with village inhabitants, native specialists and field assistants, an in-country research community and international collaborators.[6] The impetus to study the local effects of climate change was community-initiated and based on a major finding of 2003–2006 community sustainability research in which 90 per cent of survey participants expressed concern about their changing climate because it increasingly threatened both their subsistence activities and place-based cultural livelihoods (Crate, 2008a; 2006c). Our research team interviewed 33 local elders about the unprecedented changes they were observing. Based upon these data, we began a new project in December 2007. Our first summer field research in 2008 surveyed the communities at large about observations, perceptions and responses.

For the survey, we formed two focus groups in each of the four villages (one male and one female, with two representatives of several age groups: youth 18–25; middle 26–55; elder 56+) and interviewed 15 inhabitants, 5 from each of the age groups. In focus groups, we first asked participants to fill out a seven-column chart so each could get their thoughts and ideas down and so that we would have additional data for later analysis. They wrote the changes they have noticed, how long they have noticed them, what they believe the cause of each change is, how each affects their lives (ranking in order of most destructive to least), how they have adapted to each change and what time(s) of year each occurs. Once focus groups finished writing, we created a group chart on the board.

We were not able to achieve the same amount of responses in each group due to the limitation of time – focus groups were two hours long, some groups took much longer to fill out the sheets and some groups went off on tangents that were hard to return from. This was another reason why it was good to have the written forms available for further analysis. The semi-structured interviews asked the same information as the written chart, with additional questions to tease out finer points and details.

Like the focus group sessions, interviews varied in length (30–75 minutes) and depth; youth interviews tended to take less time and have less data and elders' lasted longer with more data. We also recorded participants in both focus groups and interviews when they had particularly compelling stories to tell to illustrate their points, which we summarized as follows:

(1) winters are warm
(2) the land is water
(3) lots of rain
(4) summers are cold
(5) more floods
(6) seasons arrive late

(7) lots of snow

(8) temperature changes suddenly

(9) less birds and animals

This list of the nine main changes shows that changes in water regimes are a dominant feature of what inhabitants are observing (Figure 10.2). Our follow-up conversations and interviews showed that increased water on the land and a collective 'fear of going under water' were the most prominent concerns of the communities.

Bridging Cosmology to Contemporary Issues

In this section I explain how, in the process of the research project, we are attempting to bridge Sakha cosmology to the issues most relevant to our research communities. I begin with an overview of Sakha cosmology as it relates to water, then give an example of how to develop a model based on cosmology. Lastly, I explain our recent efforts to bridge these areas.

Water in Sakha Cosmology

Water is an important part of Viliui Sakhas' spirit world. As already stated, like most place-based peoples, they consider all parts of their natural world sentient or spirit-filled. A commonly held understanding is *Uu ichchiileekh*, meaning 'water has a spirit', and according to Sakha cosmology, humans need to pay respect to that spirit when they interact with it (Kulakovski, 1979, p. 43). Rivers, lakes and all surface water sources are considered as grandmother or *ebe*. When taking water for use and/or crossing water or using it as a mode of transportation, Viliui Sakha feed the spirit of the water and say certain words to appease it. Similarly, interactions with water for subsistence have specific rituals. The success of fishing is directly related to how well the fishers speak to and serve the water spirit, for example, in the community effort of *mungkha* or lake ice fishing. When Viliui Sakha arrived at their summer home, among the spirits to whom they pay tribute to ensure a plentiful summer harvest – by hanging a symbolic *salama* – is the spirit of the adjacent lake. Viliui Sakha also call on a shaman to appease the water spirit when they work with water, for example, to drain a lake to make more land area for hay to grow (Nikolaev, 1970; Crate, 2006b).

Viliui Sakhas' creation myth begins with a world made up totally of water, which acquires its first area of land thanks to the activities of either

FIGURE 10.2 In the last 10 years, water has increased on the lands, which interferes directly with Viliui Sakha's ability to harvest enough hay to fodder their herds through winter. © S. Crate

an abaahy (evil spirit), swallow or loon. Cows, Viliui Sakhas' main source of meat and milk, are believed to have come from water. Water is also the medium to take away what is no longer wanted. For example, it takes away the bull of winter,[7] bringing the long-awaited spring (Crate, 2008a). It is also the medium that takes away death – the *uulu uuta* (water of death). Sakha place a cup of water by the deathbed to let the soul jump into the water. One of the most famous Sakha folk tales, 'Old Woman Taal Taal', teaches that water is second in power only to the earth.

Sakha proverbs are rich with references to water. Among the many examples, two are particularly suited for our purposes. The first exemplifies the sentience of water in Viliui Sakha worldview: 'You can't see water as the river goes by but if a person speaks artistic words as the river runs by, it will braid itself in response' (Kulakovski, 1979, p. 186). Another proverb that has experienced a revival in the challenging post-Soviet economic times connotes water as an intimate entity, 'Keep water close and in-laws afar' (Kulakovski, 1979, p. 187; Crate, 2006a).

Means and Methods of Integrating Cosmologies

With this base in belief and cosmology, how do we bridge to contemporary issues? I approached this task first through textual analysis of community testimonies which showed how Viliui Sakha are observing changes in the land and their birthland areas due to increasing water on the land. Here is one of many such testimonies to provide an example (male Sakha elder, b1941):

> The *otokh* (pre-Soviet homestead areas) are falling when the ice under them melts – they fall and become a bowl and water grows there and we are losing hayland – those long ago chose to live on the higher grounds, the *otokh* – and now they have all become dips down into the land – they were a little while ago small depressions in the land and now they are so deep – a person can stand in them and can't be seen.

I also found many testimonies relaying a strong emotional response, in most cases one of fear, to the increasing water on the land. Again, one example here to illustrate (female Sakha middle-aged, b1975):

> I am very scared that we are going under water – looking down from a plane you can see that the land has patches of water across it – water is coming up from below – it looks like the land is sinking down.

One approach to understanding what Viliui Sakha are seeing these climate perturbations *with*, is by using the frame of Sakhas' spiritual worldview. Again, I provide an example of one such frame developed to understand how Viliui Sakha's cosmology explains where hay comes from. *Aan Alakhchyn* (the earth deity) and the *Ereke-Jereke* (the hay-wood spirits, considered her children) give people hay in direct accordance with their observance of specific rituals, most notably the cyclical feeding of the earth spirits, the annual gifts to *Aan Alakhchyn* during the Sakhas' yhyakh (summer fertility festival), and their hard work and diligence in caring for their lands (Kulakovski, 1979, pp. 42–44). In other words, humans have more or less direct control over how abundant their hay harvest is. The climate perturbations resulting from global climate change interferes with that direct relationship. Control is no longer in the hands of the individual, kin group or community.

Considering Viliui Sakha's beliefs and cosmology, their perceptions of the local effects of global climate change and the overwhelming concern about water issues, we can develop a model to inform our research. Once we have models of how our research partners are fitting climate perturbations into their cosmological and practical understandings of how resources are given, in what areas their lives are constrained and what capacity they have to adapt, we can take the next steps towards filling out their information to facilitate positive change.

A Work in Progress: Knowledge Exchanges

In the summer of 2010 we brought together what we knew of local effects and cosmology via an exchange of knowledge to begin the important process of integrating the 'anecdotal' knowledge with how the global processes of climate change are affecting the local environment. We first gathered information on a global scale that could 'fill in the blanks' of the local climate picture in ways that empower communities towards positive social change. We understood that communities need access to appropriate information to understand that climate change is on a global scale and to decipher how local changes are due to global climate change and to other stressors (Figure 10.3). One of our collaborators, a specialist in permafrost, agreed to participate in our knowledge exchange project. In this way we were able to address specific issues more and provide simple technological advice on ways to preserve permafrost.

Although I will not go into the details of the knowledge exchange process here, I can say that, overall, our efforts were successful. Participants

FIGURE 10.3   After village inhabitants shared their personal observations of the changes locally to enrich the scientific understanding of how climate change is affecting local places and peoples, regional scientists shared their findings to bridge understandings during knowledge exchanges in the summer of 2010. © S. Crate

came away with a much better understanding of how climate change is affecting their local environment and how they can play an active role in adapting to it.

What are the immediate benefits of these knowledge exchanges? With a fuller understanding of the global implications of local changes, our research consultants could better innovate and possibly expand existing adaptive strategies to increase their coping range.[8] One great source of empowering knowledge for Viliui Sakha communities is the extent to which what they are observing as the local effects of global climate change is remarkably similar to the changes observed in other northern indigenous communities (Turi, 2000; Krupnik et al., 2002; Turi, 2002; AHDR, 2004; Helander and Mustonen, 2004; ACIA, 2005). Accordingly, this correlation can also bolster understanding among other affected communities within similar ecosystems.

Towards a Model to Integrate Cosmologies for Effective Research

There are many parts to piece together in the effort to attend to local cosmologies in the research process; here, I discuss some of them. It is important from the beginning of this research process to be sensitive not only to how our research partners frame global climate change but how we frame global climate change with our research partners. One colleague recently commented, 'Climate change has become such an overused term in Alaskan villages that I avoid it, in order not to lead every discussion into one particular direction'. Perhaps it is best not to label what our research partners are experiencing as 'climate change' but to discover and use emic (local vernacular) terms and expressions. Here, our role as cultural interpreters is key in order to tease out how our research partners frame the issues – their own culturally bound understandings, interpretations and observations. In our 2003 surveys, we did not have a problem using the Sakha word for 'climate change', perhaps because northern Russia has far fewer researchers and far less interaction with the larger world in terms of access to media and technology than does Alaska.[9]

Once we have collectively set a research agenda, our first focus of active fieldwork is to account for the emic, by assessing and documenting community observations, knowledge and perceptions about the local and global effects of climate change. Appropriate methods include focus groups, semi-structured interviews, oral history and secondary data analyses. Considering the history they have had on the land, or the centuries of experience their people have had adapting to their ecosystem, another important first step is to learn how our research partners' ancestors adapted to climate perturbations in the past (from village elders and by reconstructing climate histories from community oral history, archival and written sources[10]) and to identify what is relevant for contemporary climate challenges. Listening can take the form of daily conversations, oral history to recount past climate experiences and modes of adaptation and focus group discussions to map out collective cultural models of what is changing and why (Figure 10.4). We need to engage all community members, especially the youth, because it is important to know their assessments and opinions about climate change since they are moving into leadership roles in their communities as well as to better enable them to advance the project efforts once field research is done. With these data we can develop cultural models based on how our research partners understand climate cycles in their cosmology and contemporary lives.

With a solid account of local perceptions and a roster of useful global-scale information, we can then use the most effective modes of communication to relay that information. These may include town meetings, engaging our research partners in developing and presenting the materials for their communities. To the extent that local television broadcasting occurs, such

FIGURE 10.4 The author working with a village elder (b. 1935), one of 15 inhabitants documenting daily observations of changes in seasonality due to climate change. © Prokopiy Yegorov

presentations can also be broadcast to those who cannot attend meetings. For Viliui Sakha, one means to effectively communicate information is to develop elder knowledge programs focusing on climate change with youth first documenting elder observations and past climate perturbations and then exchanging Western science information with them.[11] It would also serve to document and disseminate within the communities of origin elder knowledge (both life experience and narrative from parents and grand-parents) about how their people adapted in the past to climate perturbations and its relevance to their contemporary climate challenges. Similarly, it would also engage village youth in the community process of grappling with global climate change.

Once community knowledge and understanding is heightened, a critical next step is the formulation of adaptive strategies. Viliui Sakha communities have adapted successfully in the past, but they, like their circumpolar indigenous counterparts, feel at an impasse in adapting to the unprecedented environmental alteration brought on by global climate change. The anecdote of the bull of winter and the cultural transformation that the loss of that story represents is testimony in itself to an uncertainty about limits of adaptation, similar to other circumpolar inhabitants' testimonies (ACIA, 2005, p. 10).

Because of the non-point nature of climate change, our awareness of and actions towards its local effects demand a multi-sited analysis to expand the context from a 'committed localism' and explore the complex interactions of the larger world system that shape the local (Marcus, 1998, p. 8). Accordingly, we need to consider connecting our research project to policy by assessing efforts at the local, regional, national and international levels for both their utility for and applicability to local community contexts, making recommendations accordingly. Once existing policy is known, the next task is to evaluate the local level of climate change policy awareness. We can then draft policy recommendations that are both realistic and appropriate, given local communities' day to day experiences with the local effects of global climate change. To inform this process, we can bring in examples of other circumpolar countries' global climate change interventions, first hand through collaborations with similar research projects and second hand through information-sharing through indigenous councils. We can then find creative ways to present those policy recommendations to the relevant bodies.

Depending on our research partners' desires, we can also work to advocate with them through whatever political channels are deemed appropriate. Sharing the work of other indigenous groups who are already advocating for themselves would empower this experience. Comparative and collaborative work with other anthropologists and their research partners can further our research partners' capacity to self-advocate. Our elder research partners' more than 50 years of personal long-term observations are potentially valuable to arctic scientists. There could be a great advantage to bringing research partners to participate in a climate conference or two, to testify and answer questions from scientists.

Recent literature has begun to address the critical intersection between the understanding that many – if not most – of our global ecological crises are a result of human attitudes, values, ethics, perceptions and behaviours and that the most effective – if not only – way to bring about a change in those qualities is through the 'reconnection of communities to their landscape and their lives as an active community'[12] (Leigh, 2005). This is congruent with the ACIA recommendations to 'facilitate local empowerment through the devolution of authority and capacity so that communities can respond more effectively given their specific contexts' (Huntington et al., 2005, p. 95). Working as a community is a challenge in some research areas. One such area is in the post-Soviet context, which has only recently experienced a break from a centralized and paternal relationship with the state. In our 2003–2006 National Science Foundation project, research partners expressed time and again their regret that they could not somehow come together and work towards their definitions of sustainability as a community, though they referred to the way they had worked together on the state farm in the Soviet period.

Our research partners also shared that, largely as a result of the economic downturn in the post-Soviet period, no-one trusted anyone outside their immediate kin group, which explains why community efforts often failed.[13] With the disbanding of the state farm, the community has lost an important site for the creation of local solidarity and communal identity, and individual and collective possibilities for taking action have shifted to other arenas. The collective must be re-imagined and retained not on the basis of a Soviet template but on some amalgamation of local loyalties and external restraints (Humphrey, 1998, p. 482). It would be fruitful for anthropologists working in post-Soviet contexts to investigate how post-Soviet villages can recapture the community activeness of the Soviet period without reinstating a socialist mode in doing so, to move toward local action on global climate change.

Research Challenges for the Social Sciences

Social scientists have yet to take an effective role in climate change research with indigenous communities. Considering the types of changes witnessed by Viliui Sakha elders and shared by their northern counter-parts, the arctic ecosystem is undergoing unprecedented change that may not allow for future habitation by people and their key plants and animals. Similarly, other climate-sensitive areas of the world and their inhabitants are under threat (IPCC, 2007). To date, adaptive capacity is considered the main mechanism to deal with those threats. However, since projections of future change inevitably portray a landscape and ecosystem unsuitable for present day place-based people's uses, researchers and indigenous communities alike are questioning the applicability of that coping strategy.

Current research on climate change impacts, understandings and responses does little to address global climate change's cultural implications. Encounters with and contemplations of the cultural implications of Viliui Sakha communities' observations and perceptions of the local effects of global climate change reveal a need to develop research projects focusing on the cognitive/perceptual orientations of communities. Here social scientists can play a unique role. We are trained as cultural interpreters, translators, advocates, educators and mediators. Many of us already work in areas of global environmental change. We can use the tools of applied, public and advocacy-oriented anthropology on behalf of our indigenous research partners. We have a solid history of successfully advocating for and with our research partners.

Awareness and empowerment are necessary first steps towards the end goal of addressing the issues of indigenous communities confronting unprecedented climate change. We need to push further by developing collaborative research projects with other social and natural scientists, engaging a multiple stresses perspective (to include socio-economic, political and other environmental challenges), integrating notions of adaptive learning, generating policy-relevant insights and linking findings to the larger question of sustainability (at the community, regional, national and global level). In order for such efforts to be sustained on the ground long after research efforts are completed, initiatives need to be based not just in the linguistic vernacular but also in the cosmological vernacular of local beliefs and perceptions. It is exactly this 'translation' process that reverses our understanding of place-based peoples. Although they are often considered the most vulnerable to the local effects of climate change, they are highly resilient via a system of language and belief.

In sorting out these issues for those most disrupted, we are doing the necessary homework to reframe and re-appropriate cultural worlds and senses of 'home' for other communities near and far who are yet to be as noticeably affected. 'Climate change is amplified in the Arctic. What is happening to us now will happen soon in the rest of the world. Our region is the globe's climate change "barometer." If you want to protect the planet, look to the Arctic and listen to what Inuit are saying' (Watt-Cloutier, 2004). Now that many of our research partners are actively listening to their elders, the time is ripe for those elders' messages to inform the world and for anthropologists to take to heart the cultural implications and our innate responsibilities to act on everyone's behalf. In the end, we discover that each culture has its own 'bull of winter' that is not only central to how that culture orients their daily and seasonal activities, worldview and cultural identity but is also part of the amalgamation of ethnodiversity which, like biodiversity, is intrinsic to the robust health and continued human, plant and animal habitation of the planet.

Notes

[1] Much of the material for this article is derived from two previously published peer-reviewed articles (Crate, 2008a; 2008b), expanded here by more recent research. Also, much of this material is based on work supported by the National Science Foundation (NSF) under grant no. 0710935, 'Assessing Knowledge, Resilience & Adaptation and Policy Needs in Northern Russian Villages Experiencing Unprecedented Climate Change Knowledge'. Any opinions, findings, conclusions or recommendations expressed in this material are my own and do not necessarily reflect the views of the NSF. I gratefully acknowledge and thank the NSF.

[2] All quotes by Viliui Sakha are anonymous, except for birth year and gender.

[3] There are several portrayals of the bull of winter in classic Sakha ethnographic texts: 'Winter, the hardest time for working people, Sakha personify in the form of a white bull with blue spots which has huge horns and frosty breath. When this bull travelled to the spacious Sakha homeland, all in nature froze and the people and animals suffered from the cold. At the end of January, winter reached its peak. The day before the end of January, a mighty eagle arrived from the south, child of the warm sky, he scooped up snow in his nest and let out a loud cry. From the eagle's cry, the bull of winter stepped back and his horns, one by one, fell off, then, as spring approached, his head rolled off. During the ice flows, the trunk of the bull of winter swims at the bottom of the Lena to the Arctic Ocean, and the ice flow takes away the spirits of dead people and herds' (Ergis, 1974, pp. 123–124).

'Jil Bull is the personification of winter in the form of a bull. Sakha believe that he comes every year from the Arctic Ocean and brings with himself cold, starvation, need, and etc. In spring, near Afanasii Day, he loses one horn, then near the second Afanasii day, he loses the other. Whether he dies in the spring or returns to the Arctic Ocean – the Sakha either forgot or did not know' (Kulakovski, 1979, pp. 45–46).

'The freeze is definitely a bull and he has 2 horns – the first falls of on the first Afanasii Day (5 March), the second on the second Afanasii Day (24 April) and on the third Afanasii (14 May) the whole body falls (these dates are according to the old calendar so in our calendar would be 19 February, 10 April, 30 April, respectively)' (Seroshevski, 1993, p. 26).

The bull of winter: Creating the world, the gods asked humans, 'Do you want winter to be longer or summer?' The humans answered, 'Ask our friends – the horse and bull.' The horse wanted summer longer because in winter its legs and hooves felt very cold. But the bull wanted winter longer because in summer heat its nose got wet. Then the Gods made winter longer and summer shorter. Having got angry, the horse kicked the bull in the nose and knocked out its upper teeth. The bull butted the horse into its side and pierced through its bile. Since that time horse have not bile and horned cattle no upper teeth' (Sivtsev, 1996, p. 131).

[4] With its protection from oceanic humidity and precipitation by high mountains to the east and south and by the cold Arctic Ocean to the north, glaciation of north-eastern and central Siberia during the last ice age lagged behind Europe. Most of eastern Siberia remained free from above-ground ice shields and provided refuge for many plant and animal species that were 'iced out' elsewhere. Siberia was affected by underground ice or permafrost, however. Mammoth, woolly rhinoceros, wild horse and musk ox remains date the permafrost formation to the last ice age (Suslov, 1961, p. 145). The eastern Siberian permafrost is a relic of the last ice age – a surrogate of the massive ice covers that were characteristic of adjacent high latitude areas. This protection also explains why Siberian permafrost extends farther south – in some cases to the same latitudes as Kiev, Paris and Vienna – than permafrost in other parts of the contemporary world (Jochelson, 1933).

[5] It is interesting to note that the Sakha word for cow, *ynakh*, comes from the Turkic word *Inak* which has the Latin root *Inachus* (Pekarski, 1959, p. 3798). Inachus was the river god and the first god of Argos in the Peloponnesus, southern Greece. As the story goes, Inachus lost track of his daughter Io. When the daughter returned to her father's stream, she caught Jupiter's [Zeus'] eye and Hera disguised Io as a cow to protect her. She saw her own reflection in her father's river and fled in terror. Still, she followed her father and sisters. 'Father Inachus himself, twin-horned, leans leftward upon his tilted urn [from which he poured his streams forth]' (Atsma, 2007).

[6] I served as project PI with funding by NSF OPP/Arctic Social Sciences from December 2007 to December 2010. I also refer to the work from here on out as 'we' since this is a collaborative project.

[7] A mythological beast whose arrival coincides with the coldest part of Sakha's winter (Crate, 2008a).

[8] Ideally, a key source of this would be down-scaling global models to show how projected climate change impacts will play out in the specific local context of our research partners.

[9] The Sakhas' limited access to information on the global scale of climate change also explains why elders' explanations for its causes are, to date, so meagre.

[10] For more on reconstructing past climate histories, see the work of Astrid Ogilvie (www.instaar.colorado.edu/people/bios/ogilvie.html) and Jones et al. (2001).

[11] Granted, the implementation of an 'elder knowledge program' may potentially be in the interest of the whole community, but it will probably be appropriated by different factions in different ways, and to different ends.

[12] By 'reconnection of communities to their landscape and their lives as an active community', Leigh means that people need to regain a relationship with the earth and with each other.

[13] We did observe some inter-village variation in terms of coming together as a community. We worked with four villages with populations of 3500, 1000 and 400 (two villages). The medium-sized village was small enough for people to know one another, yet not small enough for it to be controlled by a certain extended kin group. This was also true in the two villages of 400.

References

ACIA (2005), *Arctic Climate Impact Assessment*. Cambridge: Cambridge University Press.

AHDR (2004), *Arctic Human Development Report*. Akureyri: Stefansson Arctic Institute.

Alekseev, N. A. (1975), *Traditzionnie Religioznie Verovanie Yakutov v XIX-nachalye XX v* (Traditional Religious Belief of the Yakut from the Nineteenth to Beginning of the Twentieth Century). Novosibirsk: Science Publishers.

Atsma, A. (ed.) (2007), 'Inakhos'. www.theoi.com/Potamos/PotamosInakhos. html. Accessed 6 October, 2010.

Crate, S. A. (2002a), 'Co-option in Siberia: the case of diamonds & the Vilyuy Sakha'. *Polar Geography*, 26, 289–307.

— (2002b), 'Viliui Sakha oral history: the key to contemporary household survival'. *Arctic Anthropology*, 39, 134–154.

— (2003), 'Viliui Sakha adaptation: a subarctic test of Netting's smallholder theory'. *Human Ecology*, 31, 499–528.

— (2006a), '*Ohuokai*: a unique integration of social meaning and sound'. *Journal of American Folklore*,19, 161–183.

— (2006b), Cows, Kin and Globalization: An Ethnography of Sustainability. Walnut Creek, CA: Alta Mira Press.

— (2006c), 'Investigating local definitions of sustainability in the Arctic: insights from post-Soviet villages'. *Arctic*, 59, 115–131.

— (2006d), 'Elder knowledge and sustainable livelihoods in post-Soviet Russia: finding dialogue across the generations'. *Arctic Anthropology*, 43, 40–51.

— (2008a), 'Gone the bull of winter: grappling with the cultural implications of and anthropology's role(s) in global climate change'. *Current Anthropology*, 49, 569–595.

— (2008b), 'Walking behind the old women: sacred cow knowledge in the 21st century'. *Human Ecology Review*, 15, 115–129.

— (2008c), 'Eating hay: the ecology, economy and culture of Viliui Sakha smallholders of northeastern Siberia'. *Human Ecology*, 36, 161–174.

Crate, S. and Nuttall, M. (eds) (2009), *Anthropology and Climate Change: From Encounters to Actions*. Walnut Creek, CA: Left Coast Press.

Ergis, G. U. (1974), *Ocherki pa Yakutskomy folklory*. Moscow: Science Publishers.

Glassie, H. (1975), *All Silver and No Brass*. Bloomington: Indiana University Press.

Gogolev, A. I. (1994), *Mifologicheskii mir Iakutov: bozhestva I dukhi-pokroviteli* (The Mythological World of the Yakut: Gods and Spirit-Protectors). Yakutsk: Yakutsk State University Press.

Helander, E. and Mustonen, T. (eds) (2004), *Snowscapes, Dreamscapes*. Tampere: Tampereen ammattikorkeakoulu.

Hobsbawm, E. and Ranger, T. (eds) (1983), *The Invention of Tradition*. Cambridge: Cambridge University Press.

Humphrey, C. (1998), *Marx Went Away – But Karl Stayed Behind*. Ann Arbor: University of Michigan Press.

Huntington, H., Fox, S., Berkes, F. and Krupnik, I. (2005), 'The changing arctic: indigenous perspectives', in *Arctic Climate Impact Assessment*. Cambridge: Cambridge University Press, pp. 61–98.

IPCC (2007), *Climate Change 2007: Impacts, Adaptation and Vulnerability*. Working Group II's Summary for policymakers. Geneva: IPCC Secretariat.

Jochelson, W. (1933), *The Yakut*. New York: Anthropological Papers of the American Museum of Natural History 33(II).

Jones, P. D., Ogilvie, A. E. J., Davies, T. D. and Briffa, K. B. (2001), 'Unlocking the doors to the past: recent developments in climate and climate-impact research', in P. D. Jones, A. E. J. Ogilvie, T. D. Davies and K. B. Briffa (eds), *History and Climate: Memories of the Future?*. New York: Kluwer Academic/Plenum, pp. 1–8.

Krupnik, I. and Jolly, D. (eds) (2002), *The Earth is Faster Now: Indigenous Observations of Arctic Environment Change*. Fairbanks: Arctic Research Consortium of the United States/Smithsonian Institution – Arctic Studies Center.Kulakovski, A. E. (1979), *Nayuchni Trude* (Scientific Works). Yakutsk: Yakutsk Book Publishers.

Leigh, P. (2005), 'The ecological crisis, the human condition, and community-based restoration as an instrument for its cure'. *Ethics in Science and Environmental Politics*, 3, 3–15.

Maak, R. K. (1994), *Viliuiski Okrug* (The Viliui Okrug) (second edition). Moscow: Yana.

Marcus, G. (1998), *Ethnography Through Thick and Thin*. Princeton: Princeton University Press.

Nikolaev, S. I. (1970), *Iakuty: Nauchnyi otchet* (The Yakut [Sakha]: Scientific accounts) Yakutsk: Russian Academy of Science, Siberian Dpt. F. 5, Op. 1, delo 501.

Pekarski, E. K. (1959 [1899]), *Slovar Iakutskovo Iazika* (Dictionary of the Sakha Language (second edition). Yakutsk: Russian Academy of Science.

Peterson, D. J. (1993), Troubled Lands: The Legacy of Soviet Environmental Destruction. Boulder: Westview Press.

Rosen, A. (2007), *Civilizing Climate*. Walnut Creek, CA: Alta Mira Press.

Seroshevski, V. L. (1993 [1896]), *Yakuti*. Moscow: Rosspen.

Sivtsev, D. K. (1996 [1947]), *Sakha fol'klora: Khomyyrynn'yk*. Novosibirsk: Nauka.

Suslov, S. P., Gershevsky, N. D. and Williams, J. E. (1961), *Physical Geography of Asiatic Russia*. San Francisco: W. H. Freeman.

Troshanski, V. F. (1902), *Evolutziia Chorni Veri u Iakutof* (The Evolution of the Yakut Black Belief). Kazan: Kazan University.

Turi, J. M. (2000), 'Native reindeer herders: priorities for research'. *Polar Research*, 19, 131–133.

— (2002), 'The world reindeer livelihood – current situation. Threats and possibilities', in S. Kankaanpää, L. Müller-Wille, P. Susiluoto and M.-L. Sutinen (eds), *Northern Timberline Forests: Environmental and Socio-economic Issues and Concerns*. Jyväskylä: Finnish Forest Research Institute, pp. 70–75.

Vinokurova, U. A. (2002), *Kyn Juhugai Ayii* (Sun-Horse God Protector). Yakutsk: Bichik.

Watt-Cloutier, S. (2004), 'Climate change and human rights'. *Human Rights Dialogue*, Series 2, no. 11. www.cceia.org/resources/publications/dialogue/2_11/section_1/4445.html.

Chapter 11

Religious Perspectives on Climate Change Among Indigenous Communities: Questions and Challenges for Ethnological Research

Lioba Rossbach de Olmos

Introduction

The ecological cycle that has structured the annual pattern of Colombian Amazon Indians' lives for generations is changing. Aymara Indians complain about increasing temperatures, melting glaciers and water scarcity, and the circum-Caribbean indigenous communities of the Nicaraguan Miskitú or the Panama Cuna anticipate more frequent, stronger hurricanes (Kronik and Verner, 2010). Climate change has reached the indigenous peoples not only in Latin America but all over the world.

In the last decade, indigenous political leaders have begun to express their concerns about climate change-related impacts and to demand their participation in the international climate mitigation process and in national policies as far as their interests are concerned. Most of the nongovernmental organizations working on indigenous rights issues have integrated climate change into their agenda (IWGIA, 2010).

However, our understanding of an indigenous society's views and responses to specific climate change-induced alterations of the natural environment is still in its very early stages. We might encounter indigenous societies that do not separate nature from culture in the way Western society does (Descola, 2009). We might assume that different approaches to organizing one's life and livelihood generate not only different skills but also different perceptions of the environment (Ingold, 2009). We might encounter worldviews that express irregularities of the environment in religious or mythological indigenous terms. In communicating with such societies on local climate change impacts, it is not appropriate to provide them with only scientific knowledge about climate change. At least from the perspective of cultural anthropology, the general acceptance of a plurality of distinct cultural approaches is required (Nuttall, 2009). This chapter presents different ethnological approaches to indigenous peoples' perceptions of irregularities in the natural environment. Subsequently, it offers some examples of religious indigenous reactions to ecological disasters and advocates for the general acceptance of a plurality of local interpretations and perceptions of global climate change challenges.

Cultural Anthropology, Indigenous Cultures and the Environment

Anthropology as the science of the cultural 'other' is characterized by a long debate on the relationship between humans and their natural environment. This is because the subjects of the discipline are often indigenous populations abroad, which are very often located in inhospitable, hostile or isolated parts of the world – for example, the Inuit in the Arctic, the Aborigines in Australia or the San in the Kalahari Desert. However, it is also those regions that will be most strongly affected by human-induced climate change and that have already had to adapt to change.

With their demand for rationality and objectivity, the natural sciences have provided the paradigm for many of the earlier theoretical models in anthropology. Of particular interest is the 'culturology' of neo-evolutionist Leslie A. White (2005), who elaborated lineal stages of cultural development on the basis of the quantifiable energy consumption. Another example is the application of the biologically derived ecosystem approach by Roy A. Rappaport (1968), who considered human beings as one among different populations competing for limited natural resources, performing religious rituals in order to maintain an ecological balance. Another notable approach is the cultural materialism of Marvin Harris (1979), who considered culture to be the result of constantly optimizing human efforts of ecological adaptation. Social aspects were accorded more importance with the cultural ecology theory of Julian H. Steward (1955), who directed his attention towards the interdependence between nature and culture and the interaction with nature as an incitement for technical innovation and cultural change.

Later on, linguistics became the anthropological *Leitwissenschaft*, generating the ethnoecology or ethnoscience approach that analysed native classification patterns of animals and plants and elaborated schemes similar to the taxonomies known from biology (see Keesing, 1972). Even though specialized bulletins and surveys with a hard-core scientific orientation can still be found, in general, natural science has lost ground as a paradigm within anthropology. The more prevalent approaches are now interpretative, such as are employed in postmodern, post-colonial and globalization studies, which in most cases neither comply with the claim for inter-subjective objectivity demanded by the natural sciences nor with the corresponding search for law-like regularity within social developments.

Most of the approaches that can be considered relevant for studies related to climate change do not fit into these current tendencies in anthropology, since natural sciences do not currently provide the dominant paradigm for the study of cultures. However, there have recently been new promising attempts to relate ethnographic evidence of climate change experienced by anthropologists in their field work among indigenous and local communities with the growing scientific knowledge and the ongoing political processes related to global warming (Crate and Nuttall, 2009a). Nevertheless, in order to ensure fruitful cooperation between the climate sciences and anthropology, we must also be aware of the differences between these research fields, that is, not simply subordinate the one to the other but try to acknowledge that natural and social sciences operate at different levels when dealing with climate change (Crate and Nuttall, 2009b, pp. 394–395). For this reason, I will try to present both disciplines in a dialogue to delineate in a very general manner the type of research that should be conducted in the future. Some of the following deliberations may seem somewhat provocative. The intention is to provide a critical view of climate change issues from an anthropological – though not from a 'climate sceptic' – perspective. My discussion will focus on South America.

The Ethnoclimatological Approach: Validating Traditional Knowledge Systems

One current approach that links anthropology and climate science has been labelled 'ethnoclimatology' and is directly related to Benjamin Orlove. For many years, as an anthropologist, Orlove has been committed to environmental and climatic issues. This approach began when he and a meteorologist friend examined an interesting weather-forecasting tradition of Indian farmers from the Central Andes (Orlove et al., 2002). Every year at the end of June, these indigenous farmers climb to the top of the mountains in order to observe the star cluster of the Pleiades. The farmers forecast dry or rainy weather three months later based on whether the cluster appears to be bright or cloudy. Thus they set a time for sowing potatoes, which must be done just before the beginning of the rainy season. If the potatoes are sown too early and the rain fails to appear on time, the harvest will be poor. Meteorologist Mark Cane provided the meteorological reason for this. He discovered that the cloudy appearance of the Pleiades indicates the forth-coming arrival of the El Niño phenomenon or ENSO/Southern Oscillation (Kappas, 2009, pp. 121–135), which blurs the atmosphere above the Andes every five to six years and deflects the normal air flow, while at the same time preventing the normal October precipitation.

The traditional forecasting method of the farmers was correctly cor-related with 65 per cent of the actual weather occurrences derived from statistical data over a period of several years. Orlove and Cane considered this finding as the proof that the traditional Andean weather-forecasting method was exact enough to compare well with modern methods.

A survey on vulnerability and adaptation to climate change carried out with financial support of the Netherlands and published in 2006 identified similar systems of weather forecasting among Aymara Indians in Bolivia based on the observation of astronomical objects (sun and stars), and typical indicators in plant and animal behaviour. Festivities in the annual cycle were characterized as assuming a monitoring function. The survey explained inaccuracies in the traditional forecasting approach due to the impacts of climate change-induced variability, which were already notice-able (Ministerio de Planificación del Desarrollo, 2006, pp. 50ff.).

A similar tradition of weather forecasting has been reported from the Indian state of Gujarat. That study was not carried out by anthropologists, but by Professor P. R. Kanani from Gujarat Agricultural University. Much like farmers in the Andean region, Gujarat farmers schedule sowing dates in accordance with traditional natural indicators that they believe pres-aged the arrival of the monsoon. The practice is based on environmen-tal observations (animal behaviour or the budding of plants), but also on interpretations of mythological texts from previous centuries that were partly fixed in written records and partly transmitted by oral communica-tion (Kanani and Pastakia, 1999; Kanani, 2006). This forecasting likewise demonstrated a respectable accuracy over several years.

I consider these examples to be clear indications of existing traditional climate- and weather-related knowledge systems that merit further investi-gation in terms of their importance for natural science, but also in terms of the study of cultures. However, it has to be noted that, with respect to the examples cited above, the scientific approach used to validate these knowledge systems is restricted to the standards of exact science, that is, subordinated to the demands of objectivity of Western knowledge systems. This is, of course, an acceptable approach to validate the findings, but ignores the cultural and religious background in which these traditional knowledge systems are embedded and their strong links to cultural and religious contexts.

It was, for example, Orlove himself who ascertained that the Andean Pleiades observation coincides historically with the winter solstice. Already by the time of the pre-colonial Incan Empire this event defined the date for the *Inti Raymi* festivity, which represents one of two great celebrations of the Andean solar year. Chroniclers reported that the Pleiades (*Oncoy*) themselves were worshipped, including sacrifices, in order to assure a good harvest. This approach to weather forecasting has strong religious implications, and the question is whether it should be exposed to 'disenchantment' in Max Weber's sense, in view of the fact that the traditional Andean meteorologist sees the weather knowledge system as an integral part of his religion (Dean, 1999, pp. 36–37).

There is yet another problem to be addressed. Anthropologists have encountered traditional climate-related knowledge systems that feature a high degree of awareness of climate change indications based on environmental observations. However, these systems cannot be translated into current scientific or even popularized scientific language since their authoritative knowledge structure is totally different from the scientific one. Experts in such knowledge systems may even get confused when confronted with common climate change concepts (Marino and Schweitzer, 2009).

Perspectivism and Relativism: Different Concepts of the Environment

Another approach to the climate change problem has to take into account the classical anthropological attitude of the 'native point of view', that is, to see and perceive the world from the perspective of the other culture/cultural other. In the meantime it has been recognized that no anthropologist can understand a foreign culture without reverting to some preconceptions. That is part of what the hermeneutic circle teaches us. In any event, the attempt to understand other cultures on their own terms remains an anthropological challenge. To mention just one prominent example, I will briefly describe the indigenous perspectivism of the Brazilian anthropologist Eduardo Viveiros de Castro (1998), who demonstrated that certain indigenous peoples from the Amazon Basin traditionally did not, as we do, consider human beings as human beings, animals as animals and spirits as spirits (in case we believe in spirits). Rather, under certain circumstances, they saw spirits as hunters of humans, while they thought that animals see humans as both spirits and animals, and see spirits themselves as humans. This represents a kind of perspectivistic ontology. A similar debate stems from Philippe Descola (1992; 2009) who believes that the distinction between nature and culture might be relevant for scientific analysis but does not exist in the view of the world of Amazon Indians, who consider the relation between culture and nature as a kind of continuum.

In this context, however, I would like to exemplify the anthropological perspective of 'the native point of view' with a case study more directly related to climate issues that may occur in this or a similar manner as a result of anthropogenic environmental changes such as global warming. The case refers to a mudslide that occurred on 6 June 1994 as a result of an earthquake near the Nevado del Huila (a volcano of the Central Andean Cordillera of Colombia, 5,364 m above sea level) and destroyed large parts of the Cauca Province, killing around 1,000 Nasa or Paez Indians of the Tierradentro Region. After several decades of land rights struggles, for which the Nasa Indians and their Regional Indigenous Council of the Cauca were famous, the mudslide motivated a group of shamans to start a process of religious rethinking. They criticized the inconsiderate destruction of the vegetation during the earlier land fights, particularly the wild riverine vegetation, which they considered to be the homes of important spirits. After more than a century, the shamans revitalized an old complex ritual, the *saakhelu*, which was designed to 'cure' their territory (Drexler, 2004; 2007).

The shamans applied the concept of healing to the environment, a concept restricted to living creatures in our own culture. Their fundamental principle is an understanding of the environment as an animated nature that includes inorganic material such as stones or mountains. As an intrinsic part of complementary opposites – masculine/feminine, left/right, hot/ cold, positive/negative energies, domesticated culture/sacred savagery (which in the conception of the Nasa do not constitute a strict dualism but a continuum) – humans are obliged to fulfil duties of reciprocity towards the environment. This is done by offering gifts in return for things that humans take from the environment. If this offering is not made, nature falls ill, heats up and must be cooled down. Otherwise, it generates 'black clouds', that is, negative energies that have to be driven away.

The 2002 performance of the *saakhelu* ritual was characterized not only by the repetition of the marriage of the mythical parent couple of the sun and moon, and the exchange of ritually cured seeds that rain magic guaranteed would thrive and prosper, but by another ritual. This time, the accumulated negative energy was driven into the interior of the volcano Nevado de Huila, where it had to be cooled down and cured afterwards. The shamans considered the cooling ritual necessary since the earth has been heated up due to repeated deforestation and slashing and burning of great areas of land. This heating up generates movements of the earth (such as the catastrophe on 6 June 1994), thus requiring a regular cooling-down ritual.

It is quite possible that the current issue of global climate change means something to some groups of Nasa shamans. However, the outcome might be something that could be called climate syncretism, in which global warming is subordinated under their own shamanistic logic. This kind of indigenous appropriation of scientific discourse may occur more frequently than currently believed and has to be studied further.

Climate Change and the Challenge of Interculturality

The obvious fact that the anthropological requirement to take the native point of view might lead to a problematic cultural relativism that tends to accept even very exotic visions as plausible explanations of the world was criticized by Kay Milton as early as the 1990s (Milton, 1997). Let me briefly note that 'cultural relativism' is the anthropological attitude that seeks not to assess foreign cultures according to the anthropologist's own values but to understand them in their own terms and approach all of them with equal respect. According to Milton, extreme cultural relativism impedes an intercultural perspective, or the comparative approach to various cultures, because it always takes one single culture as its frame of reference. But Milton focuses above all on the immanent claim that cultural relativism has to apply to all cultures in a similar way, while she believes that some knowledge systems, such as the Western natural sciences, are better prepared to understand and manage the external world. Regarding global warming she thinks, 'Other cultural perspectives . . . may attribute it to the actions of spirits, or a divine creator. Or accepting some degree of human responsibility they may regard it as retribution, imposed by some higher authority, for the failure of their society to maintain its ancient traditions' (Milton, 1997, p. 487). And this is indeed what anthropologists may find in the field, as the Nasa shamans have made clear.

Milton's solution to this predicament is twofold, and is what I would like to present as a third anthropological approach to climate change. On the one hand, she resorts to a mediating concept, allowing every culture its own interpretation of the world, originating from the same sense-based perception of the surrounding environment. That means that the perception is the same in all cultures and valid at an intercultural level, while only the interpretation of the perceived environment is different and culturally defined. On the other hand, every interpretation of the environment has to be seen as an outcome of direct contact with nature and of resolving concrete problems in such a way that the truth of any knowledge system can only be validated by its effectiveness in resolving problems. This seems to be convincing. However, Milton's position regarding the first part seems doubtful in the light of recent outcomes of neurosciences that question – I can here only briefly refer to this – the separation of perception and interpretation, due to the fact that every perception itself includes interpretation. Furthermore, this perception – and here we have another insight from recent transcultural neuroscience studies published in popular scientific journals (Northoff, 2009) – shows strong cultural influences, as demonstrated by different experiments with European and Asian probands. This is not surprising to most anthropologists. However, anthropologists also know that the particular visions of spirits or ghosts (with or without the consumption of drugs), which constitute an integral part of every well-trained shaman's experience, are a kind of perception excluded under this perception/interpretation scheme.

Even the evidential value of knowledge by means of its capacity to solve practical problems is tricky. On the one hand, the above-mentioned weather forecasting traditions show a notable accuracy, but are embedded in religious concepts that would have difficulties meeting with approval under a Western style of thought. On the other hand, by the 1970s, anthropology was already undergoing an intensive debate over magical practices and their inherent logic and rationality, which appeared clearest when magic failed to work (Kippenberg and Luchesi, 1978). Furthermore, in the past, human resilience – not collapse – has usually been the response to environmental challenges. We are aware of very few cultures, such as the Maya from Mesoamerica or the settlers of the Easter Island (Rapa Nui), that vanished from the earth, presumably due to over-exploitation of their natural resources. But even in these cases, the possible causes are too manifold to reduce them to one culturally bound self-made problem (McAnany and Yoffee, 2009). And would it not be our own 'superior' Western civilization itself that fails to offer successful solutions to man-made problems when it solves one kind of problem – that is, providing energy – while at the same time generating new ones – namely, global warming?

Anthropogenic Dimensions of Climate (Change) Policy

Such protests do not change the fact that cultural relativism *relativizes*. Things are even more complex since any cultural differences noticed by revealing how things could be viewed from another angle are always different only in comparison to the observer's own culture. But it is within the same reflection of the own and the other that the proper culture of the anthropologist is also submitted to a process of relativism, which might also relate to the global warming discourse. I believe it does not undermine the understanding of the urgent need for global climate protection nor relativize the relevant aspects of the scientific discourse on climate change to contrast it with more traditional concepts and popular understanding. Here I see a desideratum of anthropological research. We should bear in mind that, after being grasped first as a philosophical and anthropological concept, and then as a geographical one, climate has been 'scientificated' as an interacting system of physical and recordable components that can only be understood as mathematical average values. The understanding of the climate in terms of natural science needs to be broken down to tangible aspects such as temperature, precipitation, insolation, drought and so on to become meaningful to humans. There are, certainly, a growing number of studies and attempts to predict specific impacts of climate change on a regional level (IPCC, 2007; for Latin America, see also Kronik and Verner, 2010). However, global climate is a highly condensed scientific construction with temporal and spatial scales that are nearly only comprehendable at a mathematical and statistical level. Furthermore, many aspects are based on scientific results that, in the end, are translated to human consensus. Strictly speaking, there are no 'natural' parameters for determining statistical measures regarding climate conditions; they have to be agreed upon. For instance, the standard time framework for meteorological observation is 30 years, which may not be long enough for an adequate description of climate that shows variations at much longer time scales (Stehr and von Storch, 1999, p. 26). Just to mention one current example: on 9 December 2009, the German newspaper *Frankfurter Allgemeine Zeitung* quoted Carlo Jäger from the Potsdam Institute for Climate Impact Research, who explained that the generally recognized peak for acceptable global warming, the 2°C target, has to be understood as an unexpressed agreement and not a scientifically verified value. 'The 2 degree limit appeared almost by chance', Jäger was quoted as saying (Müller-Jung, 2009). However, this limit has not only yielded a broad effect but is considered to be an invariable truth.

On the immediate human level, climate research will probably never be put into practice according to Kay Milton's requirements of proving the value of the knowledge systems in resolving concrete problems, since climate research can only calculate risks and will never be able to identify single incidences as direct impacts of climate change. From the perspective of cultural relativism, there are some questions like this, and it would be interesting to conduct surveys – some have already been done (Behringer, 2007) – of the cultural history or even ethnographies of climate research. I do not believe that an anthropological reflection on the culture of climate research must necessarily result in a sceptical deconstruction of the issue. The current constitution of our world demands a pluralistic way of thinking: we should be aware that the climate is a scientific construction, but it is also a human construction and there are different ways of perceiving it. We should, in any event, take measures to protect it. The only relativism that might be applicable is the provision that climate protection should not only meet the aim of climate mitigation or protection per se but also the further objectives of general sustainability. The reduction of our oil consumption would meet this target, while emissions trading might not.

After all, we must consider the issue of global climate change as children of our time. International climate policy is as much an expression of globalization as it is its obstetrician. News reports constantly clarify that the threats of climate change transcend frontiers and continents, and that the issue of justice has to be addressed globally. The climate problem has motivated the establishment of a global environmental regime that is relatively powerful compared to, for instance, its 'little sister', the Biodiversity Convention. In concert with worldwide networking via the internet and perhaps even more powerful than the coordinated management of the recent international financial and real estate crisis, the present debate on the global warming crisis suggests that we have the global climate under control in good as well as bad ways. In brochures, campaigns and bulletins, we look at visual representations of the globe from above, which suggest visually as well as discursively that we can ruin the earth or save it. I am concerned about our almost almighty claim of control, which we should think about more profoundly. In contrast to this is the statement of Walter Álvarez Quispe,[1] a Kallawaya, a representative of an ethnic group in Northern Bolivia and at the same time of a famous group of Indian healers. Quispe quite humbly confirmed in an interview recorded on 12 May 2007[2] that he had observed indications of climate change caused by humans, but he also insisted that it is part of human existence to be always confronted with a changing environment. This dual perspective, which sees nature as ever-changing but also identifies climate change as anthropogenic, is typical of the traditional indigenous Andean view of cyclical occurrences of profound changes and radical renewals. In Quechua, the most important traditional language of the Andean region, the word *pachakutik* expresses this repeated change and can be translated as 'time of transition', 'cataclysms' or 'convulsion of the earth' (Bouysse-Cassagne, 1988). It can refer to violent historical events, to religious incidents such as the Biblical Flood described by Christian Evangelicals or even to natural catastrophes such as volcanic eruptions.

Quispe has also been trained as a medical doctor in Cuba and considers the knowledge of Kallawaya healers – which was declared an Intangible Cultural Heritage of Humanity by the UNESCO in 2003[3] – to be religious, as well as scientific and medical. His professional background represents a kind of biography that is increasingly common among indigenous representatives, and symbolizes a new kind of anthropological challenge. Indigenous communities are no longer isolated and self-contained populations abruptly affected by global warming. Many communities are connected to the globalized world and have had experience in dealing with different discourses, but without renouncing their own culture – as represented by Quispe himself.

A New Stage of the Applied Anthropology

In this context, I would like to introduce the fourth and last anthropological approach as presented by Conrad P. Kottak (1999) under the rubric 'New Ecological Anthropology'. He proposed a cultural mediation – an agency for processes of cultural change – based on an understanding that 'change always proceeds in the face of prior structures (a given sociocultural heritage)' (Kottak, 1999, p. 34). Anthropology also accounts for this applied style of science, in its categorization of previous experiences such as 'action anthropology' (Schlesier, 1980), when scholars support indigenous claims and furnish experts to courts of justice; or 'development anthropology' (Schönhuth, 2003), when scholars introduce anthropological methods in development cooperation; or 'collaborative anthropology' (Lassiter, 2005), when studies are designed with research partners. There is already a number of these kinds of studies in the realm of climate change. The outcome of the Arctic Climate Impact Assessment (Symon, 2005) includes corresponding surveys on the observations by indigenous populations of growing indications of climate change and related impacts on livelihoods in terms of hunting, fishing and herding. In recent publications, anthropologists in a dialogue with indigenous representatives broke down climate change impacts to the level of daily life in terms of food security and so forth. A study of this type, on climate change and indigenous women, has recently been produced in Colombia (Ulloa et al., 2009), while Crate and Nuttall (2009a) have edited a comprehensive overview of studies on anthropology and climate change proposing that anthropologists serve as mediators between indigenous and local communities affected by climate change and relevant political decision makers (Crate and Nuttall, 2009c).

Furthermore, we have to take into account processes related to the growing national and international recognition of the rights of indigenous peoples who follow their own agenda under the United Nations, particularly the Permanent Forum on Indigenous Issues. Indigenous representatives are participants in international climate negotiations and intervene as far as their interests are concerned, even if their influence is limited. They articulate positions on climate impacts, sequestration, adaptation, Clean Development Mechanisms, carbon sinks or Reducing Emissions from Deforestation and Degradation (REDD); they also constantly reference culture and religion. One example of this was when they started their caucus meeting at the Copenhagen COP (Conference of the Parties) with a prayer. Although indigenous peoples had limited ability to directly address the COP plenary, 'Mother Earth' appeared as a kind of intercultural symbolic stand-in to remind people of their cultural and religious commitment to nature.

A Dream(ed) World of Plurality

It is here that I believe Kottak's New Ecological Anthropology and the concept that change always proceeds in the face of prior structures is far from being fulfilled. In the meantime, indigenous communities will be recognized as bearers of traditional knowledge on weather forecasting, as victims of climate change impacts or as actors of adaptation to climate change. However, there is still the problem that their knowledge and abilities are only of interest as far as they are related to climate change. Their knowledge and abilities are often decontextualized, and I wonder if this is right. The strength of indigenous knowledge and abilities lies precisely in the religious fundament, in the concern about equilibrium and in the reciprocal relationship to nature. At the same time, we must consider global cultural diversity, including different conceptual access to the environment that urges us, from an anthropological point of view, to assume a pluralistic openness. This pluralism can serve as a mirror for a climate debate that, due to the severity of expected impacts, might produce blind spots. There should be more anthropological research to investigate the climate-related access of indigenous populations to the environment. This research should encourage pluralistic concepts that include those religious or cultural aspects.

My dream(ed) world of plurality as a cultural anthropologist is a climate researcher who enters into a dialogue with a traditional West-African rainmaker (Sanders, 2003) and who sees a rainmaking ritual highly interspersed with sexual symbolism. It is not about convincing the climate researcher of the effectiveness of the ritual but about reminding him that other people in other cultures have totally different access to that part of the environment that we in the West call 'climate'.

Notes

[1] More information about Álvarez Quispe can be found at: www.minedu.gov. bo/utlsaa/ciencias_sociales/la_cosmovision_andina.php. Accessed 5 January 2010.

[2] The interview was conducted by Jose Francisco Olmos, with questions on climate change provided by the author of this chapter.

[3] See www.unesco.org/culture/ich/index.php?RL=00048. Accessed 27 December 2009.

References

Behringer, W. (2007), *Kulturgeschichte des Klimas*. München: C. H. Beck.

Bouysse-Cassagne, T. (1988), *Lluvias y Cenizas: Dos Pachacuti en la Historia*. La Paz: Hisbol.

Crate, S. A. and Nuttall, M. (eds) (2009a), *Anthropology and Climate Change: From Encounters to Actions*. Walnut Creek, CA: Left Coast Press.

— (2009b), 'Epilogue: anthropologist, science, and climate change policy', in S. A. Crate and M. Nuttall (eds), *Anthropology and Climate Change: From Encounters to Actions*. Walnut Creek, CA: Left Coast Press, pp. 394–400.

— (2009c), 'Introduction: anthropology and climate change', in S. A. Crate and M. Nuttall (eds), *Anthropology and Climate Change: From Encounters to Actions*. Walnut Creek, CA: Left Coast Press, pp. 9–36.

Dean, C. (1999), *Inka Bodies and the Body of Christ. Corpus Christi in Colonial Cuzco, Peru*. Durham, NC: Duke University Press.

Descola, P. (1992), 'Societies of nature and the nature of society', in Adam Kuper (ed.), *Conceptualizing Society*. London and New York: Routledge, pp. 107–126.

— (2009), 'Human natures'. *Social Anthropology/Anthropologie Sociale*, 17, 145–157.

Drexler, J. (2004), 'Die Heilung des Territoriums. Das Saakhelu-Ritual der Nasa (Páez) von Tierradentro (Cauca, Kolumbien)'. *Indiana*, 21, 141–173.

— (2007), '"Unser kühles Territorium": Das indioamerikanische Konzept der Territorialhygiene am Beispiel des Ressourcenkrisenmanagements der Nasa (Páez) des kolumbianischen Tierradentro'. *Indiana*, 24, 291–315.

Han, S. and Northoff, G. (2008), 'Culture-sensitive neural substrates of human cognition: a transcultural neuroimaging approach'. *Nature Reviews Neuroscience*, 9, 646–654.

Harris, M. (1979 [2001]), *Cultural Materialism: The Struggle for a Science of Culture*. Lanham: AltaMira Press.

Ingold, T. (2009), 'The wedge and the knot: hammering and stitching the face of nature', in S. Bergmann, Scott, P. M., Jansdotter Samuelsson, M. and Bedford-Strohm, H. (eds), *Nature, Space and the Sacred*. Surrey and Burlington: Ashgate, pp. 147–161.

IPCC (2007), *Climate Change 2007: Impacts, Adaptation and Vulnerability. Contribution of Working Group II to the Fourth Assessment Report of the Intergovernmental Panel on Climate Change*. Cambridge: Cambridge University Press.

IWGIA [International Work Group of Indigenous Affairs] (ed.) (2010), *The Indigenous World 2010*. Copenhagen: IWGIA.

Kanani, P. R. (2006), 'Testing of traditional methods of weather forecasting in Gujarat using the participatory approach', in A. V. Balasubramanian and T. D. Nirmala Devi (eds), *Traditional Knowledge Systems of India and Sri Lanka*. Compass series on Worldviews and Sciences, Vol. 5. Chennai: Centre for Indian Knowledge Systems, pp. 125–144.

Kanani, P. R. and Pastakia, A. (1999), 'Everything is written in the sky! Participatory meteorological assessment and prediction based on traditional beliefs and indicators in Saurashtra'. *Eubios Journal of Asian and International Bioethics*, 9, 170–176.

Kappas, M. (2009), *Klimatologie: Klimaforschung im 21. Jahrhundert – Herausforderung für Natur- und Sozialwissenschaften*. Heidelberg: Spektrum.

Keesing, R. M. (1972), 'Paradigms lost: the new ethnography and the new linguistics'. *Southwestern Journal of Anthropology*, 28, 299–331.

Kippenberg, H. G. and Luchesi B. (eds) (1978), *Magie. Die sozialwissenschaftliche Kontroverse über das Verstehen fremden Denkens*. Frankfurt am Main: Suhrkamp.

Kottak, C. P. (1999), 'The new ecological anthropology'. *American Anthropologist*, 101, 23–35.

Kronik, J. and Verner, D. (2010), *Indigenous Peoples and Climate Change in Latin America and the Caribbean*. Washington: The International Bank for Reconstruction and Development and The World Bank.

Lassiter, L. E. (2005), *The Chicago Guide to Collaborative Ethnography*. Chicago/London: University of Chicago Press.

McAnany, P. A. and Yoffee, N. (eds) (2009), *Questioning Collapse: Human Resilience, Ecological Vulnerability, and the Aftermath of Empire*. Cambridge: Cambridge University Press.

Marino, E. and Schweitzer P. (2009), 'Talking and not talking about climate change in Northwestern Alaska', in S. A. Crate and M. Nuttall (eds), *Anthropology and Climate Change: From Encounters to Actions*. Walnut Creek, CA: Left Coast Press, pp. 209–217.

Milton, K. (1997), 'Ecologies: anthropology, culture and the environment'. *International Social Science Journal*, 154, 477–495.

Ministerio de Planificación del Desarrollo, Programa Nacional de Cambios Climáticos, Bolivia (2006), *Vulnerabilidad y Adaptación al Cambio Climático en las Regiones del lago Titicaca y los Valles Cruceños de Bolivia.*

Müller-Jung, J. (2009), 'Warum sollten maximal zwei Grad die Welt retten?', *Frankfurter Allgemeine Zeitung*, 9 December 2009.

Nordhoff, G. (2009), 'Der Chamäleon-Effekt'. *Hirn und Geist*, 6, 14–19.

Nuttall, M. (2009), 'Living in a world of movement: human resilience to environmental instability in Greenland', in S. A. Crate and M. Nuttall (eds), *Anthropology and Climate Change: From Encounters to Actions.* Walnut Creek, CA: Left Coast Press, pp. 292–310.

Orlove, B., Chiang, J. C. H. and Cane, M. A. (2002), 'Ethnoclimatology in the Andes. A cross-disciplinary study uncovers a scientific basis for the scheme Andean potato farmers traditionally use to predict the coming rains'. *American Scientist*, 90, 428–435.

Rappaport, R. A. (1968), *Pigs for the Ancestors. Ritual in the Ecology of a New Guinea People.* New Haven: Yale University Press.

Sanders, T. (2003), '(En)gendering the weather: rainmaking and reproduction in Tanzania', in S. Strauss and B. Orlove (eds), *Weather, Climate, Culture.* Oxford and New York: Berg, pp. 83–102.

Schlesier, K. H. (1980), 'Zum Weltbild einer neuen Kulturanthropologie. Erkenntnis und Praxis. Die Rolle der Action Anthropology. Vier Beispiele'. *Zeitschrift für Ethnologie*, 105, 32–66.

Schönhuth, M. (2003), *Entwicklung, Partizipation und Ethnologie. Implikationen der Begegnung von ethnologischen und partizipativen Forschungsansätzen im Entwicklungskontext.* Habilitation thesis, University of Trier.

Stehr, N. and von Storch, H. (1999), *Über Klima, Wetter, Mensch.* München: C. H. Beck.

Steward, J. H. (1955), *Theory of Culture Change. The Methodology of Multilinear Evolution.* Urbana: University of Ilinois Press.

Symon, C. (ed.) (2005), *Arctic Climate Impact Assessment.* Cambridge: Cambridge University Press.

Ulloa, A., Escobar, E. M., Donato, L. M. and Escobar, P. (eds) (2009), *Mujeres indígenas y cambio climático. Perspectivas latinoamericanas.* Bogotá: Fundación Natura.

Viveiros de Castro, E. (1998), 'Cosmological deixis and Amerindian perspectivism'. *Journal of the Royal Anthropological Institute*, 4, 469–488.

White, L. A. (2005[1949]), *The Science of Culture. A Study of Man and Civilization.* New York: Percheron Press/Eliot Werner Publications.

Chapter 12

Vulnerable Coastal Regions: Indigenous People under Climate Change in Indonesia

Urte Undine Frömming and Christian Reichel

Introduction

In this chapter[1], we will examine consequences of climate change by investigating the situation of 'indigenous or local groups'[2] living in the particularly vulnerable coastal regions of Indonesia. Two general questions will be considered: (1) What kind of local knowledge exists both for predicting, and for adapting to, climate-related events and for preventing catastrophic effects through sustainable practices? (2) What are the perceptions of current environmental change and in what sociocultural and/or cosmological ideas are they rooted?

Cultural–scientific research for mitigating climate change and for adapting to its expected consequences (possibly catastrophes) is still very limited and is dominated by the paradigm of the natural sciences:

> Given the massive, worldwide problems that are to be expected under climate and environmental change and the fact that a large part of the world's population is not (yet) subject to the technocratic worldview, it is imperative to complement the existing technological and economical oriented problem solutions with alternative perspectives – narratives that integrate the entanglement of humans and their environment (Bergmann and Gerten, 2010, p. 5).

The political reaction to the global discussion on climate change is still mostly based on common solutions that are scientifically developed and institutionally certified. These solutions do not do a good job of reflecting the local frame of reference or the most basic related changes that are revealed through the interpretation of nature and society by the local population. Here, in contrast, we assume that catastrophes are dealt with based on the social, cultural and geographical contexts in which they occur, and the experiences that one has with them. Locations that experience tropical storms frequently enough to generate expectations that they will regularly occur face considerably less of a mental and practical challenge than locations where tropical storms are rare (Welzer, 2009). A fundamental understanding of the cultural interpretation, processing and treatment of climate change and its related catastrophes is necessary in order to both develop more effective alternative action strategies for the future and gain the population's support in the process (Crate and Nuttall, 2009). If these strategies are not considered in catastrophe management, it is highly probable that those affected will not be reached or that they will boycott services.

For many indigenous societies, the impact of climate change is not a problem of the future; it is already being felt, and the impacts will be imminent if no concrete counteractive measures are undertaken. Indigenous groups of Indonesia are especially vulnerable to the direct and indirect consequences of climate change, such as tropical storms, floods, tidal waves and coral bleaching. Although these groups have done the least to trigger anthropogenic climate change, they already have to face its indirect consequences, including poverty, marginalization and discrimination (Crate and Nuttall, 2009). Thus, there have been reasonable demands that equalization payments be offered to the so-called third world, a topic that was also the subject of negotiations at the Climate Conference in Cancun in 2010. In addition, there is a need to systematically analyse the cultural techniques, strategies and discourses (Bergmann, 2010) used by local people in the conservation of nature, and to integrate these ideas into programmes for managing resources and protecting the climate. The people of Indonesia have lived for centuries with numerous natural threats – earthquakes, tidal waves and volcanic eruptions. Through their longstanding experience of repeated natural catastrophes or extreme events,[3] various groups have developed protective systems rooted in cultural and religious beliefs (Bergmann and Gerten, 2010); these systems protect the environment, and thereby the local population.

Our research areas are particularly suited to this examination of 'old Indonesian' (see note 2) cultural techniques regarding natural catastrophes, because sections of the coastal population are strongly tied to the environment through various beliefs about sacred places that play a crucial role in their spiritual orientation. This has implications for their use of natural resources. However, these orally transmitted cultural techniques are being or are in danger of being suppressed, not only due to mission-ary activities of orthodox Islam and Christian churches but also because of national and international interests such as raw material extraction, destructive forms of fishing and a tourism industry that is not culturally and ecologically adapted to the environment. These pressures are intensi-fying due to an increasing coastal population, multiple utilization interests and continuing resource depletion. The resulting frustration and disorien-tation of many local residents often trigger resource-related conflicts that can turn violent (Reichel et al., 2009).

In this chapter we provide an overview of several protective mechanisms and resource management strategies developed by indigenous peoples; these may at first seem to be completely contrary to Western strategies of regimentation, but in our opinion they offer in their efficiency at least a few lessons that can be integrated into politically negotiated global strat-egies for preserving natural resources and protecting against the con-sequences of climate change. This would suggest the need for further systematic research in other vulnerable regions in order to document local protective strategies, as well as to categorize, visualize and/or map them as necessary.

Anticipated Consequences of Global Warming for Inhabitants of the Coral Triangle

It is important to note that the effects, consequences and causes of cli-mate change will by no means be the same throughout the world. Instead, these factors will manifest themselves at different regional scales through interactions with ecological, economic and social frameworks that are con-text specific (Dietz, 2006). Projections suggest that particular climate-sen-sitive regions in Indonesia will face consequences earlier and on a much stronger scale than the global average. The frequency and strength of cli-mate-related natural hazards in these areas will increase rapidly as a result (UNEP-WCMC, 2006). The negative consequences of climate change are especially noticeable in the Coral Triangle. Here, one can expect an increase in natural disasters due to a rise in the magnitude and frequency of climate-dependent natural threats such as tropical storms, rising sea lev-els and coral bleaching. The effects of these sweeping phenomena on local populations will be exacerbated by various social, ecological and economic factors, such as the population explosion on the coasts, as well as the asso-ciated shrinking of resources through destructive fishing methods. It will be increasingly difficult for more and more people to survive in the coastal regions (Reichel, 2008).

This habitat destabilization will likely result in millions of climate refugees, a situation that will put particular pressure on nearby countries such as Australia and New Zealand to accept these refugees. People are migrating and will migrate due to the indirect effects of climate change: because they cannot find work, because natural resources are becoming ever more scarce and because their basic subsistence is no longer secure. Migration generally represents socio-political pressure that will increase with further global warming, possibly leading to new conflicts (Welzer, 2009).

In order to gain the best possible insight into the local perspective, our ethnographic research was carried out using both qualitatively and quantitatively different methods. The foreground research included participative observation, semi-standardized interviews and group interviews. We also conducted comparatively applied research based on the methodology of multi-sited ethnography (Marcus, 1995). After carrying out field research in each region over a period of four months (Undine Frömming in Nusa Tenggara; Christian Reichel in Central Java and South Sulawesi), we were able to gain some insight into local people's perceptions of, and responses to, climate change. The connections and differences between the three study regions were also considered. While the Segara Anakan Lagoon (Central Java) is situated on the border of the Coral Triangle, the Islands of Flores (Nusa Tenggara) and the Taka Bonerate Atoll (South Sulawesi) are situated in the middle. This marine area stretches from the Philippines in the south to the Lesser Sunda Islands of Indonesia in the west and the Solomon Islands in the east (see Figure 12.1).

Due to its special geographical position connecting the Indian and Pacific oceans and its geologically formative history,[4] the Coral Triangle is a hotspot of biodiversity.[5] Mangrove swamps and coral reefs distinguish the coasts in this region. As a result of their high biodiversity and productivity, these coasts are among the most valuable natural resources in the world. It is precisely this combination of reefs and swamps that provides the best natural defence against storms and waves; together they lessen the effects of erosion and offer protection against tropical storms and tsunamis. When intact, mangrove swamps and coral reefs can absorb between 70 and 90 per cent of wind-generated wave energy, thus serving as an effective buffer between humans and the sea (UNEP-WCMC, 2006). For local inhabitants, the economic use of the sea is enormously important in terms of both nutrition and employment. More than 120 million people are directly or indirectly dependent on fishing. It provides not only their primary source of protein,

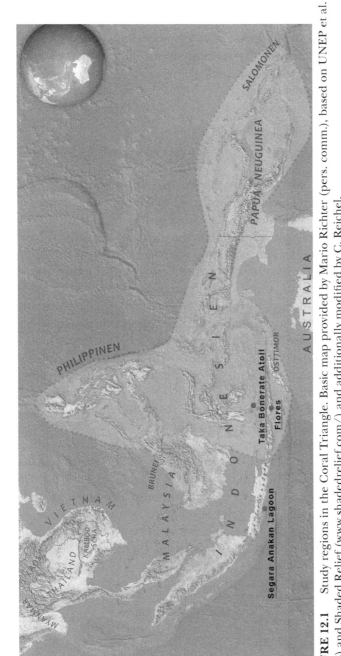

FIGURE 12.1 Study regions in the Coral Triangle. Basic map provided by Mario Richter (pers. comm.), based on UNEP et al. (1988) and Shaded Relief (www.shadedrelief.com/) and additionally modified by C. Reichel.

but also the main source of work in coastal regions (Unsworth and Clifton, 2010). However, this means of subsistence is under severe threat. In addition to the destructive exploitation of natural resources, global warming represents the greatest danger to these coastal ecosystems (Allen and Werner, 2002). In the last 30 years, some 35 per cent of mangrove swamps have disappeared worldwide, and it is predicted that by 2030, some 60 per cent of all coral reefs will be destroyed (UNEP-WCMC, 2006).

Indigenous Conceptions of Nature in Indonesia

In order to understand the significance of climate change for indigenous groups in Indonesia, one must first recognize that, for many, nature represents a central point of orientation in society, in constituting its values, norms and beliefs, as well as its identity. This relationship with nature is not only religious, but also iconic and symbolic. Within the traditional conception of many Indonesian cultures, there was no specific word for nature itself. This alone points to the special significance of nature; it was not perceived as being an object. Therefore, these indigenous cultural connotations of nature cannot be easily categorized under classical Western conceptual systems. A central aspect of old Indonesian conceptions of nature is the recognition of nature's dominance. This inverts the occidental understanding of the power dynamics between humans and their environment: in the conceptual world of the inhabitants of Flores, the idea of humanity dominating nature would be entirely absurd. The entire culture is informed by the concept of 'natural forces' that counterbalance social spheres, in which humans can communicate with these forces through sacrificial rites, oracles and incantations, thus creating an equilibrium between people and natural forces (cf. Frömming, 2006, pp. 33f.).

Indonesian conceptions of nature involve a complex and dynamic network of meanings and relationships. All natural locations – especially noteworthy ones such as mountains, rivers and the ocean – are seen to be inhabited by gods and spirits; therefore, these locations are also invested with a series of taboos.

Trespass Taboos

Many Indonesians, due to fear of natural or ancestral spirits, still obey religious taboos against trespassing in specific areas. As much as possible, Floresians avoid travelling alone in natural environments, because these are outside the control of the living, belonging instead to the realm of nature spirits and the ancestors. If travel alone cannot be avoided – for example, when an individual is hunting wild boar or gathering plants and berries – then the individual brings along small sacrificial offerings such as eggs, tobacco, rice or betel nuts to apologize for trespassing in the realm of the spirits. This zone only roughly corresponds to the concept of 'wilderness'. This taboo against trespassing is based on a conception of specific natural environments as spaces inhabited by gods and spirits, indicating a conceptualization of nature that is culturally based instead of being rationalistic or 'objectively given' (Moscovici, 1968; Luig and Schultz, 2002).

The natural world is seen as parallel or in opposition to the human world (Luig and von Oppen, 1997, pp. 7f.), and it manifests itself by projecting influences 'which emanate from it and with which humans stand in a responsive relationship. Natural disasters are seen as warnings or punishments from the gods, in response to social misconduct' (Frömming, 2006, pp. 27ff.). Here, natural threats are viewed not only as a source of danger (the scientific viewpoint) but also in their cultural construction as the acts or signs of the ancestors and nature spirits. These have a social and cathartic function (Frömming, 2006, p. 50). Such local strategies result in two important side effects: on the one hand, humans avoid potentially dangerous locations, and on the other hand, coastal ecosystems remain intact (i.e. unaffected by anthropogenic intervention), thus offering effective protection against tidal waves and tsunamis.

Cultural Techniques for Handling Natural Threats

In general, one can differentiate cultural techniques for handling natural threats into three general categories: (1) prediction, (2) protection and (3) coping strategies and interpretation. These strategies are connected to a specific local environmental knowledge base as well as codes of conduct regarding nature and the forces that inhabit these natural spaces.

For prediction, various oracles and weather observations are used to predict the coming monsoon or potential natural catastrophes. Beyond these weather forecasts, animal sacrifices are also used to predict the future of the clan according to the shape of the sinews and the appearance of the liver. Protective strategies can be divided into short term (such as how to behave in seismic danger zones) and long term (such as environmental protection measures for preventing natural catastrophes). These approaches involve knowledge about dangerous natural environments that has been acquired over generations. Often passed on in the form of myths, this knowledge creates the basis for a repertoire of collectively shared social practices that aid in strengthening a society's resilience. Often this knowledge is based on the wisdom expressed by elders and healers (*dukun*), who command great respect. The third category, strategies to cope with and interpret natural catastrophes after the event, covers collective rituals, including sacrificial ceremonies and the cult of the ancestors. These strategies help to frame the catastrophic event in an explainable and logical sense and therefore help individuals and groups to overcome its traumatic impact.

Of course, modern geophysical techniques have supplanted these old Indonesian cultural practices, and not all traditional codes of conduct can guarantee protection against natural disasters. A few of these human behaviours can be very hazardous in themselves, such as believing that the gods and spirits of dangerous natural environments can protect people or refusing to abandon graves and holy places that lie in danger zones. Ritual behaviours performed in danger zones during natural catastrophes are another major risk factor. The populace is also made vulnerable by their coastal settlement patterns and the positioning of main roads, frequently built along the shoreline itself.

The Islands of Flores (Nusa Tenggara). Conceptions of the Ancestors and the Afterlife, and their Role in Nature Conservation

Flores is situated in eastern Indonesia and belongs to the small Sunda Islands. The island is 14,125 km^2 and has about one million inhabitants. Muslims were not able to gain a strong foothold in this remote island region. Over 90 per cent of the inhabitants are Christians and – because of Portuguese missionary activities in the sixteenth century – almost exclusively Roman Catholic. Pre-Christian rituals and belief systems are still alive in Flores, however. Though often entangled with Christian belief systems and rituals, they are relatively resistant to influences from Christianity (Kohl, 1988; Schröter, 2002). There are roughly 26 volcanoes on Flores, 14 of which are active. Tsunamis that result from seaquakes and volcanic eruptions regularly affect the island (Monk et al., 1996; Rynn, 2002).

In Flores, as well as many other parts of Indonesia, there is a prevalent belief that the ancestors (*ebu nusi*) continue their existence in the natural world, especially on mountains and volcanoes, where they 'live' in villages – in other words, they have their own parallel world (Arndt, 1929/1931; Forth, 1998; Frömming, 2006). But it is also thought that they

FIGURE 12.2 House for the ancestors, Flores. © S. Ziarno

sometimes spend time in other natural locations, especially in certain trees or in the deep jungle, but also in mountains and the ocean. Now and then, they 'visit' the villages of the living, resting for a while in the local ancestral shrines (Figure 12.2), especially when called on by the Floresians during ceremonies to remember and honour ancestors, like the Reba festival (Figure 12.3).

Hence, beliefs about the afterlife play a key role within the Floresian conception of nature. In believing that the ancestors continue their existence in various natural environments, and by performing rituals to honour them, one comes to terms with mortality, an idea which might otherwise overwhelm human consciousness. At the same time, this conception overcomes the dichotomy between nature and humanity. Here, the ancestors connect humans to the natural world, functioning as mediators between social reality and natural (as well as supernatural) forces, and thus as guarantors of a conservational approach to natural environments. The eschatological dimension of ancestor worship is closely interwoven with social relevance: volcanoes are not only moral agents, but also legislative ones. This means that nature – in the form of either angry or benevolent ancestors, or natural spirits and gods – can either punish or bless human activities. Because nature is seen primarily as the territory of the dead, or as conceptually equivalent to the dead – 'the mountain is the forefather' – then

FIGURE 12.3 Reba ceremony – calling the ancestors and natural spirits, Flores. © U. Frömming.

every encroachment upon the natural world implies contact with powerful spirits and gods.

In the conceptualization of the Floresians, one sphere is represented by the terms *nitu zale* or *nua nitu*; these indicate the 'lower realm of the *nitu*' or the '*nitu* place', such as mountains, cliffs, springs,[6] rivers, trees and the sea. This is in contrast to the *déwa zeta*, or the 'upper realm of the *déwa*'; these *déwa* are the 'heavenly gods', who are differentiated into the *déwa langit* or 'sky god', *déwa bulan* or 'moon goddess', *déwa mata hari* or 'sun god', and *déwa bintang* or 'star gods'. The *déwa* are considered to be much less influential than the *nitu*, at least in the 'old Indonesian' context. Thus, missionary Paul Arndt mentions that the nature spirits or *nitu* are frequently cited before the gods or *déwa* (Arndt, 1956, pp. 423f.).

Flores Seaquake Case Study: Ritual Handling of a Catastrophe

We will now briefly discuss a seaquake and its ritual handling in Larantuka, a town in the north of Flores. Before the 2004 Indian Ocean disaster, when a seaquake was followed by a tsunami, Indonesia's second-largest seaquake in a century occurred at the island of Flores on 12 December 1992. With a Richter magnitude of 7.5, it devastated the town of Maumere and the coastal regions. The seaquake also resulted in a tsunami, 26 metres high, which caused particularly heavy damage to the northeast coastal regions of Flores as well as the offshore island of Babi. The last two rituals to ward off catastrophes took place on 12 December 1992 and on 27 February 1979, when the harbour town of Larantuka was flooded by a tsunami. In these ceremonies, an invocation to stop the tidal wave was addressed to the ancestral spirits, who, according to the local people of Larantuka, live on the volcano. At the same time, the people begged forgiveness for any offence they may have caused the ancestors. In the local dialect of Larantuka, this is called a 'ceremony to ward off misfortune or catastrophes' and an 'invocation of the ancestral spirits for help' ('Upacara menjauhkan penduduk dari bencana alam').

The ceremony to ward off catastrophes is usually led by the king or the king's son (the *Don Se*), or else the village chief. It takes place in the morning, like most ceremonies, and lasts until midday. The sacrificial offering may be put in the traditional ceremonial house known as the *korke*; otherwise, it is placed on a large sacrificial stone, in a large tree or on the grave of the king – all at the foot of the volcano. The leader of the ceremony, chosen by the king, sings special *pantun* poems in the local Lamaholot language. After the ceremony, all the participants share in eating the sacrificial animal. In general, the sacrificial offerings include a pig, a goat, a chicken, a chicken egg, betel nuts, tobacco, lantar leaves to be used as cigarette papers, palm wine, red rice, red coconuts, a machete and a knife.

Beyond the aforementioned reasons, another intention of this ceremony is to unite the villagers who live around the volcano. Furthermore, the local inhabitants believe they inhabit land that belongs to the ancestors, which is why these must be ceremonially honoured and appeased.

The Mangrove-fringed Segara Anakan Lagoon, the Fish Nursery and Feeding Grounds for Central Java

Site Description

Until the mid-1970s, the local population consisted almost entirely of Javanese fisherfolk who arrived in the fifteenth and sixteenth centuries. Over the past few decades, this region has seen the additional arrival of Sundanese farmers, who now make up around 10 to 15 per cent of the population (Duewel, 1994).

Located on the southern coast of central Java, the Segara Anakan Lagoon has a total area of 238 km^2, and is surrounded by Java's largest contiguous mangrove region. This area combines diverse habitats such as mangrove swamps, marshlands and open waters, resulting in an ideal breeding and feeding zone for many commercially useful species of fish and crab. Therefore, the lagoon represents a highly productive ecosystem with exceptional ecological and economic significance not only for local fisheries but also for more distant coastal and oceanic fisheries. However, intensive and occasionally destructive fishing, cutting mangrove trees for firewood, opening new clearings for settlement and agriculture, and building ponds for shrimp farming have destroyed large parts of the natural habitat.

The Religious Frame of Reference – The Interwoven Concept between Islam and Kejawen

Although most rural Javanese do adhere to the basic tenets of Islam, a great many are still influenced by the spiritual and ethical values of *kejawen*, as well as the religious syncretism of the *abangan*. In this complex blend, Islam becomes interwoven with elements from Buddhism and Hinduism as well as a traditional Javanese belief in supernatural agents such as gods, ancestors and the spirits that emanate from the natural environment itself. For example, fisherfolk place great emphasis on the *Nyai Ratu Kidul* or 'Goddess of the South Sea' (Schlehe, 1998). These conceptions have a decisive influence on the use of natural resources. For example, some Javanese still believe that fishing in itself disrupts the natural balance. Therefore, this destabilization needs to be counteracted by the strict observance of religious regulations and prohibitions. Specific times and places are assigned a particular significance because of their spiritual importance not because of goal-oriented, utilitarian considerations; at these times and places, certain practices are to be avoided with regard to fishing and agriculture (Reichel et al., 2009).

An example of this would be the *wetonan* cycle, a traditional religious calendar system that still influences contemporary economic activities. The five days of the *pasaran* cycle – known as *legi, pahing, pon, wagé* and *kliwon* – were originally used to define local market days; these are combined with the seven days of the week from Monday to Sunday, known as *senin, selasa, rebo, kemis, jumat, setu* and *minggu*. This produces a calendrical cycle of 35 combinations, each associated with certain meanings that lead to specific commandments and prohibitions. Particular significance is placed on the pasaran day known as kliwon. Many fishermen believe that if kliwon falls on a Tuesday or Friday, one should not go fishing, because the ancestral spirits travel around on these days and breaking this taboo could lead to accidents.

Furthermore, various locations around the Segara Anakan Lagoon are subject to restrictions on resource exploitation because they are considered to be the homes of ancestral spirits, and it is forbidden to disturb them through fishing or woodcutting. For example, in the south-western part of Nusa Kambangan Island, which blocks the Segara Anakan Lagoon up south to the Indian Ocean, is a region known as *solok pring*, *solok bokong*, *solok besek*: woodcutting is forbidden here, and one should not visit during the twilight hours of morning and evening. There is a belief that if anyone breaks this taboo of the *buta ijo* or 'forest spirit', then the whole village could become cursed. In the past, someone who broke this rule might have lost all social status and could even have faced complete ostracism; the local *kuncen*, who was in charge of maintaining the traditions, would have enforced this.

The Taka Bonerate Atoll, South Sulawesi. A Hot-Spot of Biodiversity with Supra-Regional Importance

With an area of 2220 km^2, Taka Bonerate is the largest atoll in Indonesia and the third largest in the world. It is located in the Flores Sea, between the south-west tip of Sulawesi and the island of Flores. The atoll includes more than 60 different reefs as well as 21 islands made of durable sandbanks. Some 6,000 people inhabit seven of these islands.

The inhabitants of Taka Bonerate are mostly fisherfolk and traders, and generally belong to one of two ethnicities – the Bajau and the Bugis – which are differentiated by both language and culture. Since the 1980s, the region has seen increasing numbers of non-local fishermen, who threaten coral reef fish stocks with destructive fishing methods involving dynamite and cyanide. Some members of the local population then copy these methods.

The Religious Frame of Reference – The Interwoven Concept between Islam and the Belief in Local Sea Spirits

The Bajau of Taka Bonerate also have various rules of conduct, as well as times and places in which the exploitation of natural resources is either restricted or forbidden in order to avoid damaging relations with the supernatural spirits of the sea. Although the Bajau nominally declare themselves to be Muslims, their religious worldview is still marked by a parallel belief that the sea is inhabited by *dewa* (gods), *hantu laut* (sea spirits) and *jinn* (demons), who exist in a specific hierarchy and possess different powers. At the top of this hierarchy is *dewa laut*. He possesses more power than all the other supernatural beings and controls the outcome of all activities taking place at sea. When *dewa laut* interacts with human beings, he takes on the form of *ombojanngo*, the four-armed octopus.

Many Bajau avoid all locations where they believe the sea god *dewa laut* appears in this form, because fishing or even just passing through these areas would anger him, provoking him to afflict the entire village with illnesses or natural disasters such as tsunamis and catastrophic floods. This taboo includes two areas in Taka Bonerate, which have transregional significance due to their high biodiversity: the Taka Mariam reef, where an old cannon from the Dutch colonial period was apparently sunk in the sea, and the Taka Gantarang reef, whose waters supposedly contain ceramics from a Chinese junk that ran aground. According to Bajau beliefs, the community needs to guard (*piara*) the artefacts at these location, because they represent a direct connection between human beings and the supernatural sphere of the gods. The size of these taboo zones corresponds to the strength of the power residing in these objects.

An important part of the conceptual, behavioural and religious framework of the Bajau worldview is the belief that under the multiplicity of things, there exists a cosmic order that influences all aspects of life, connecting everything together. This 'order' or 'unity' is called *semangat*. According to the Bajau, excessive or single-minded fishing activities could destabilize this order. To avoid this, the people of the atoll use a fishery system named *silelebbas* that precisely delineates permissible seasons for all market-oriented fishing activities, while conforming to the life cycles of these maritime species. The year is roughly divided into three distinct fishing seasons, covering all species destined for market sales. One season is for fish, another is for sea cucumbers and a third is for clams. During the fish season, for example, only fish can be sold at market, while clams and sea cucumbers are harvested purely at subsistence levels. Disobeying these regulations is a violation of the accepted moral order; these rules are enforced by the *panglima menteng*, who can mete out punishments such as ostracism from society.

Cultural Techniques for the Sustainable Use of Natural Resources and the Prevention of and Adaptation to Natural Hazards

Local knowledge includes numerous strategies concerning the prevention and management of climate-related natural dangers and catastrophes as well as sustainable resource management. Although some of these religious restrictions, such as taboo areas or calendar systems, may seem inefficient from a Western scientific perspective, others bear a striking resemblance to modern strategies. In fact, some even seem innovative because they draw upon the latest research.

At first sight, traditional local strategies for managing natural resources may not have the goal of maintaining ecological equilibrium; nonetheless, they are often more sustainable than top-down imposed programmes. Furthermore, they discourage people from entering potentially dangerous regions. As a result, ecosystems remain intact and can present an effective form of protection against tidal waves and tsunamis.

The state management of natural resources and natural hazards is often very inflexible, and in countries like Indonesia, where even distant peripheral regions are regulated by centralized state organs, there can be massive delays (and bureaucracy) that prevent an adequate response to the changing dynamics of local environmental situations. In view of the fact that Indonesia's fishing grounds stretch across over 17,500 islands with 81,000 kilometres of coastline containing 60 per cent of the population, the state simply does not have the necessary administrative and technical resources for implementing a management system that could be flexible enough to keep up with constantly changing ecological conditions (Briggs, 2003).

Because the effects of the global phenomenon of climate change can only be understood by their impact at a local level, incorporating the knowledge of local people offers new possibilities for developing sustainable resource management strategies and facing natural catastrophes in an appropriate way. Although more research in this field will be a challenge because of the regional differences, we assume according to Berkes (2003), Folke (2005) and Turner (2003) that, compared to conventional strategies, these possibilities have various advantages, such as the following.

1. Local strategies are in general developed by relatively small groups of community residents. This is an ideal setting to develop regulatory measures by group consensus with the aim to implement them effectively in several national and international adaptive governance strategies for social–ecological systems (see Folke et al., 2005).
2. Local strategies implemented by small, decentralized groups can be more flexible and effective in reacting to the changing dynamics of local conditions.
3. Administrative costs are much lower, because implementation and monitoring are not entirely dependent on external staff such as park rangers or police.

4. Because each local strategy has been adapted to a specific ecosystem and to the necessity of maintaining a permanent source of food – often over a very long period of time – one can learn from a rich body of local knowledge concerning natural phenomena, such as weather conditions and the life cycles of resident species. This localized knowledge informs a series of religious taboos and socially defined permissions, often resulting in a sustainable system for using natural resources.
5. In contrast to governmental strategies that often focus on the exploitation of ja few specific natural resources, local strategies generally include a much broader palette. This allows local people to compensate for variations in the quantity and quality of available resources, giving them a wider range of opportunities for sustaining themselves.
6. In contrast to the destructive exploitation of natural resources designed to obtain the highest yield for the smallest investment, even if it leads to the complete loss of a particular resource, local management strategies generally adapt themselves to the dynamics of the resource. The utilization of a particular species thus becomes more or less intensive according to the prevalence of that species (Turner et al., 2003; Berkes et al., 2003).

Local knowledge may allow people to react flexibly to looming environmental changes, reducing their vulnerability and strengthening their resilience in the face of catastrophic events such as tsunamis, shrinking maritime resources and climate change. In their increasing awareness of this more progressive approach, those in charge of resource management have been abandoning their attitude of trying to take control of changes in order to keep systems as stable as possible and thus maintain equilibrium. Under the banner of 'resilience', the new approach is to focus on gathering competencies that can help in adapting to future changes, in order to cope with change and even incorporate it constructively. One example for such an approach is the Indonesian–German cooperation project called SPICE (Science for the Protection of Indonesian Costal Ecosystems), which is organized from the German side by the Leibnitz Centre for Marine Tropical Ecology in Bremen. SPICE aims to provide an interdisciplinary and international scientific basis for the protection and sustainable use of tropical coastal ecosystems in close cooperation with partners in the tropics (Glaser et al., 2010).

Following the concept of social–ecological resilience, local knowledge is a category that describes how societies understand uncertainties, disturbances and surprises, as a trigger of a recursive learning process that makes them sustainable for the long term (see Berkes et al., 2003; Bohle, 2007; Voss, 2008; Smith and Stirling, 2010).

Irregularities that arise are not considered to be insurmountable or life-threatening attacks, but rather the beginning of a transformation process in which people reshape their interdependency with their natural foundations using a far-sighted, sustainable approach (Turner et al., 2003; Berkes et al., 2003; Gallopín, 2006; Bohle, 2007; Voss, 2008). However, it would also be wrong to romanticize these local strategies as a 'paradisiacal environmental consciousness' and assume that their mere existence could guarantee that natural resources will not be overexploited. The opposite would also be wrong. Every local knowledge base is constantly changing, exists to different extents among various members of the community and is embedded in its own natural, social and cultural context.

According to all cultural systems, local knowledge focused on resource management is in constant flux, which incorporates the reality that adaptation to a changing environment can result in equally destructive resource exploitation strategies. Changes that occur in the naturally existing biological environment through the disappearance of particular fish species and the consequent decrease in overall catches, or in the social environment through new connections to extra-regional markets (which also opens new economic perspectives), also change the local knowledge base.

It is also important to consider that, through the process of 'glocalization' (Robertson, 1995), the global environmental and climate protection discourse impacts local ideas and religious interpretations of climate change. But local knowledge can conversely enter the global discourse through indigenous movements that advocate greater autonomy and land rights. This happens in the friction-full space between empowering other knowledge bases and creatively adapting or expanding one's own body of knowledge (Appadurai, 1986; Tsing, 2005).

Besides improving sensitivity towards social-anthropological research, this awareness could play a decisive role in the development of culturally determined protective zones and catastrophe plans. Catastrophe zones, mapped with the help of ethnographic fieldwork, include the constitutive societal influences of natural dangers with regard to religious meanings and local agents, who are able to provide diverse sustainability strategies combined with cultural techniques (Böhme et al., 2004) in order to protect against hazards or extreme events in the long term. In consideration of local perspectives, cultural integrity may be guaranteed, which therefore produces an efficient complement to Western early-warning systems. This may also reduce the impact of catastrophes, more effectively protecting human life. The conceptual expansion for specific challenges related to climate change under this form of adaptive governance is currently in its early stages. This also applies to areas of cultural-ecological resilience activities such as the management of natural hazards in south-east Asia's coastal areas in times of global environmental and climate change.

Notes

[1] Parts of this text were published in German in Frömming (2005).

[2] At least since the beginning of the twentieth century, there is no longer a well-defined difference between indigenous or 'old Indonesian' groups and 'young Indonesian' groups. The direct confrontation with Christianity that was brought to the villages by missionaries, the expansion of Islam and, most notably, the intervention of colonialism led to manifest changes and an intermixture of indigenous and Christian or Islamic belief systems (see Schröter, 2002). However, Karl-Heinz Kohl (1988) has nevertheless noted the resistance of indigenous religion to this contact, especially in the Nusa Tengarra region. Waldemar Stöhr (1965) considers the following groups to continue to belong to the old Indonesian ethnic groups: those located on the isolated islands or in the jungle regions that are difficult to access, such as the Niasser of the Island Nias, the Toba-Batak of Sumatra, the Ngadju-Dajak and Iban from Kalimantan (Sarawak), the Toradja of Sulawesi, the Ngada of Flores, and the Wemale of the Molukk Island. We do not consider indigenous or local knowledge that we describe in this chapter as a fixed structural character but rather as a globally connected flow of knowledge grounded in historical religious belief systems (see Eichborn, 2001; Lölke, 2002; Pottier et al., 2003).

[3] Whether an event is understood as a catastrophe depends on the rating system of the cultural group in which those affected live. Different agents that experience the catastrophic event therefore define the concept differently. For those who are affected, catastrophes are considered to be damaging events that either disrupt or at least severely interfere with their ability to 'read the world'. This relates to every form of cultural interpretation that enables people to orient themselves in the surrounding world, determine their actions and create a sense of context. The resulting range of interpretations makes it possible for people to understand their current situation and react appropriately. In this sense, catastrophes are events that cannot be integrated into the traditional constructs of interpretation; instead, they require that these constructs either be changed significantly or re-established (Blumberg, 1986; Groh et al., 2003, p. 15).

[4] During the Miocene Epoch, 10 to 15 million years ago, plate tectonic processes brought about a collision of the Asian and Australian land masses, resulting in a mixture of the respective flora and fauna and favourable conditions for the unique evolution of different plant and animal species.

[5] The ocean in this area has the highest level of biodiversity anywhere. For example, 75 per cent of all coral species and over 3,000 species of reef fish are located here (Allen and Werner, 2002).

[6] Schröter (1997, p. 47) mentioned female spring spirits called *nitu*.

References

Allen, G. and Werner, B. (2002), 'Coral reef fish assessment in the "coral triangle" of southeastern Asia'. *Environmental Biology of Fishes*, 65, 209–214.

Appadurai, A. (1986), *The Social Life of Things: Commodities in Cultural Perspective.* Cambridge: Cambridge University Press.

Arndt, P. (1929/1931), 'Die Religion der Ngad'a (West-Flores, Kleine Sunda-Inseln)'. *Anthropos*, 24, 817–861; *Anthropos*, 25, 353–405, 697–739.

— (1956), 'Krankheit und Krankheitsursachen bei den Ngadha (Mittel-Flores)'. *Anthropos*, 51, 417–446.

Bergmann, S. (2010), 'Dangerous environmental change and religion: how climate discourse changes the perception of our environment, the spiritual fabrication of its meaning and the interaction of science and religion', in S. Bergmann and D. Gerten (eds), *Religion and Dangerous Environmental Change.* Münster: LIT, pp. 13–38.

Bergmann, S. and Gerten, D. (2010), *Religion and Dangerous Environmental Change: Transdisciplinary Perspectives on the Ethics of Climate Change.* Studies in Religion and the Environment, Vol. 2. Münster: LIT.

Berkes, F., Colding, J. and Folke, C. (2003), *Navigating Social-Ecological Systems. Building Resilience for Complexity and Change.* Cambridge: Cambridge University Press.

Blumberg, H. (1986), *Die Lesbarkeit der Welt.* Frankfurt am Main: Suhrkamp.

Bohle, H.-G. (2007), 'Leben mit dem Risiko – Resilience als neues Paradigma für die Risikowelten von morgen', in C. Felgentreff and T. Glade (eds), Naturrisiken und Sozialkatastrophen. Berlin: Spektrum, pp. 435–441.

Böhme, H., Barkhoff, J. and Riou, J. (eds) (2004), *Netzwerke. Eine Kulturtechnik der Moderne.* Köln: Böhlau.

Briggs, M. (2003), *Destructive Fishing Practices in South Sulawesi Island – East Indonesia and the Role of Aquaculture as a Potential Alternative Livelihood.* Bangkok: APEC Grouper Research and Development Network.

Crate, S. and Nuttall, M. (2009), 'Introduction: anthropology and climate change', in S. Crate and M. Nuttall (eds), *Anthropology and Climate Change. From Encounters to Actions.* Walnut Creek, CA: Left Coast Press, pp. 9–36.

Dietz, K. (2006), *Vulnerabilität und Anpassung gegenüber Klimawandel aus sozial-ökologischer Perspektive. Aktuelle Tendenzen und Herausforderungen in der internationalen Klima- und Entwicklungspolitik.* Discussion paper 01/06 of the project 'Global Governance und Klimawandel', Berlin.

Duewel, J. (1994), *Socio-Economic Assessment of Segara Anakan Lagoon and Environs.* Asian Development Bank Technical Assistance Consultant's Report.

Eichborn, S. (2001), *Lokales Wissen in der Entwicklungszusammenarbeit (EZ): Soll alles bleiben wie bisher?* Diskussionspapiere 77 (Das Arabische Buch) des Fachbereichs Wirtschaftswissenschaft, Fachgebiet Volkswirtschaft des Vorderen Orients. Berlin: Freie Universität.

Folke, C., Hahn, T., Olsson, P. and Norberg, J. (2005), 'Adaptive governance of social-ecological systems'. *Annual Review of Environment and Resources*, 30, 441–473.

Forth, G. (1998), *Beneath the Volcano: Religion, Cosmology and Spirit Classification Among the Nage of Eastern Indonesia.* Leiden: The Royal Institute (KITLV) Press.

Frömming, U. (2005), 'Der Zwang zum Geständnis. Friedensrituale und Mythologie im Kontext von Naturkatastrophen auf Flores (Ostindonesien)'. *Anthropos*, 100, 379–388.

— (2006), *Naturkatastrophen. Kulturelle Deutung und Verarbeitung.* Frankfurt am Main: Campus.

Gallopín, G. C. (2006), 'Linkages between vulnerability, resilience and adaptive capacity'. *Global Environmental Change*, 16, 293–303.

Glaser, M., Baitoningish, W., Ferse, S., Neil, M. and Deswandi, R. (2010), 'Whose sustainability? Top-down participation and emergent rules in marine protected area management in Indonesia'. *Marine Policy*, 34, 1215–1225.

Groh, D., Kempe, M. and Mauelshagen, F. (2003), *Naturkatastrophen. Beiträge zu ihrer Deutung, Wahrnehmung und Darstellung in Text und Bild von der Antike bis ins 20. Jahrhundert.* Tübingen: Gunter Narr.

Kohl, K. H. (1988), 'Ein verlorener Gegenstand? Zur Widerstandsfähigkeit autochthoner Religionen gegenüber dem Vordringen der Weltreligionen', in Zinser, H. (ed.), *Religionswissenschaft. Eine Einführung.* Berlin: Reimer, pp. 252–273.

Lölke, U. (2002), 'Zur Lokalität von Wissen. Die Kritik der *local-knowlegde*-Debatte', *Anthropologie und Internationale Zusammenarbeit.* Hamburg: Institut für Afrikakunde, p. 21.

Luig, U. and von Oppen, A. (1997), 'Landscape in Africa: process and vision. An introductory essay'. *Paideuma. Mitteilungen zur Kulturgeschichte*, 43, 7–45.

Luig, U. and Schultz, H.-D. (2002), *Natur in der Moderne. Interdisziplinäre Ansichten.* Berliner Geographische Arbeiten. Berlin: Humboldt-Universität, p. 93.

Marcus, G. (1995), 'Ethnography in/of the world system: the emergence of multi-sited ethnography'. *Annual Review of Anthropology*, 24, 95–117.

Monk, K. A., Fretes, Y. and Reksodiharjo-Lilley, G. (1996), *The Ecology of Nusa Tenggara and Maluku.* Hong Kong: Periplus Editions Ltd.

Moscovici, S. (1968), *Essai sur l'histoire humaine de la nature.* Paris: Flammarion.

Pottier, J., Bicker, A. and Sillitoe, P. (eds) (2003), *Negotiating Local Knowledge: Power and Identity in Development.* London: Pluto Press.

Reichel, C. (2008), *Lokales Wissen als Möglichkeit nachhaltiger Ressourcennutzung und des Schutzes vor Naturkatastrophen. Am Beispiel der Segara Anakan Lagune (Zentral Java) und des Taka Bonerate Archipels (Süd-Sulawesi) – Indonesien.* Master thesis, Freie Universität Berlin, Institut für Ethnologie.

Reichel, C., Frömming, U. and Glaser, M. (2009), 'Conflicts between stakeholder groups affecting the ecology and economy of the Segara Anakan region'. *Regional Environmental Change*, 9, 335–343.

Robertson, R. (1995), 'Glocalization: time–space and homogeneity–heterogeneity', in F. Mike (ed.), *Global Modernities*, London: Sage Publications, pp. 25–44.

Rynn, J. (2002), 'A preliminary assessment of tsunami hazards and risk in the Indonesian region'. *Science of Tsunami Hazards*, 20, 193.

Schlehe, J. (1998), *Die Meereskönigin des Südens, Ratu Kidul. Geisterpolitik im javanischen Alltag.* Berlin: Reimer.

Schröter, S. (1997), 'Topographie der Geschlechter bei den Ngada in Indonesien', in G. Völker (ed.), *Sie und Er. Frauenmacht und Männerherrschaft im Kulturvergleich*, Ethnologica 22, 41–50.

— (2002), 'Jesus als Yamsheros. Die Aneignung des Katholizismus in einer indone-
sischen Lokalgesellschaft'. *Petermanns Geographische Mitteilungen*, 36–41.

Smith, A. and Stirling, A. (2010), 'The politics of social-ecological resilience and
sustainable socio-technical transitions'. *Ecology and Society*, 15, 11. www.ecology-
andsociety.org/vol15/iss1/art11/.

Stöhr, W. and Zoetmulder P. (1965), 'Die Religionen Indonesiens', in C. M.
Schröder (ed.), *Die Religionen der Menschheit*, Vol. 5.1. Stuttgart: Kohlhammer.

Tsing, A. L. (2005), *Friction. An Ethnography of Global Connection*. Princeton:
Princeton University Press.

Turner, B. L., Kasperson, R. E., Matson, P. A., McCarthy, J. J., Corell, R. W. et al.
(2003), 'A framework for vulnerability analysis in sustainability science'.
Proceedings of the National Academy of Sciences of the United States of America, 100,
8074–8079.

UNEP (United Nations Environment Programme) and IUCN (International
Union for Conservation of Nature and Natural Resources) (1988), *Coral Reefs of
the World Vol. 2: Indian Ocean, Red Sea and Gulf*. UNEP Regional Seas Directories
and Bibliographies. Nairobi, Gland and Cambridge: UNEP and IUCN.

UNEP-WCMC (2006), *In the Front of the Line: Shoreline Protection and Other Ecosystems
Services from Mangroves and Coral Reefs*. Cambridge: UNEP World Conservation
Monitoring Centre.

Unsworth, R. and Clifton, J. (2010), *Marine Research and Conservation in the Coral
Triangle*. New York: Nova Science Publishers Inc.

Voss, M. (2008), 'The vulnerable can't speak. An integrative vulnerability approach
to disaster and climate change research'. *Behemoth*, 1/3, 39–71.

Welzer, H. (2009), *Klimakriege. Wofür im 21. Jahrhundert getötet wird*. Frankfurt am
Main: Fischer.

Chapter 13

Jaichylyk: Harmonizing the Will of Nature and Human Needs

Gulnara Aitpaeva

Introduction: Polysemy as an Indicator of Multidimensional Phenomena

This chapter examines the historical and contemporary dimensions of *jaichylyk*, the Kyrgyz spiritual practice related to weather. This analysis is based on epic literature and oral history, and describes the traditional foundations of jaichylyk; the bearers of this spiritual capacity; and its goals, related rituals, techniques and other properties. Other world cultures have practices similar to jaichylyk. A reconstruction of the jaichylyk knowledge system based on a targeted study of the epic *Manas* and epic tales of other Turkic and Altai peoples (see Mamytbekov, 1993, p. 160; Verbitskyi, 1893, p. 64; Potanin, 2005, pp. 773f) should also enable the elucidation of modern-day scientific parallels and paradigms.

The word *jaichylyk* refers to a traditional practice of the Kyrgyz people that is designed to change the weather. A *jaichy* was someone who had specific knowledge and abilities to impact the weather and the environment. If it did not rain for a long time, and livestock and the harvest would suffer as a result of drought, the practice of jaichylyk was designed to invoke rain. If it rained for a very long time and it was impossible to dry hay, for example, this practice was aimed at stopping the rain. If an enemy needed to be stopped, the jaichy would work to invoke a tempest or a blizzard. Similarly, if clear blue skies could bring a desired victory, the jaichy would perform certain actions to bring them about.

The underlying word *jai* has several meanings in the Kyrgyz language. Jai denotes the summer, as one of the four seasons (Akmoldoeva, 2009, p. 24; Abduldaev and Isaev, 1984, pp. 280–281). At the same time, jai means 'space' in the broadest sense of the term, and – depending on the context – it can mean one particular point or the entire universe. Jai also indicates a state of calmness and order, and it refers to spreading something, such as knowledge or carpets.

Subordinate vocabulary can be created from each of the four meanings of the word *jai*. However, it is not by chance that the same word characterizes different phenomena, conditions and actions. This is a typical example of the traditional Kyrgyz philosophy that is encoded in the language (Aitpaeva, 1999, pp. 3–5). In Kyrgyz, multiple meanings always signal that the item being referred to has a number of different qualities, and the multiple meanings also denote the root fusion or initial affinity of all these qualities.

We can see that by referring simultaneously to time and space using the same word, the Kyrgyz ancestors were able to capture quite clearly the main quality of these concepts, which is their inextricable connection. To be precise, the initial oneness of time and space (Melnikov, 2006) was captured in the Kyrgyz language, and according to the polysemantic word *jai* – denoting a state of calmness and order – the spreading (unfolding, circulating, propagating) of specific materials with different properties (material–spiritual, heavy–light, allowed–forbidden, new–old, etc.) directly depends on the objective flow of time and space.

Following the underlying word jai, its derivative jaichylyk (jai + chylyk) also has several meanings, basically peace and well-being (Abduldaev and Isaev, 1984, p. 283).

My hypothesis in this chapter is that jaichylyk, understood as humans influencing the weather, contains all of the major meanings of the word jai. Time, space, a state of calmness and order, as well as the action of spreading are represented here in their initial oneness, or root fusion. Time and space are thus coordinates in which jaichylyk takes place. Jai as calmness and order represents the rhythm of the coordinates. It was only after one found one's exact position in these coordinates and tuned in to their rhythm that jai, or the spreading of some desired impact, could begin. Based on the same principle, I argue that a clear connection between the practice of human influence upon the weather and a prosperous world existed in the traditional Kyrgyz society.

The Epic Concept of Jaichylyk

Focus on *Manas*

Currently, one of the most important sources of traditional knowledge and practices associated with the Kyrgyz people, including those related to weather and climate, are Kyrgyz epics. These can be divided into two groups, the epic trilogy *Manas* and some 'small' epics (Akmataliev, 2002, pp. 3–40).

The centrepiece of the Kyrgyz oral tradition is the great *Manas* epic, which contains up to 500,000 lines. More important than the size is the fact that the telling of the *Manas*, along with the individuals who do the telling (the *manaschy*), played an important part in the traditional Kyrgyz society (van der Heide, 2008, pp. 141–149). Because it has occupied such a special place in the intellectual and emotional world of Kyrgyz, the *Manas* is often the basis for comparison with the rest of the oral tradition. Compared with the *Manas* story, other epic folk poems have been affectionately called *kenje*, which means both 'junior' and 'small'. However, despite the kenje status of other stories, their average size is often from 1,000 to 17,000 lines. It is also important to note that the small or junior label given these other epics does not refer to their age. Several epics date back to the same period as the *Manas*. To roughly date these epics, Kyrgyzstan celebrated the 1,000-year anniversary of *Manas* in 1995. The first episodes of *Manas* were recorded by Kazakh researcher Chokan Valikhanov (Valikhanov, 1986, pp. 241–250) in 1856 and Russian scholar Vladimir Radlov in 1862–1869 (Radlov, 1885).

Jaichylyk practices are described in both kinds of epics. This chapter focuses on the *Manas*, as it is the cornerstone and the pivot of the Kyrgyz people's entire epic heritage. It is named after its main hero, who engaged in a severe struggle against foreign enemies (Kalmaks and Chinese) and was able to unite the scattered Kyrgyz tribes, thus creating one nation with its own territory.[1]

As the longest epic in the world, the *Manas* contains enormous amounts of information accumulated over centuries. In the twentieth century, scholars and writers emphasized the vast scale and encyclopaedic nature of this epic (Kadyrbaeva, 1980; Moldobaev, 1995; Akmoldoeva, 2009; Akmataliev, 2002, pp. 3–130; Asankanov and Bekmuhamedova, 1999, pp. 37–54). A prominent writer, Chyngyz Aitmatov, introduced the epithet 'ocean-like *Manas*' (Aitmatov, 1994). In the twenty-first century, another feature of the ancient epic – apart from its encyclopaedic nature, which addresses various aspects of traditional livelihoods – is of paramount importance: the *Manas* is no longer just a symbol of antiquity and a repository of collective folk knowledge, but is an actively evolving phenomenon. New versions of the epic have appeared which differ significantly from its classical versions (Umot uulu, 2009). Additionally, new manaschy have appeared, that is, the chanters of the epic and bearers of the epic knowledge (Aitpaeva, 2006, pp. 118–123; Aitpaeva et al., 2007, pp. 264–282; Aitpaeva and Egemberdieva, 2009, pp. 55–65, 74–79; Kadyrov, 2009). Astoundingly, the emergence of the new versions and chanters takes place in accordance with the epic-based thinking, which has little, if anything, to do with the contemporary rationality. Academic science typically treats the epic as an object of study, but not as an independent entity capable of restoring itself, transitioning from epic reality to social reality.[2]

What is Jaichylyk in the Epic World?

When the Chinese came close as one solid wall,
The day was dark and the night was bright,
And it was wet in some areas.
When he beheld a host of foes,
Almambet performed jaichylyk.
And then the highland was covered with hail,
And the valleys were flooded with rain.
The clouds dashed across the sky,
And the thunder roared in the heaven.
The Chinese who attacked so defiantly
Were locked up on the ground,
They dreamed of seeing the sun.
The whole battlefield was covered with snow
And the snowdrifts were as tall as a spear,
And then the countless Chinese, the Manjurs,
Turned into weeping girls.[3]

This is an excerpt from the chapter of the *Manas* called *Chong Kazat* ('Great March'), which describes when the Manas-led Kyrgyz tribes went on a military march to the stronghold of the Chinese, Beijing. A drastic change of the weather was 'performed' by Almambet, a staunch fellow-fighter of Manas. There is no description of jaichylyk, or the process of affecting the weather. All we know is that 'Almambet performed jaichylyk'. There are more detailed descriptions of jaichylyk in the entire text, and yet no clear details are provided as to how humans actually influenced nature. This is not typical of the epic since it describes other traditions, rituals and practices in numerous minor details. In this context, we may assume that the paucity of description has to do with the specific nature of jaichylyk itself. In fact, the epic tale presents jaichylyk as secret knowledge and a closed ritual.

According to the *Manas* epic, only a very few people can actually cause an impact on the weather and nature at all. As a rule, these are men who were specifically trained for this purpose:

> Without trying to sound audacious,
> I can turn summer into winter.
> I can make the Chinese dressed in light garments
> Weep like girls.
> The reason I can do it is,
> I came to the Kyrgyz all light-handed,
> And I came in, having studied the craft of sorcery.

These words were pronounced by Almambet, who is one of the most tragic heroes in the classic versions of the Kyrgyz epic. His father was Chinese, and he was raised among the Chinese, but he then joined the Kyrgyz when he began to shape his personal philosophy and make a spiritual quest. Despite being half-Chinese, Almambet was the main jaichylyk expert among the Kyrgyz. He studied the craft of jaichylyk in China when he was among his 'own people'. Much in the way that the epic contains no details about the practice itself, it is difficult to find any particulars about the school where jaichylyk was taught. It is known that it was located in the vicinity of Beijing, and the epic stresses that an *ajydaar*, a dragon, conducted all selection and training. As described by Kuban Almabekov, a manaschy coming from a family of epic chanters (Almabekov, 2009, pp. 46–50), this detail is sufficient to understand how sensitive and viable a young man had to be in order to be recruited for the school. Men had to be able to survive the selection process and stay alive during the actual training.

Jaichylyk as a 'Super-Weapon'

The epic contains scenes, for example, in which Almambet disperses the clouds so others may enjoy a fight between two strong wrestlers. However, in the heroic epic that focuses on the struggle of the Kyrgyz people for their independence and territorial integrity, the main reason for deploying jaichylyk is military. Enemy attacks, intelligence operations and the need for stealth all are reasons for affecting the weather and environment with jaichylyk. Jaichylyk is an epic 'super-weapon' that was available only to highly qualified experts. The power of this weapon was enormous. Indeed, one jaichy who went through the 'dragon's school' could stop thousands of warriors in their tracks, cause confusion among the winners of a battle or defeat the enemy's best fighters. If there were two students of the 'dragon's school' in two opposing armies, the result of a battle largely depended on them.

The 'Great March' featured numerous armies, strong warriors and spies, but also two jaichy locked in a fight: Shypshaidar and Almambet. Shypshaidar won this battle. He dispersed the clouds invoked by Almambet, stopped rain showers and calmed the winds, counteracting the natural disasters that Almambet had called up and sending them back against the Kyrgyz. The 'Great March' ends tragically. Manas was wounded and then died from his injuries at his place of birth, while Almambet and other warriors were killed by the sniper shots from Shypshaidar.

Based on the hypothesis that the word *jai* contains all connotations of the word, we can explain Shypshaidar's victory by the fact that the battle of the jaichy took place in an area that was alien to the Kyrgyz but native to the Chinese. The epic also tells us that Almambet was defeated because he had studied the craft of jaichylyk for less time (several months) than Shypshaidar.

A Description of the Basic Principles and Components of Jaichylyk

A few years after the death of 54-year-old Manas and his warriors, the Kyrgyz, according to a law governing vendettas, embarked on a march towards Beijing to avenge the deaths of their fellow tribesmen. The sons of Manas and Almambet were among the new warriors. The first person who entered a battle with the Kyrgyz was Muradyl, a Chinese jaichy:

> He flung a jai stone into the lake,
> And started conjuring the sun,
> The master of the clouds, Buurakan,
> Calling his name,
> The master of the place, Jelshamal,
> Calling his name,
> And he brought in the winter clouds,
> In the summertime.
> Muradyl, a big Chinese warrior,
> Pronounced incantations endlessly.
> Fog appeared in the gorge,
> And black clouds became thick
> From behind the mountain peaks.
> Ice-cold hail poured down immediately

Upon the highlands,
The earth started twisting, accompanied by noise,
And ice-cold hail was falling down.
Invisible to the eye,
Black mist was floating low on the ground.
The earth was not to be seen,
The earth split apart, making a roar,
And water was flowing noisily
Down the hollows and dimples.
The black rock fell off,
And the cliff was carried away . . .
The summer day was turned into a cold day,
The leader's face was covered
With ice which was four fingers thick.
Fourteen war horses
Were rushing about and neighing like foals.
All their bridles were torn off sharply,
And the spacious world became small.
The surface of the ground was covered with snow,
Starting from the saddles of the horses.
All animals hiding in the clefts and gullies
Were dying struck by the hail.

This is one of the most comprehensive descriptions as to how jaichylyk actually worked. Muradyl's first action was throwing (directing) a special stone, *jai-tash*, into the lake. The second thing he did was to pronounce *duba*, or verbal formulas, to address the relevant forces of nature. Jai-tash and duba are two basic components in influencing the weather and nature. They can be found in the actions of all jaichy in the epic.

The scene above clearly illustrates the conceptual basis of jaichylyk: (1) the jaichy entered a place–space and became one with their natural surroundings (lake); (2) they entered time and become harmonious with the prevalent force of the place–space (sun); (3) they turned to the spirits of nature (clouds, areas) and (4) they used a natural object (stone). In other words, jaichylyk is based upon the concepts of reciprocity and cooperation and – at some point – oneness between humans and the natural world. Only by contacting the forces of nature and their spirits and gaining their support could a human being influence the weather and environment. In the epic notion of jaichylyk, there is no human dominance over or management of nature. Jaichy, as experts who went through the 'dragon's school' and were well acquainted with the forces they dealt with, would have no intention of dominating or managing nature.

Returning to the scene involving Muradyl, it should be mentioned that Kulchoro, the son of Almambet, was able to counteract Muradyl's powerful influence upon nature. Kulchoro's mother learned the lessons of her husband's death very well. She prepared her son for revenge and sent him to study the secrets of jaichylyk at a very young age. According to the epic, Kulchoro's power was partly accounted for by Almambet's ritual stone.

The *jai-tash* (jai stone) is an integral part of the ritual for influencing the weather and nature. If the jai-tash is a mandatory accessory of this practice, and if it is one of the two visible pillars on which the practice is based, it would be fair to assume that the nature of this stone reflected the nature of the practice itself. According to the folklorist Zair Mamytbekov, this stone was of animal origin (Mamytbekov, 1993, p. 150). It was found in the stomachs of both domestic and wild animals, such as sheep, horses, cows or argali. It could also be found in the stomachs of some wild beasts, namely bears and wolves (Aliev, 1995, pp. 194–195).

Why was a Stone used in the Epic's Description of the Jaichylyk Practice?

The four elements of nature – earth, water, air and fire – have long been known to humans.[4] The jaichylyk ritual needed to include these four elements in the quest to become harmonious with nature. A stone is a solid substance like the earth. Presumably, a stone is used as a stand-in for the earth or at least one of the four elements. In the case of jaichylyk, a solid substance (a stone) is always conjoined with water or another liquid substance. Even if we simply throw a stone into water, a visible reaction will take place. And if we throw, immerse or pour water onto a stone as a part of a ritual, that is, with a clear intention and in a certain fashion, the reaction will, most probably, be as expected. Why and how should a stone be of animal origin, however? According to the epic, Chinese leaders would station animals such as *ak kulja* (white argali) and the *kuu tulku* (cunning fox) along with the *ordok* (duck) on the Kyrgyz border to protect it. If needed, these 'border guards' could perform the functions of jaichy. In the epic world, humans and animals are very close to each other, oftentimes interchangeable. A stone extracted from the stomach of an animal or beast is different from a stone that, for instance, was resting at the bottom of a river or in a mountain gorge. It is different, first of all due to the fact that it went through (lived through) the life cycle of a warm-blooded mammal, which could also be a human. In this case, we may assume that jai-tash – as an equivalent of the earth on the one hand, and as a piece of a warm-blooded mammal on the other – conjoins various elements of nature. An object of such origin fits perfectly in the epic concept of jaichylyk. Indeed, this ritual performance is built on the interaction of natural phenomena, one of which is a human being.

The second basic pillar of jaichylyk is the duba or verbal formula. In the scene involving Muradyl, we can see who the duba is meant for – Buurkan, the master of clouds, and Jelshamal, the master of the place. According to the Kyrgyz traditional perspective, calling such forces by their names is a very serious venture. Knowing the names of natural forces and how to call them in a way that they can hear and respond to is presumably one of those bits of knowledge taught in the 'dragon's school'. Detailed wordings of duba are difficult to find in the epic, which once again indicates their secret nature (Mamytbekov, 1993, p. 75).

All relevant epic scenes focus not so much on the ritual itself, but rather on the reasons for performing it and its ramifications. Apart from military purposes, one fundamental reason for employing the ritual practices of jaichylyk is when communities experience a disaster that they cannot handle on their own and need a powerful ally, such as nature itself. In this situation, jaichylyk results in those weather changes and changes in nature that the community in need would like. Jaichy, or the mediators between the human world and the natural world, bridge the gap between cause and effect. Jaichy serve their people and rulers. And when these people and rulers fight with one another, jaichy also enter the fight. Those who can make nature their ally and those who are well acquainted with the language of natural forces, such as hurricanes, ice blizzards, earthquakes and mountain rivers, will win this fight. In other words, the victors are those most skilful and precise in entering time and space and harmonizing with nature.

The idea of jaichylyk as *ayan*, or secret knowledge, runs like a golden thread through the epic. Only the chosen ones, or those who are able to withstand the dragon's lessons, can access it. The dragon is the embodiment of might and mind pertaining to natural forces. The jaichylyk knowledge system is, presumably, a knowledge system governing interactions between humans and other natural forces and based on the principle of reciprocity.

All epic scenes involving jaichylyk are strictly limited in time and space. Any effect on nature occurs when there is a request, and ends along with the problem that was supposed to be solved by 'sending the request'. Most probably, this spatial-temporal limitation is one more piece of knowledge that jaichy are taught.

Jaichylyk in the Oral History of the Present-Day Kyrgyz

Jaichylyk as a Branch of Kyrgyzchylyk

Today any Kyrgyz person is generally familiar enough with the epic *Manas* to sustain a conversation about it. However, this is not true of jaichylyk. If you want to learn about the traditional practices of influencing the weather, you must meet either with the elders who may remember the past, or with those whose professional and/or spiritual interests are related to traditional culture. Currently, oral history and the knowledge of the epics are unique but accessible sources of traditional practices.

Jaichylyk is similar to *manaschylyk*, or the reciting of *Manas*, while the two are different branches of the same cultural and natural phenomenon that the Kyrgyz labelled *kyrgyzchylyk* (Aitpaeva and Molchanova, 2007, pp. 377–394; Aitpaeva, 2008, pp. 66–82; Koshaliev, 2008). During Soviet times, kyrgyzchylyk – a complex of various traditions, rituals and practices pertaining to the Kyrgyz people – was destroyed and brutally eliminated from all areas of Kyrgyz life. This was for ideological reasons, as traditional thinking and behaviour expressed through customs, rituals and practices were rooted deeply in the spiritual and religious realms. During the 70 years that the Kyrgyz spent in a totally atheistic state, much was destroyed or lost. However, in 1992, after the USSR disappeared from the world map and a new country called Kyrgyzstan had appeared, a process of restoring and resuscitating kyrgyzchylyk in its various forms began. Traditional practices such as healing, manaschylyk, pilgrimages to sacred sites and many other activities returned to daily life, and are currently undergoing a new renaissance.[5] In this context, jaichylyk should be seen as a separate issue, considered more a part of people's memories than in their actions.

Jaichylyk as Lost Knowledge

Our village, Tash Aryk, in Naryn province, had one jaichy, and his name was Jaichy. When he was born he had a different name, but people kept calling him Jaichy. He was a very gifted person, and the belief was that this gift was from God. He could change the weather. Sometimes, when the village would decide to move to the mountains, and the weather would turn nasty or it would start raining, he would perform a ritual, and the weather would return to normal, and the rain would stop. Jaichy died not so long ago, when he was about 85 or 86. His relatives and children are still alive, and they still live in our village. None of his children inherited their father's gift. There are no jaichy like him these days.

(Archive of the Aigine Cultural and Research Centre, 2010)[6]

This story was shared by Kubanychbek Tezekbayev, a leader of the organization called Uluu Kyrgyz Ordo, which works to restore ancient spiritual practices and traditional sports. The following story comes from the oral collection of Cholponbek Abykeev, a writer and a person who possesses extensive knowledge about the past:

In the Issyk-Kul valley, in Ton, there lived a famous visionary named Osmonaaly. He died almost yesterday, in 1957. He had knowledge of jaichylyk and jylanchylyk (snake studies). He could call up rain at any time and stop it. I spoke with some people who had witnessed these weather changes. When there was no rain for a long time, farmers would approach Osmonaaly, and then due to his duba they would be able to invoke rain. He was the last real jaichy, there are no longer any people like him nowadays.

(Archive of the Aigine Cultural and Research Centre, 2010)

We were able to hear the beginning and the end of both stories ('there lived one jaichy, but there are no longer any people like him nowadays') in three regions of the country from 2006–2010. Jaichy lived 70, 100 and very many years ago. Jaichy could have been alive quite recently – only 50 years ago – like Osmonaaly, but 'there are no longer any people like him nowadays'. In present-day oral stories we clearly see some sort of an inclination to describe jaichylyk as lost knowledge that has already disappeared, along with its bearers.

When talking about 'such jaichy', the interlocutors imply high-level practitioners, similar to those we encounter in the epic. 'Such jaichy' were able to turn a summer day into a winter day, to stop rivers, to move mountains apart, to speak with snakes and so on.

In the opinion of Kuban Almabekov, a manaschy from birth, the last jaichy similar to the ones we see in the epic was Berdike, who worked under Atake Baatyr at the end of the eighteenth and the early nineteenth centuries (Saparaliev, 2006, pp. 580–581). Currently there are no written or oral sources that could either confirm or refute this opinion.

In 2010, Kuban told a story about Berdike, which he heard in childhood from his grandfather, manaschy Almabek in Issyk-Kul province:

> When Atake's troops were surrounded by ten thousand Kokhand fighters in the vicinity of the Chychkan gorge (close to a modern Toktogul hydropower station), Berdike performed jaichylyk. He took his jai-tash out, plunged it into the water and started pronouncing duba, causing heavy showers and severe mudslides. Back then about one thousand Kokhand fighters died, and the rest had to withdraw. Atake's troops were saved, and they did not allow the Kokhands to move to the north of the Kyrgyz territory.

Another story about the same jaichy was told in Talas province, in 2006. Although the jaichy's name was forgotten, the name of his leader, Atake, was still remembered:

> Once, a peasant whose corn crops could perish because of a drought under the scorching sun heard about Atake's troops that were approaching his area. There was a jaichy among them, and the peasant went out in their direction to meet them. The farmer spoke with Atake, saying the following: 'It hasn't been raining for a long time, and all my crops may perish. Ask your jaichy to call up the rain one time.' And Atake responded: 'It won't be good if the farmer's year-long efforts are wasted.' Then he looked at his jaichy as if asking him to find a way to help the farmer, and then started moving further. A response to the request followed when Atake and his people moved away as far as two mountain ridges from the farmer's field. This is where the greatness of Atake and the high skills of his jaichy should be appreciated. The rain was falling down along the line of Atake's horse's rump, and only the hemline of his gown became wet. The hemline of his gown was hanging below his horse's rump, and that's why it became wet. But the leader himself was dry. This is a jaichy who knows his business very well.

> (Archive of Aigine CRC, 2008)

In the stories about Berdike we can see the level of modern-day expectations as regards jaichy. This individual should be an epic-like specialist possessing epic-like powers, while his impact should be immediate and his skills should be precise. This example of the line along which Berdike's rain fell and which only got the horse's legs and the hemline of Atake's dress wet is a cultural symbol of preciseness that jaichy should possess. Jaichylyk should be accurate in terms of time and strictly limited to the space where it is anticipated. It should not affect those areas where it is not needed.

Reasons for the Loss of 'Epic Jaichylyk'

If we follow the opinion that Berdike was, so to speak, the last of the Mohicans, this would mean that jaichylyk started disappearing approximately around the mid-nineteenth century. This was long before the Soviet social system was established.

Berdike's example gives rise to some thoughts as to why jaichylyk knowledge was lost. Notably, Berdike used the super-weapon against the Kokhand army. The Kokhand Khanate and Tsarist Russia were the last outside enemies of the Kyrgyz people. Understanding jaichylyk as a secret and formidable super-weapon helps connect the epic concept of jaichylyk with present-day reminiscences. When fighting for their fatherland and independence, jaichy would serve the high and noble cause, moving mountains if needed. Motherland, territorial integrity and independence were the fundamental values of the Kyrgyz nomadic society. Given the traditional way of life, the need to procct these values was conducive to sustaining and reproducing the knowledge of jaichylyk.

In the contemporary oral history, Berdike's activities are not related to Islam, nor are they opposed to it. There is the assumption that Berdike worked outside the Islamic system. We would be able to judge more accurately to what extent Berdike as jaichy was inside or outside the Islamic paradigm based on duba, or his verbal spells. However, duba were always the most secretive part of a jaichylyk ritual, and today it is almost impossible to find out the verbal formulations of Berdike's duba.

At the same time, by the beginning of nineteenth century, Islam had already been introduced to the Kyrgyz. As a folk practice that had been shaped long before the emergence of Islam and before it was spread among the Kyrgyz in particular, jaichylyk still falls in the area of 'active tension' between kyrgyzchylyk and Islam (Toktogulova, 2007, pp. 252–258; 507–517). Unquestionably, a traditional practitioner who directly contacted natural forces by bypassing the Almighty was not acting according to Islamic tenets. Jaichy who changed the environment assumed the role of the Almighty. Needless to say, when Islam arrived in the country, the roles and skills of jaichy inevitably had to be altered. Instead of receiving training from the epic dragon, they had to study the Qur'an. Jaichy had to accede to the restrictions of Islam, and as a result, they lost their epic greatness and freedom.

In modern oral histories, the phenomenon referred to as *jaichy-moldolor* (mullahs) is represented rather widely. These are Islamic clergymen who know Muslim duba. This phenomenon should be viewed as a consequence of one of the practices of kyrgyzchylyk being subsumed by Islamic principles. In a broader context, this is a concrete and extremely interesting example of what scholars call 'folk Islam' (Light, 2007, pp. 476–497; Schubel, 2009, pp. 279–288; Aitpaeva and Egemberdieva, 2010, pp. 25–42). Asylbek Sarygulov from Manas village, Talas province, told us:

> Jaichy are those who are knowledgeable about Muslim duba. Apart from the Qur'an, mullahs also have a book of incantations, Azeimkan. When biting winter frosts set in, they [jaichy-mullahs] dig out a cellar in the ground and lie there for forty days, reading this book.
>
> (Archive of Aigine CRC, 2008)

In this elderly man's report, there is no mention of the fact that jaichylyk was a pre-Islamic practice, and there is no division between jaichylyk and Islam. In this case, influencing the weather is a component of Islamic practices. Such syncretic understanding is another distinctive feature of present-day collective memory about jaichylyk.

The main area for jaichy-moldolor activities is people's everyday lives, illustrated by the perishing crops and the farmer helped by Berdike. Every region features stories about different jaichy-moldolor who helped people. There are also stories demonstrating that jaichylyk was used as a weapon in inter-personal relations and as a means of intimidating the disobedient. The very existence of such stories suggests sacred knowledge is becoming profane. Presumably, this occurs as a result of the loss of such knowledge.

However, the principle of using time and space in a strict, targeted and limited fashion as a basic principle of jaichylyk is well preserved in the memories of traditional knowledge custodians.

> I lived at one time with a man named Jarmambet. I never saw what he was doing, but I heard a lot about it. Once, people were moving their livestock from Talas to Aksy. When they passed Ketmen-Tube, the sun was scorching hot. Then they approached mullah Jarmambet asking him to do something about the heat. Jarmambet pronounced duba over one stone and flung it into a spring. From that moment, the heat subsided, and the sun was not so hot by the time they got to the market and sold

their livestock. It even rained a little. However, in the market Jarmambet was very anxious and hurried back, saying that the time was about to be up. When he returned, he walked briskly to the spring and pulled his stone out. This is when he calmed down. Duba is performed for a specific time period, for some precise number of days or hours. Jaichy may face horrendous ramifications unless a stone is removed within this period of time and unless the activity of duba is stopped.

(Archive of Aigine CRC, 2009)

Thus, under the influence of Islam, the paradigm within which jaichy used to work has changed, narrowing their scope of activities and reducing the significance of the scale, but the internal principles governing time and space remain intact.

Therefore, both historical and religious factors restricted the use of jaichylyk. The significant historical milestones that influenced this process were the union with Russia (a few northern tribes did that in 1855), the award of the status of an autonomous province (1924) and the shift to a Soviet republic (1926). Becoming a part of the Soviet system and having a fixed territory resulted in the weakening of outside threats on the one hand and a loss of the traditional nomadic lifestyle on the other. As has been described above, one of the main areas where jaichylyk was used involved wars with external enemies. Additionally, the nomadic lifestyle was rooted in and fully interconnected with the natural seasons and cycles. Nomadic life required deep and systematic knowledge of nature, an understanding of the human place in the holistic natural system and congruent actions. From this perspective, nomadism was fertile ground for growing of jaichylyk.

These factors, connected with religion, or more specifically the establishment of Islam (in the tenth and eleventh century, during the time of Kara Khanate) combined later with Soviet atheism operated to restrict and eliminate jaichylyk.

Jaichylyk in the Context of Global Changes

In the section on the epic concept of jaichylyk, I emphasized that the *Manas* epic is a living and evolving phenomenon. This statement would have been difficult to prove some 10–12 years ago; today it is possible due to a new understanding of the Kyrgyz spiritual culture and folklore. In the section on jaichylyk in present-day oral history, I stressed that the knowledge and

FIGURE 13.1 Jaichy Kalyiman of Issyk-Kul province, Kyrgyzstan, at a sacred site. © Aigine CRC

practices that enabled jaichy to influence weather had been lost and that there is no reason to think any differently today. And yet, based on field observations and in light of the current restoration of the epic *Manas*, the question arises as to whether or not it is possible to revive jaichylyk in the epoch of global change, including climate change.

'Naturalness' and Spirituality as the Basis for Jaichylyk

A woman named Kaliyman Danakeeva, born in 1940, resides in the village of Kichi-Jargylchak, in Issyk-Kul province (see photo, Figure 13.1). Those who know her call her '*jaichy apa*', or a 'granny jaichy'. While she does not deny that she does jaichylyk, it is extremely difficult to learn anything about Kaliyman's jaichylyk activities, in full accordance with the traditional understanding of jaichylyk as secret knoweldge. There are some people whom she has told about jaichylyk, but they are bound by a promise not to share this information.

However, Kaliyman's past and her current lifestyle are not a secret. The village of Kichi-Jargylchak is located on the southern shore of Lake Issyk-

Kul, far from large towns and resort areas. However, Kaliyman does not live in the village. She lives year-round surrounded by mountains in a place called Cholok Kiya. She comes down to the village only when there is a need to do so, for instance, to attend funerals or wedding ceremonies. Kaliyman's husband died eight years ago. She has children and grandchildren, and they spend some time with her, but most of the time she lives alone in the mountains, taking care of her family livestock.

In the case of Kaliyman, jaichylyk is closely related to the epic *Manas*. Her father was a great teller of the story. She has never chanted the epic herself in public, although she does so in her dreams. When she was a young woman, Kaliyman suffered from epilepsy, and she was taken to a mental hospital many times. Such disorders are quite common among many bearers of kyrgyzchylyk at certain stages of their lives.[7] Normally, medical treatment in such cases does not help (Aitpaeva, 2009, pp. 254–265). Similarly, it was not medical treatment that helped Kaliyman, but rather her seclusion in the mountains and accepting the task that she had received from the spirit of Manas. Once he came to her in a dream and gave her a cup with kumis, saying the following:

If you drink this cup of kumis, you will find a coin at the bottom. Take it. When you go to the water, you will find a mirror there. Take it. There is a dagger in the barn where you keep your animals. Take it as well and use it for the benefit of the people.

(Archives of Aigine CRC, 2009)

Thus, she received ritual items, such as a mirror and a dagger. She also has jai-tash, or a ritual stone. Since she received this message, Kaliyman has performed jaichylyk, healing people and counselling them in various difficult life situations. To perform any ritual, she uses an old edition of the book *Manas*. Her neighbours say that if Kaliyman turns up in the village for some occasion, people ask her to call up rain, particularly on hot days. And it does start raining in some limited area for a short while.

There are a few key aspects in Kaliyman's life that help us understand the nature of jaichylyk better. The first is the space where she spends most of her life, the natural environment. It is not an exaggeration to say that Kaliyman lives in nature. The second aspect is the time in which Kaliyman lives: it is also more natural than social. She has a hard time living even in the remote village that is a part of greater society. The third is the path that led her to jaichylyk: this is an ancient traditional path, by which one is chosen and taught to carry out a certain spiritual mission (Aitpaeva, 2009, pp. 254–256). Kaliyman never attended any classes by moldo (mullahs) or any other person. In terms of traditional culture, she learned – and keeps acting – under the tutelage of spirits, primarily the spirit of Manas. There is no doubt that although she lives in the mountains all alone, Kaliyman does not live in solitude. She does not feel intimidated by mountain nature. She feels she is an organic part of a bigger natural world.

Kaliyman's example makes it clear that jaichylyk is a phenomenon that exists in the state of interrelation and intercommunication of humans, spirits and nature. These key aspects – co-existence with nature and spirits, in other words, 'naturalness' and spirituality – prepared the ground from which Kaliyman's jaichylyk stems. This is very ancient ground, and the epic jaichylyk also stems from there. In this context, it is evident that jaichylyk is the knowledge of nature and spirits, including the spirits of nature. Oral narratives often confirm this observation. Thus, a famous jaichy from the village of Tepke, Issyk-Kul province, Manake, was extremely knowledgeable about the stars. Mukai, a jaichy from Talas province, used to say that just as we see road signs along the road, he can see many signs amid the clouds that tell him what weather to expect. The Kyrgyz referred to such people by saying '*tabiyattyn tilin bilchu*', or 'they knew the language of nature'. This was not a metaphor, but rather a literal statement. In accordance with oral history, before the Soviet era and during its early years, almost every community had its own jaichy, a mediator between the human and natural communities. Today, Kaliyman is a rare person in the country as a whole.

When People are Helpless, Nature Helps

However, a process of restoring ancient traditional practices in Kyrgyzstan, including jaichylyk, is currently underway. Considering that Kyrgyzstan is an economically undeveloped, post-Soviet country, the process is taking different shapes and forms.

The renaissance of jaichylyk in the country has not yet been studied scientifically. Non-systematic practices of influencing weather have taken place in a few traditional communities such as Kut Ordo, Kyrgyz Uluu Ordo and Bata. The practitioners work in the field of kyrgyzchylyk and have little to do with science in its Western meaning. However the word *ilim* – science – is often used by kyrgyzchylyk practitioners. As a rule, the leaders of such communities are spiritual messengers. The common quality and specific task of such leaders is study through spiritual messages. According to their logic and understanding, certain chosen people get messages from a spiritual realm, interpret messages and then undertake necessary actions (Aitpaeva, 2008, pp. 78, 80). The exact process of getting information and its interpretation is called ilim. The experiences of spiritual leaders (and the communities behind them) involve discovering a spiritual realm as a diverse, multidimensional and multilevel phenomenon: it could be *Aalam* (Universe), *Jaratkan* (Creator), *arbaktar* (spirits of widely known or unknown ancestors) and others.

In December 2004, an event that has been characterized by its participants as jaichylyk took place in Talas.[8] Two people were involved in the event. Both were knowledgeable about traditions, but neither had experience in influencing the weather. These individuals were not engaged in politics, members of any political party nor part of the opposition. However, as citizens of Kyrgyzstan, they thought it was totally unacceptable to prolong the country's president's third term in office. As spiritual practitioners, they believed it was important to work first with any task or issue at a spiritual level, and thought that the political overthrow of the president might be spiritually predetermined. In their opinion,[9] at the beginning of 2005, when the issue of the president's term in office was expected to be resolved, the president was not supposed to enter Manas Ordo, a sacred site that is home to Manas Mausoleum (Aitpacva ct al., 2007, pp. 26–30). In order to prevent the president from going to the sacred site, the two men turned to nature as an ally and used the weather as a weapon. At the same time, they did not have the skills or knowledge to perform jaichylyk. They had never studied the discipline, did not have any ritual-related items, nor did they have any special duba. In that situation, they opted for the most simple and ancient, and yet the most widespread, ritual among the Kyrgyz, called '*tilek kyluu*'. '*Tilek kyluu*' means 'to make a wish'. The essence of the ritual is as follows: at a certain location and at a certain time, a wish should be sent directly, without any intermediaries, to the highest force(s) or spirits in which a person believes. Around noon, in an open space, not far from the Manas Mausoleum, two people made a wish. The words and thoughts directed to *Jaratkan* (the Creator) were their duba. In accordance with what the participants had hoped for, the response was rapid. The clear weather suddenly turned cloudy, and it started snowing heavily. The mountain road was covered with snow, and the president had to cancel his visit to Manas Ordo. For the participants of the weather ritual this meant that '*tilek kabyl boldy*', or the wish was accepted.[10]

Was that a jaichylyk ritual? In terms of certain formal features, it was not, as there was no jai-tash or duba, and there were no ritual accessories themselves. The general tilek-kyluu ritual in this case was somewhat specialized. If we take the position of the participants and assume that this was a jaichylyk ritual, then this ancient weather practice was aimed at influencing the political situation in Kyrgyzstan. This case, given its disputable nature, clearly demonstrates the social component of jaichylyk.

Moral Responsibility of Jaichylyk

According to the writer Cholponbek Abykeev, Osmonaaly, a jaichy from the southern shore of Lake Issyk-Kul, died in 1957, leaving no apprentices or successors. He had two sons. When his fellow villagers asked him why he was not teaching his sons the art, Osmonaaly used to say that none of his sons, based on their personalities, matched the mission of jaichy. His elder son was '*kara murtoz*' (hard-edged), and he might abuse the sacred knowledge, while his younger son was '*ak konul*' (of mild nature), and others could abuse his knowledge. Osmonaaly used to tell his friends that he had a successor, a boy from the neighbouring village, and that he was waiting until the boy turned 12 to begin to instruct him. However, before the boy reached the age when he could become an apprentice, Osmonaaly was bitten by a snake and died.[11]

The principles of sternness and selectivity have been mentioned quite frequently in present-day narratives about jaichylyk. Kaliyman's children do not have the right to touch her ritual items. There are dynasties of epic jaichy (Almambet-Kulchoro), although in written sources and oral history, no information has been found for jaichy dynasties.

Manaschy Kuban Almabekov, the keeper of knowledge regarding the 'last jaichy, Berdike' and one of the few people who knows the epic jaichylyk, claims that only those with well-developed and solid moral principles were able to master jaichylyk. Jaichy were morally responsible for using and disseminating this knowledge. In today's language, jaichylyk implies traditional technologies that had their own goals and areas of application. In the past, jaichylyk could be aimed at fulfilling opposite functions, as is the case with nuclear technologies in the modern world. Thus, it entails a moral responsibility.

A lack of attention to the issue of moral responsibility can be seen in the operational scope of modern spiritual messengers. One of the participants of the Talas ritual took part in a few other group campaigns aimed at changing the weather. He reported that there was always some impact following their actions. However, he also noticed that this impact took place not only in those areas where they were desired, but also manifested itself in various absolutely unexpected ways. This observation compelled him to recognize his lack of knowledge regarding jaichylyk, and he put an end to his amateur experiments.

The experience of this spiritual practitioner shows once again that jaichylyk represents a profound systemic knowledge that must be learned. This knowledge is required, in the first place, to restrict the impact to a certain time and space. When one makes an impact at one location, the entire system will, inevitably, be involved. One should be able to see the whole system to foresee all possible consequences and to prevent them in case they arise. Before initiating this type of change, one should clearly know how and when it should end. Probably, the mystery of jaichylyk lies in the area of controlling time and space – which is precisely the knowledge that has disappeared.

But it is clear that in a time of global change, when people increasingly feel, face and realize their own helplessness, there is a growing need for practices like jaichylyk.

Disappearance of Jaichylyk as a Harbinger of Global Changes

The purpose and values of jaichylyk are integrated in the word itself. If we recall the four basic meanings of the term, jaichylyk denotes the spread of calm and orderly time and space. It would be logical to assume that this is the social and cultural mission of jaichylyk. As natural and spiritual knowledge given to humans, it was meant to harmonize the needs of the people with weather and environmental conditions. Jaichy could call up snowfalls and gales, or bring in sunny weather in order to meet people's needs. In fact, through changing the weather and environment, jaichy could balance the state of affairs, be it a military battle or a drought that would diminish crop yields. Jaichy did not affect the climate, that is, weather in the long-term perspective. This is confirmed by the basic principle of their activities, which involved strict control over time and space. Practitioners knew their capabilities and limits through very close ties with nature and spirituality.

Jaichylyk as a cultural phenomenon started to disappear long before the world realized that global environmental and climate changes were underway. If one type of a plant or animal species disappears in nature, this signifies some breakdown in a particular ecosystem. The disappearance of jaichylyk from the Kyrgyz culture was a signal of a breakdown in the 'naturalness' and spirituality of Kyrgyz.

As mentioned above, there are currently just a few jaichy practitioners in the country, along with non-systematic group experiences where it is practiced under spiritual guidance. Similar to their ancestors, the modern Kyrgyz people have realized that when faced with undesirable weather, human beings are unable to alter the situation single-handedly. Climate change and a systematic crisis in society have forced the Kyrgyz to look to the past and remember the concepts, notions and practices that would help make life more normal.

Harmonizing nature with human needs is at the very core of jaichylyk philosophy. This philosophy is based on the concepts of reciprocity and local action coupled with global responsibility, and is an approach adopted by indigenous cultures throughout the world (Rappaport, 1979, pp. 27–42; Cajete, 2000, pp. 58–66; Pere, 2006, pp. 145–147; Tuxteneva et al., 2006, p. 446; Crate and Nuttall, 2009, p. 187; Mamyev, 2009, pp. 101–105). The crucial importance of the ongoing process of jaichylyk restoration in Kyrgyzstan, with all its imperfections and lack of special knowledge, is in restoring the philosophy of reciprocity and responsibility. Regaining 'naturalness' and establishing a link with spiritual realm(s) or other living beings are significant steps for humans in order to deal with climate change. In the past, the Kyrgyz used jaichylyk productively to lessen the impacts of frost or drought. Today, facing global climate instability, it is reasonable to educate people in the philosophy of jaichylyk, rebuild its spiritual technology and modify ancient knowledge for current needs.

Notes

[1] There are many versions of the epic with one common plot, all of which are referred to as classic versions. This section relies on the versions of Sayakbai Karalayev and Diykanbai Almabekov.

[2] The tragic events that took place in Kyrgyzstan in April 2010 demonstrated that Manas, the epic hero, became an actual spiritual support and a leader of those who went out to protest the anti-popular regime.

[3] This and subsequent translations of the epic by Gulnara Aitpaeva and Aleksander Grishuk.

[4] 'Not so many people think about it, but what seems hidden behind these elements are four structural types of substances and four conditions of substances: earth–matter; water–liquid; air–gas; and fire–plasma' (Kadyrov, 2008, p. 7).

[5] Aigine Cultural Research Center (CRC) has been doing extensive field studies and documentation of the Kyrgyz traditional practices and knowledge with the financial support of The Christensen Fund of California since 2005.

[6] This and further interviews are from the archive of the Aigine CRC, 2006–2010, which is partly presented on the web resource: www.tk.aigine.kg. This and all subsequent translations of the interviews by Gulnara Aitpaeva.

[7] For example, at the stage of awareness, spiritual solidification and search (see Umetbaeva, 2007, pp. 226–252).

[8] Talas is a town in north-west Kyrgyzstan which is the administrative centre of Talas province.

[9] The story was shared by both participants of the experiment, and there are slight differences between the two stories. For the purpose of this chapter, the motives we report are those that were common to both stories.

[10] In 2005, the first president had to leave not only his position, but also the country.

[11] Notably, jylanchylyk, or snake studies, was his specialty along with jaichylyk. Most probably, in the case of Osmonaaly, influencing the weather and being a snake-man were different manifestations of undivided spirituality.

References

Abduldaev, E. and Isaev, D. (eds) (1984), *Definition Dictionary*, Vol. 1. Frunze: Mektep (in Kyrgyz).

Aitmatov, C. (1994), *Manas is the Epos-Ocean*. Bishkek: Ilim (in Russian).

Aitpaeva, G. (1999), 'Polysemy as an indicator of the Kyrgyz world comprehension', in American University in Kyrgyzstan (AUK) (ed.), *The Nature of University Education and Research: Conference proceedings*. Bishkek: AUK, V.2, pp. 3–5 (in Russian).

— (2006), 'The phenomenon of sacred sites in Kyrgyzstan', in *Conserving Cultural and Biological Diversity: The Role of Sacred Natural Sites and Cultural Landscapes*. UNESCO: Paris, pp. 118–123.

— (2008), 'Searching new paradigms in ancient practices'. *Anthropological Yearbook of European Cultures*, 17, 66–82.

— (2009), 'Spiritual mission, health and sacred site worship in Kyrgyzstan', in S. Bergmann, P. M. Scott, M. Jansdotten Samuelsson and H. Bedford-Strohm (eds), *Nature, Space and the Sacred. Transdisciplinary Perspectives*. Surrey: Ashgate, pp. 249–264.

Aitpaeva, G., Aldakeeva, G. and Egemberdieva, A. (2010), 'Common followers of Islam or phenomenon of mullahs in Kyrgyzstan', *Ethnographic Observation*, N5, 25–42 (in Russian).

Aitpaeva, G. and Egemberdieva, A. (eds) (2009), *Sacred Sites of Ysyk-Kol: Spiritual Power, Pilgrimage and Art*. Bishkek: Maxprint.

Aitpaeva, G., Egemberdieva, A. and Toktogulova, M. (eds) (2007), *Mazar Worship in Kyrgyzstan: Rituals and Practitioners in Talas*. Bishkek: Maxprint.

Aitpaeva, G. and Molchanova, E. (2007), 'Kyrgyzchylyk: searching between spirituality and science', in G. Aitpaeva, A. Egemberdieva and M. Toktogulova (eds), *Mazar Worship in Kyrgyzstan: Rituals and Practitioners in Talas*. Bishkek: Maxprint, pp. 377–394.

Akmataliev, A. (2002), *The History of Kyrgyz Literature*. Bishkek: Sham (in Kyrgyz).

Akmoldoeva, S. (2009), *The Universe of Manas*. Bishkek: Arabaev National University Press (in Russian).

Aliev, S. (1995), 'Jai-Tash', in A. Karypkulov (ed.), *Encyclopaedia of Manas*. Bishkek: Akyl, pp. 194–195 (in Kyrgyz).

Almabekov, K. (2009), 'As long as you respect the earth and water, they will give you their blessing', in G. Aitpaeva and A. Egemberdieva (eds), *Sacred Sites of Ysyk-Kol: Spiritual Power, Pilgrimage and Art*. Bishkek: Maxprint, pp. 46–50.

Asankanov, A. and Bekmuhamedova, N. (1999), *Akyns and Manaschis – Creators and Keepers of the Kyrgyz People Spiritual Culture*. Bishkek: Sham.

Cajete, G. (2000), *Native Science Natural Law of Interdependence*. Santa Fe: Clear Light Publishers.

Crate, S. and Nuttall, M. (eds) (2009), *Anthropology of Climate Change From Encounters to Actions*. Walnut Creek, CA: Left Coast Press.

Kadyrbaeva, R. (1980), *The Genesis of the Epic 'Manas'*. Frunze: Ilim (in Russian).

Kadyrov, D. (2008), *Philosophy of Common Field*. Bishkek: Gulchynar (in Russian).

Kadyrov, J. (2009), *Bubu Mariam*. Bishkek: Biyiktik (in Kyrgyz).

Koshaliev, K. (2008), *Purity Will Save the World*. Bishkek: Poligrafcombinat (in Kyrgyz).

Light, N. (2007), 'Participation and analysis in studying religion in Central Asia', in G. Aitpaeva, A. Egemberdieva and M. Toktogulova (eds), *Mazar Worship in Kyrgyzstan: Rituals and Practitioners in Talas*. Bishkek: Maxprint, pp. 476–487.

Mamyev, D. (2009), 'Ecological principles of traditional culture', in I. Jernosenko (ed.), *Ecology and Culture*. Gorno-Altaisk, Barnaul: Artika (in Russian).

Mamytbekov, Z. (1993), *Reflection of Life and Struggle of Kyrgyz People in the Epic 'Manas'*. Bishkek: Ilim (in Kyrgyz).

Mclnikov, G. (2006), 'Fractal unity of time and space'. Available online at http://nauka.izvestia.ru/blogs/article69912/print.html (in Russian).

Moldobaev, I. (1995), *'Manas' is the Historical and Cultural Monument of Kyrgyz*. Bishkek: Kyrgyzstan (in Russian).

Pere, R. T. (2006), 'A celebration of Maori sacred and spiritual wisdom', in C. Laudine, *Aboriginal Environmental Knowledge Rational Reverence*. Cornwall: Ashgate, pp. 143–157.

Potanin, J. (2005), *Essays of North-Western Mongolia*. Gorno-Altayisk: Bai (in Russian).

Radlov, V. (1885), *Examples of Folk Literature of Northern Turkish Tribes*. St. Petersburg: Publishing House of Imperial Academy of Science (in Russian).

Rappaport, R. (1979), *Ecology, Meaning and Religion*. Berkeley, CA: North Atlantic Books.

Saparaliev, D. (2006), 'Atake', in U. Asanov (ed.), *Kyrgyzstan. National Encyclopaedia*. Bishkek: Al-Salam, pp. 580–581 (in Kyrgyz).

Schubel, V. (2009), 'Islam's diverse paths: seeking the real Islam in Central Asia', in G. Aitpaeva and A. Egemberdieva (eds), *Sacred Sites of Ysyk-Kol: Spiritual Power, Pilgrimage and Art*. Bishkek: Maxprint, pp. 279–288.

Toktogulova, M. (2007), 'Syncretism of religious beliefs (*kyrgyzchylyk* and *musul-manchylyk*)', in G. Aitpaeva, A. Egemberdieva and M. Toktogulova (eds), *Mazar Worship in Kyrgyzstan: Rituals and Practitioners in Talas*. Bishkek: Maxprint, pp. 507–517.

Tuxteneva, S., Xalemba, A., Sherstova, L. and Doblynskyia, O. (2006), 'Spiritual culture', in D. Funk and N. Tomilov (eds), *Turkish Peoples of Siberia*. Moscow: Nauka, pp. 429–461 (in Russian).

Umetbaeva, T. (2007), 'The worst illness is Kyrgyzchylyk', in G. Aitpaeva, A. Egemberdieva and M. Toktogulova (eds), *Mazar Worship in Kyrgyzstan: Rituals and Practitioners in Talas*. Bishkek: Maxprint, pp. 226–252.

Umot uulu, J. (2009), *Aikol Manas I*. Bishkek: Biyiktik (in Kyrgyz).

Valikhanov, C. (1986), *Selected Papers*. Moscow: Nauka (in Russian).

van der Heide, N. (2008), *Spirited Performance: The Manas Epic and Society in Kyrgyzstan*. Amsterdam: Rozenberg.

Verbitskyi, V. (1893), *Altai Non-Russians*. Moscow: Moscow University Press.

Chapter 14

Environment, Climate and Religion in Ancient European History

Holger Sonnabend

This chapter deals with the role of religion in climate and environmental change from a historical point of view, according to the research and findings of the comparatively new research branch called historical ecology or, in German, *Umweltgeschichte* (environmental history) (Hughes, 2006; Thommen, 2009, pp. 11–20). The foundation of the European Society for Environmental History (ESEH) in 1999 is one example of the growing interest of scholars in this subject.

The main question of this chapter is how did people in the past respond to environmental changes such as climate change or devastating changes like disasters and natural hazards. The following reflections will concentrate on ancient history, defined as the time of the ancient Greeks and Romans and the history of the ancient Mediterranean world, with a brief look at subsequent European history. Several scholars have conducted instructive studies of climate history from 1000 AD up to the present (see Glaser, 2008; Behringer, 2010). I do not want to miss the opportunity to emphasize that environmental history has one great advantage in this respect: historical events have happened already, and historians therefore find themselves in the comfortable situation of analysing developments based on recorded facts. Having said that, it is also important to remember that history can provide answers that can be influential for current and future developments. Thus, we can also expect answers to the question of what role religion has played, and can continue to play, with respect to global environmental and climate change.

When speaking of ancient times, both pre-Christian and Christian, we must consider that people's daily lives were informed by religion (Latte, 1960; Nilsson, 1967/1974; Sonnabend, 2008). Nature and religion were also closely connected: nature was full of traces of gods and deities in the worldview of ancient peoples (more commonly in Greece than in generally more pragmatic Rome). Everything in nature had religious implications, and everything in religion had nature-related implications. Ancient people saw gods at work everywhere. The Roman author Petronius (*Satyricon*, 17) had a sense of humour and said: 'The earth is so full with the presence of divine powers that it is easier to find a god than a human being'. Accordingly, religion and cults were strongly organized and administered, with numerous temples and priests whose duty it was to explain the signs that the gods sent to earth (see Latte, 1960; Kerényi, 1995; Sonnabend, 2008).

There is no reason to doubt that there were many and also significant environmental changes in ancient times, including changes in climate, coastlines, sea level and so on. There were a considerable number of reported natural disasters such as earthquakes and volcanic eruptions (the famous eruption of Mount Vesuvius in 79 AD was only one of many such events). Interestingly, there are also several examples of dangerous anthropogenic environmental changes, as in the mining industry – which, incidentally, led to religiously inspired reactions. The Roman author Pliny the Elder wrote in the middle of the first century AD that Roman mining (especially in Spain and Italy) was an attack on *tellus*, which here does not simply mean 'the earth' but also has a religious connotation, as the Goddess Earth, the Goddess Tellus. Pliny also calls the earth *sacra parens* in the same context, that is, *holy mother* (an expression that Christians later adopted for the mother of Jesus Christ).

Another example of man-made environmental changes accompanied by religiously inspired resistance was the construction of channels. There were six attempts in antiquity – from the sixth century BC to the second century AD – to construct a channel at the Strait of Corinth (the modern channel was constructed at the end of the nineteenth century). Economically, the channel would have offered a great advantage for shipping and navigation. But many people believed that human beings should not intervene in the divine plan, and in the end no channel was built (Sonnabend, 1991). This prominent example demonstrates the close relationship between nature and religion in antiquity, specifically the connection of religion to environmental change: religious concerns prevented people from approving man-made environmental change.

But what about climate change and religion in antiquity? Regarding this relationship, we can offer two statements. First, the written sources contain few – at least no direct – reflections on climate, although the term *klima* derives, like so many other words, from the ancient Greek language, and Greek scientists (Parmenides) had discovered the existence of seven distinct climate zones by the sixth century BC, encompassing the Mediterranean world and also the northern and southern borderlands (Hempel, 1999). There are not many written sources on (long-term) climate, but there are a number on weather phenomena (wind, rain, snow, sunshine and so on, deriving from the everyday life of farmers).

Second, we know from research into the natural sciences (dendrochronology, isotope climatology) and also from agricultural studies that there was some significant climate changes from the ninth century BC until the third century AD In general, the Mediterranean was and is characterized (both in historical and present times) by mild and humid winters and hot and dry summers (Hempel, 1999). Between 850 and 600 BC, however, there was a rather cold and wet period. In contrast, in the first century BC, people enjoyed a period that was dry and warm. Thereafter, lasting until 150 AD, climate changed again, and there was a colder period with much rain and lower temperatures. From 150 to 230 AD (during the time of the slowly disintegrating Roman Empire) it was again warmer and drier. But these changes have not been extraordinary compared to ice ages or the currently anticipated rate and degree of global warming (Maise, 1998; Thommen, 2009, pp. 27–30).

Although ancient sources contain little information about climate and climate change, there are some examples of reflections about climate change in relation to religion. I would like to introduce three such cases here:

1) The problem of man-made (and at the same time climate change-induced) alluvial deposits that caused estuaries of major rivers to dry up, especially in the coastal regions of Asia Minor. A Greek source from the second century AD (Pausanias 7,2,11) describes this as follows:

> The people of Myus left their city on account of the following accident. A small inlet of the sea used to run into their land. The river Meander turned this inlet into a lake, by blocking the entrance with mud. When the water, ceasing to be sea, became fresh, gnats in vast swarms bred in the lake until the inhabitants were forced to leave the city. They departed for Miletus, taking with them the images of the gods and their other movables, and on my visit I found nothing in Myus except for a white marble temple of Dionysus. A similar fate to that of Myus happened to the people of Atarneus, under Mount Pergamus.

What does this example show? First, people responded to climate change by leaving their city and moving elsewhere. Second, they took special care of the images of their gods while leaving, because they believed the gods were the guarantors of the persistence of the community and because they were responsible for their fate.

2) The old myth of the Great Flood also illustrates the influence of disaster and climate change on religion (Caduff, 1986). Note that the Bible was not the first place that this story was mentioned. The story of a Great Flood that destroyed a large part of earth and of mankind was a widespread oral tradition in the ancient East by the second millennium BC (note the ancient Assyrian-Babylonian epic of Gilgamesh). The ancient Greeks' version of Gilgamesh or Noah is the myth of Deukalion.

The historical structure of this myth runs as follows: there must have been a real flood, possibly in Mesopotamia as noted in the famous epic of Gilgamesh (Renger, 1996). In the myth, this historical flood developed to a huge, destroying flood, with a dual message: first, the wrath of God or the gods can be terrible. Second, disaster can have a beneficial effect, because people improved in a moral sense. The historical flood thus developed to an element of religious belief and as a way to give religion power over the people. Religion was used as an instrument to explain dangerous environmental change, but in turn religion was also transformed by such changes.

3) The experience of environmental change influences not only the *content* of religion but also the *form*, the *ritual*. If there was a natural disaster in ancient Rome, such as a thunderstorm or a flood, the priests gathered people for common prayers or ritual walks around the walls of the city (Sonnabend, 1999, especially pp. 119–158). When Roman power increased, Romans felt responsible for the ritual handling of catastrophes that had occurred in their empire, and so they used to walk around the walls as stand-ins for the victims. This took place until they came to the point that they had to walk almost every day, which made them realize that this ritual had negative effects on the economy and everyday life. In the end, they asked the gods and the priests for dispensation, which was fortunately granted.

In general, there were two ways of interpreting environmental change and natural disasters in antiquity. First, the religious explanation was that these changes or disasters were signs of the gods or even punishment, as indicated by the preceding examples. An alternative approach was provided by scholars, who searched for explanations and who found (like Thales and Aristotle) non-religious, reasonable, rational explanations. We *can* speak of rationality, although the ancient concept in this regard differed from modern concepts – for example, ancient philosophy did not yet have the capacity to recognize the modern implication of purposive rationality (Dodds, 1973; 2001). Who were the 'winners', the religious traditionalists or the scientific modernists? The winners were the former, because people preferred the security of religious interpretation to rational scientific analysis. It was easier to appease the gods (by prayers and rituals) than to appease anonymous powers. Additionally, the Christians, who in the fourth century AD became the leading religious power in the Roman Empire, cultivated religious explanations and punished those who insisted on scientific explanations. As a result, it took many centuries before rational science was able to establish itself. But religion has retained its influence if we consider the way many people respond to dangerous environmental changes even today. For example, the ancient perception of catastrophes as wrath or sign of the gods is still alive in modern Greece, and is even expressed with the same word – *theomenia* (concerning the origin of this expression see Meier, 2003, p. 47).

This phenomenon may underline the necessity of integrating historical experience in the modern handling of natural disasters. History certainly offers us a range of human experiences in this respect. But more importantly, the fact that religion was historically more important than science should not be rejected as a completely old-fashioned view now overcome by modern rationality. In fact, religion can – as history shows – give people more confidence than scientific research. If climate change and other natural disasters are going to play an increasingly important role in the future, there may be some value in decision makers considering not only technocratic solutions, but also solutions that reflect religious sensitivities.

References

Behringer, W. (2010), *Kulturgeschichte des Klimas. Von der Eiszeit bis zur globalen Erwärmung.* München: C. H. Beck.

Caduff, G. A. (1986), *Antike Sintflutsagen.* Göttingen: Vandenhoeck & Ruprecht.

Dodds, E. R. (1973), *The Greeks and the Irrational.* Berkeley: University of California Press.

— (2001), *The Ancient Concept of Progress* (reprint). Oxford: Clarendon Press.

Glaser, R. (2008), *Klimageschichte Mitteleuropas. 1200 Jahre Wetter, Klima, Katastrophen.* Darmstadt: Primus.

Hempel, L. (1999), 'Klima', in H. Sonnabend (ed.), *Mensch und Landschaft in der Antike. Lexikon der Historischen Geographie.* Stuttgart: Metzler, pp. 260–263.

Hughes, J. D. (2006), *What is Environmental History?* Cambridge: Polity Press.

Kerényi, K. (1995), *Antike Religion.* Stuttgart: Klett-Cotta.

Latte, K. (1960), *Römische Religionsgeschichte*. München: C. H. Beck.

Maise, C. (1998), 'Archäoklimatologie – Vom Einfluss nacheisenzeitlicher Klimavariabilität in der Ur- und Frühgeschichte'. *Jahrbuch der Schweizerischen Gesellschaft für Ur- und Frühgeschichte*, 81, 197–235.

Meier, M. (2003), 'Zur Wahrnehmung und Deutung von Naturkatastrophen im 6. Jahrhundert n. Chr.', in D. Groh et al. (eds), *Naturkatastrophen. Beiträge zu ihrer Deutung, Wahrnehmung und Darstellung in Text und Bild von der Antike bis ins 20. Jahrhundert*. Tübingen: Gunter Narr, pp. 44–64.

Nilsson, M. P. (1967/1974), *Geschichte der griechischen Religion* (2 volumes, third edition). München: C. H. Beck.

Renger, J. (1996), 'Vergangenes Geschehen in der Text-Überlieferung des alten Mesopotamien', in H.-J. Gehrke and A. Möller (eds), *Vergangenheit und Lebenswelt*. Tübingen: Gunter Narr, pp. 9–60.

Sonnabend, H. (1991), 'Der Mensch, die Götter und die Natur. Zu den antiken Kanalbauprojekten am Isthmos von Korinth', in M. Kintzinger, W. Stürner and J. Zahlten (eds), *Das Andere Wahrnehmen*. Köln and Weimar: Böhlau, pp. 47–59.

— (1999), *Naturkatastrophen in der Antike. Wahrnehmung, Deutung, Management*. Stuttgart: Metzler.

— (2008), 'Religiosität – Antike', in P. Dinzelbacher (ed.), *Europäische Entalitätsgeschichte*. Stuttgart: Kröner, pp. 117–135.

Thommen, L. (2009), *Umweltgeschichte der Antike*. München: C. H. Beck.

Index

CPSIA information can be obtained at www.ICGtesting.com
Printed in the USA
LVOW01s1158150114

369526LV00010B/91/P

9 781472 505569